# AMERICAN LIBRARIES 1730-1950

# AMERICAN LIBRARIES
## 1730-1950
### KENNETH BREISCH

NORTON / LIBRARY OF CONGRESS VISUAL SOURCEBOOKS
IN ARCHITECTURE, DESIGN AND ENGINEERING

W.W. Norton & Company

NEW YORK AND LONDON

LIBRARY OF CONGRESS, WASHINGTON, D.C.

For information about permission to reproduce selections from this book, write to Permissions, W. W. Norton & Company, Inc., 500 Fifth Avenue, New York, NY 10110

For information about special discounts for bulk purchases, please contact W. W. Norton Special Sales at specialsales@wwnorton.com or 800-233-4830

Manufacturing by Versa Press
Book design by Kristina Kachele
Production manager: Christine Critelli
Digital Production Manager: Joe Lops

ISBN: 978-0-393-73160-6

W. W. Norton & Company, Inc.,
500 Fifth Avenue, New York, N.Y. 10110
www.wwnorton.com

W. W. Norton & Company Ltd.,
15 Carlisle Street, London W1D 3BS

0 9 8 7 6 5 4 3 2 1

Acknowledgments
I would like to thank Ford Peatross and Helena Zinkham and their colleagues in the Prints and Photographs Division of the Library of Congress who helped me access the collections that compose the visual core of this book, as well as Aimee Hess in the Library of Congress Publishing Office. I also thank my editor, Nancy Green; Qingyun Ma, Dean of the School of Architecture at the University of Southern California; and other faculty members and friends at USC, including Trudi Sandmeier and Ami Murphy. Special thanks to my graduate research assistant, Kathryn Horak, who early on helped with the research for this book. The Graduate Research Scholar Program at the School of Architecture of the University of Southern California made her work possible. I also acknowledge the School of Architecture for its financial assistance toward the realization of this endeavor, and especially Daniel Greenberg and Susan Steinhauser, lovers of libraries both, whose very generous contribution towards the publication of this book made it possible. Finally, my special thanks, as always, go to Judy Keller, my wife and best friend for these past forty years, as well as to my parents, Walter and LaVerne Breisch.

Aimee Hess, Editor and Picture Editor, Publishing Office; Becky Clark, Director of Publishing; Phil Michel, Digital Conversion Coordinator; Helena Zinkham, Chief, Prints & Photographs Division, and C. Ford Peatross, Director, Center for Architecture, Design, & Engineering; with support from reference librarians and catalogers in Prints & Photographs Division and the Library of Congress Duplication Service.

# CONTENTS

# FOREWORD

The subjects of architecture, design, and engineering are threaded throughout the monumental collections of the Library of Congress, the nation's oldest federal cultural institution and the largest library in the world. In 2003, W. W. Norton and the Library of Congress inaugurated the Visual Sourcebooks series to serve as an entry point into these vast and varied resources, and to provide a treasury of select visual material, much of it in the public domain, for students, scholars, teachers, researchers, historians of art, architecture, design, and technology, and practicing architects, engineers, and designers of all kinds. These books serve not only to introduce researchers to the illustrations selected by their authors, but also to build pathways to adjacent and related materials, and even entire archives—to millions of photographs, drawings, prints, views, maps, rare publications, and written information in the general and special collections of the Library of Congress, much of it unavailable elsewhere.

The images in this book are available for browsing and downloading from www.loc.gov/pictures, the Prints and Photographs Division's online, searchable catalog, which includes the hundreds of thousands of high-resolution photographs, measured drawings, and data files in the Historic American Buildings Survey, Historic American Engineering Records, and the Historic American Landscape Survey. I encourage readers to visit the Library's website at www.loc.gov, which is a portal to its amazing collections. With over 86 million visits a year, it serves audiences ranging from school children to the most advanced scholars throughout the world.

Opposite: 2-069, p. 90.

Since the publication of *Barns* in 2003, W. W. Norton and the Library of Congress have published nine additional volumes in the Visual Sourcebooks series: *Canals, Theaters, Lighthouses, Bridges, Public Markets, Dams, Cemeteries, Railroad Stations,* and *Eero Saarinen: Buildings from the Balthazar Korab Archive. American Libraries 1730–1950* is the eleventh, and last, of this enduring series. Bringing this well-received series to conclusion with a book about libraries—both their function and beauty—is an especially fitting high point for the Library of Congress—the national library of the United States.

Carla D. Hayden
The Librarian of Congress

# HOW TO USE THIS BOOK

The introduction to this book provides an overview of the history and evolution of libraries. It is a broad view inspired by the depth and quality of both visual and textual information in the Library of Congress collections. The balance of the book, containing more than 450 images, is organized into six sections that focus on specific aspects and representations of American libraries across three centuries. An afterword section introduces recent library design developments. Figure-number prefixes designate the section.

Short captions give the essential identifying information, where known: subject, location, creator(s) of the image, date, and Library of Congress reproduction number, which can be used to find the image online. Below is a list of the collections from which most of the images in the book were drawn.

| | |
|---|---|
| ADE | Architecture, Design, and Engineering drawing series |
| AIA/AAF | American Institute of Architects / American Architectural Foundation Collection |
| BIOG FILE | Biographical File |
| CMHA | Carol M. Highsmith Archive |
| CGC | Cass Gilbert Collection |
| DETR | Detroit Publishing Company Collection |
| DIG | Digital copy of an original print or drawing; also, a "born-digital" photograph |

| | |
|---|---|
| FSA | Farm Security Administration/Office of War Information Collection |
| GEN COLL | General Collections |
| GSC | Gottscho-Schleisner Collection |
| HABS | Historic American Buildings Survey |
| HORY | Theodor Horydczak photograph collection |
| LC | Library of Congress |
| LOT 2749 | Washington, D.C., School Survey, 1899 |
| LOT 3585 | Library planning albums, 1895–1910 |
| LOT 3752 | Denver, Colorado, public library branches, 1931 |
| LOT 4484 | Copies of American and European library plans, 1900–1920 |
| LOT 4760 | Exterior and interior views of the U.S. Library of Congress, 1895–1897 |
| LOT 5183 | Large photos emphasizing Library of Congress architectural details, 1897–1900 |
| LOT 6437 | Public and other Libraries, ca. 1900 |
| LOT 8871 | Libraries in army camps and naval installations, 1918–1919 |
| LOT 8908 | Libraries in twenty-two states and the District of Columbia, 1900–1905 |
| LOT 9643 | Views of St. Louis, Missouri, 1890–1933 |
| LOT 9823 | Historic buildings in or near Lindsborg, Kansas, ca. 1900 |
| LOT 11337 | Charles Henry Currier Collection, 1887–1910 |
| LOT 11549 | Exterior views of U.S. libraries, mostly university, 1970s |
| LOT 12562 | Library of Congress Thomas Jefferson Building, ca. 1900 |
| LOT 13440 | American Library Association, Library War Service activities, during World War I |
| LOT 13714 | Oversize miscellaneous photographs and prints, 1870–1940 |
| NYWTS | New York World Telegram & Sun Newspaper Photo Collection |
| P&P | Prints & Photographs Division, Library of Congress |
| PAN US GEOG | Panoramic Photographs Collection, subseries United States Geographic |
| PR 06 CN 375 | WPA Federal Architecture Project exhibition photos, 1930s |
| PR 06 CN 446 | Lantern slide lecture on libraries, early 1900s |
| STEREO U.S. GEOG FILE | Stereograph Photo file, subseries United States geographical |
| U.S. GEOG FILE | Geographical file, subseries United States |

Opposite: 3-043, p. 127.

[The library] is neither a storehouse of books nor a refuge for the idle; neither is it primarily a civic monument. It is alive with activity. It should be designed with simple refinement, fulfilling the desire for something beautiful; yet friendly in its expression of welcome to all, not aloof nor cold, nor trite and commonplace in its architecture. Now and then some new building shows a striking originality, a new and efficient arrangement of plan, a refreshing exterior; it is a pioneer in the advance."
—Joseph L. Wheeler and Alfred Morton Githens, *The American Public Library Building* (1941)

# INTRODUCTION: THE LIBRARY IN AMERICA

The *idea* of the library has long captivated architects and authors and their imagined libraries have served as provocative and visionary metaphors for our desire to possess and control knowledge. These range from the Enlightenment-driven imagery of the French architect, Etienne-Louis Boullée (1728–1799) to the dark, enigmatic visions of Jorge Luis Borges (1899–1986; IN-001) and Umberto Eco (1932–2016), or, more recently, the reveries of Alberto Manguel (1948– ).[1] The visible ordering of books in tangible, if somewhat less visionary, spaces frequently serves as a physical reflection of this ambition. A pioneering example of this, and one of the most impressive of mid-nineteenth-century libraries, is the iconic British Museum Reading Room (1854–1857; IN-002). As conceived by Antonio Panizzi, the Keeper of Printed Books (1837–1856), and designed by Sydney Smirke (1798–1877), this comprised a monumental space surmounted by a yawning cast-iron dome. At the center of this panoptic invention sat the librarians, commandingly elevated above their readers. Circling the periphery were 20,000 commonly consulted volumes set in numbered alcoves, organized by subject matter (IN-003). Flanking this room, and intended to hold the bulk of the collection, were the first freestanding iron book-stacks. Twenty-four to thirty-two feet in height, these stacks originally supported some twenty-five miles of shelving (IN-004).[2]

Six years earlier, the equally significant Bibliothèque Ste.-Geneviève (1844–1850; IN-005–IN-006) had opened in Paris. As described by its architect, Henri Labrouste

Opposite: AF-011, p. 295.

IN-001. La salle des planètes (an interior view of the hexagonal hall of planets at the Library of Babel). Erik Desmazières, artist. Etching from suite inspired by Jorge Luis Borges's novel *La Biblioteca de Babel*. P&P,LC-DIG-ppmsca-06666.

(1801–1875), "the names of the principal authors and writers whose works [were] preserved in the library, had been inscribed across the facade, "in the part of the upper story corresponding to the interior shelves containing the books. . . . This monumental catalogue," he noted, formed "the principal ornament of the facade, just as the books themselves are the most beautiful ornament of the interior."[3] The iconic forms of these two great archetypes would serve as indelible influences on the evolution of the library in America.

Whether ensconced in variations on these European prototypes in ivy-covered campus citadels or white Carnegie temples, or overseen, in the popular imagination, by matronly librarians casting their feminine aura over their patrons, American libraries

are imbued with their own mythology. While new technologies appear poised to supplant the library's traditional form, it is still strongly modulated by the geometry of the book and the spaces that architects have devised to store and display it. The fundamental requirements of a library have remained remarkably stable over time: ample shelving for storage of collections; quiet, comfortable, and well-lit places to read or to access a computer; stations for the distribution of books and information to patrons; and spaces for a wide variety of administrative activities. No matter their size or scope, libraries persist as powerful sites of discovery, imagination, and, at times, comfort. As Alberto Manguel has observed, "No one stepping for the first time into a room made of books can know instinctively how to behave, what is expected, what

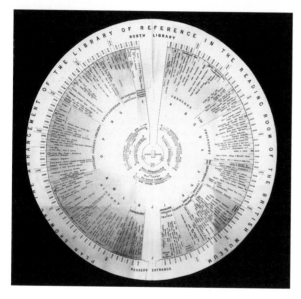

IN-002. British Museum Reading Room, London, England. Sidney Smirke, 1854–1856. In Edward Edwards, *Memoirs of Libraries, Including a Handbook of Library Economy*, vol. 2 (London, 1859), p. 701. GEN COLL,LC-DIG-ppmsca-15551.

IN-003. Diagram of the arrangement of the reference books by topic in the British Museum Reading Room, London, England. Sidney Smirke, architect, and Anthonio Panizzi, librarian, 1854–1856. P&P,LC-DIG-ds-06538.

IN-004. Bookstacks, British Museum Library, London, England. Sidney Smirke, 1854–1856. Donald Macbeth, photographer, ca. 1906. P&P,LOT 4484,LC-DIG-ds-06609.

IN-005. Bibliothèque Ste.-Geneviève, Paris, France. Henri Labrouste, 1844–1850. From *Revue générale de l'architecture et des travaux publics* (Paris, 1852), vol. 10, pl. 23. P&P,LC-DIG-ds-06552.

IN-006. Bibliothèque Ste.-Geneviève, Paris, France. Henri Labrouste, 1844–1850. In Edward Edwards, *Memoirs of Libraries, Including a Handbook of Library Economy*, vol. 2 (London, 1859), p. 674. GEN COLL,LC-DIG-ppmsca-15552.

is promised, what is allowed. One may be overcome by horror—at the clutter or the vastness, the stillness, the mocking reminder of everything one doesn't know, the surveillance—and some of that overwhelming feeling may cling on, even after the rituals and conventions are learned, the geography mapped, the natives found friendly."[4]

Foremost among libraries in America is the Library of Congress (LOC), whose collection comprises more than 162 million items, including more than 38 million cataloged books and print materials; some 70 million manuscripts; 14 million photographs; the greatest collection of rare books in North America; and the largest accumulation of legal materials, films, maps, sheet music, and sound and video recordings in the world.[5]

This book documents the history of library design in this country through images of American libraries that can be found in the Prints and Photographs Division of the LOC. The visual documentation that appears in this book necessarily has limitations. A census conducted by the United States Bureau of Education in 1900, for example, lists nearly 5,400 "public, society, and school libraries" with holdings of more than 1,000 books in the United States. As of April 2016, the American Library Association estimated that there were nearly 120,000 libraries of all kinds in the country, and over 16,500 public library buildings alone, the vast majority of them erected since World War II.[6] Images of very few of the later buildings appear in the Prints and Photographs Division, so we conclude the visual survey of libraries in 1950; a small sample of representative library images in the Afterword attempts to fill this gap.

# EARLY COLLECTIONS

While analogous to many of today's requirements, the needs of America's first libraries were somewhat less complex. During the eighteenth century even the largest of these collections numbered no more than a few thousand volumes simply stored on wooden shelves attached to one or more walls in a room set aside for the purpose in a larger building or residence. Before 1850, freestanding, purpose-built libraries were rare. Until the onset of the twentieth century, most private and subscription libraries, as well as public institutions, occupied the back room or upper story of a town hall or post office, the basement of a church or meeting house, or some out-of-the-way corner of a local store.

The earliest library building in America was raised in Philadelphia in 1745 by James Logan, who had a simple wooden structure erected to house a personal collection of several thousand volumes, which he made available to scholars and other interested readers (see 1-013). Three years later, the gentleman architect Peter Harrison (1716–1774) designed the more widely acclaimed Redwood Library in Newport, Rhode Island (see 1-026–1-029). Here, reading tables and the book collection shared a single one-story room set in a diminutive temple articulated with Doric columns supporting a classical pediment inspired by the work of the sixteenth-century Italian architect Andrea Palladio (1508–1580).[7]

Between 1750 and the end of the eighteenth century, only the Library Company of Philadelphia (1790) and the New York Society Library (ca.1795) were likewise able to erect their own edifices. In Philadelphia, the amateur architect William Thornton (1759–1826) introduced a two-story reading room bounded on four sides with floor-to-ceiling bookcases bisected by a light iron gallery that provided access to its upper shelves. Reflecting a typology that stretched back to earlier European prototypes, such as the Ambrosian Library in Milan (1603–1609) or the Arts End of the Bodleian Library at Oxford (1610 and 1613), variations on this form of hall library, or *Saalbibliothek*,[8] remained popular throughout the nineteenth century and the first half of the twentieth, especially for the conspicuous display of America's most valuable private collections, in buildings such as the J. Pierpont Morgan Library in New York City (McKim, Mead & White, 1902–1906) and the Folger Shakespeare Library in Washington, D.C. (Paul Philippe Cret, 1928–1932) (see 1-019–1-023).

In 1825, Thomas Jefferson transformed this hall library type into a centralized, two-story rotunda, which marks the construction of the first freestanding academic library in the country. This formed the secular focus of his new campus for the University of Virginia (see 2-003). While the lower floors of this edifice were given over to other activities, the book collection was ordered on the second story and surrounding gallery beneath a celestial dome modeled on that of the Pantheon in Rome, as was the building's exterior form.[9] A little more than a decade later, Robert Mills (1781–1855) proposed a rotunda plan for the reading room for a new library for South Carolina College (1836–1840, now the University of South Carolina (see 2-007–2-009). With its low-pitched gables and columnar porches, the South Carolina library reflected the Greek Revival style, an architectural fashion inspired in part by the rediscovery of classical Greek architecture during the middle of the eighteenth century. Its linear alcove system of shelving, which is attributed to Mills, was modeled on the library that Charles Bulfinch (1763–1844) designed for the Library of Congress, which was situated in the United States Capitol and opened in 1824.[10] While the American versions are two stories in height, this type of linear library arrangement descended from earlier European medieval and Renaissance institutions, such as Michelangelo's famous Laurentian Library (opened 1571) in Florence, or the University Library in Leiden (1795; IN-008). Two

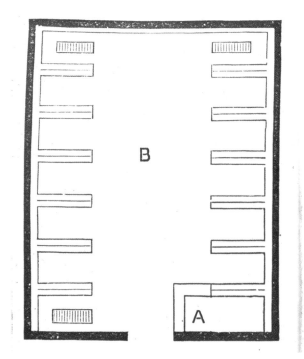
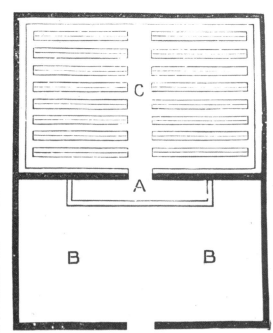

IN-007. Ideal plans for two linear libraries, with an alcove library to left, and a closed stack library with a reading room, delivery desk, and freestanding shelves to right. Original source unknown, mid-19th century. P&P,LC-DIG-ds-06547.

IN-008. Leiden University Library, founded 1595. Jan Cornelis Woudanus, delineator, 1610. P&P,LOT 3585,LC-DIG-ds-06510.

unidentified plans in the LOC depict variations on typical early linear library plans: one with book alcoves projecting from the edge of the room, and the other with freestanding shelves set in the center of a book room that is separated from a reading area with a delivery desk (IN-007).[11]

During these same years, Harvard College turned to a Gothic model for its first freestanding library building, Gore Hall (1837–1841), an edifice constructed to replace the aging and outmoded book room that had been located over the chapel in Harvard Hall since it was erected in 1766 (see 2-010–2-011). Borrowing its form from King's College Chapel in Cambridge, England, this imposing structure, which was designed by Richard Bond (1798–1861), was arranged to accommodate 100,000 volumes (the largest collection in the country at the time) in two-story alcoves similar to those at South Carolina College. Reflecting the Gothic style of a medieval cathedral, these flanked a 35-foot-high nave.[12] Over the following two decades, similar linear alcove schemes were erected by several dozen other educational institutions and private library associations in this country. These included the New York Society Library, for its second and third buildings (1840 and 1856), Yale College (1842–1846; see 2-012–2-014), and the Boston Athenaeum, which by the time it opened in 1859 was the largest and wealthiest subscription library in the country, possessing a collection that rivaled Harvard's. Thomas Ustick Walter (1804–1887) also adopted this paradigm for the Library of Congress in 1852–1853, replacing its earlier quarters in the Capitol building—which had been destroyed by fire in 1851—with this country's first fireproof cast-iron book room (see 3-007–3-008).[13]

A more unusual experiment in book storage appeared during the same period in the design of Thomas Tefft (1826–1859) for Lawrence Hall at Williams College (1846–1847). The basement level of this octagonal structure was divided into half a dozen wedge-shaped work and study rooms, while the collection—which occupied the upper two-thirds of the edifice—was shelved in wooden book-cases that radiated outward from a central reading area. According to the Unitarian minister and author Edward Everett Hale (1822–1909), who later collaborated with Tefft on a design for a new building for the American Antiquarian Society (1852–1853) in Worcester, Massachusetts, the "general idea" for this panoptic configuration was derived from the French librarian Benjamin Delessert (1773–1847), who had earlier proposed a much larger version of this scheme as a means of expanding the Bibliothèque Royale in Paris.[14]

## THE PUBLIC LIBRARY MOVEMENT

In 1848, John Jacob Astor left a bequest of $400,000 for the foundation and support of a free public reference library in New York City. While it remained private, this gesture nonetheless helped to trigger the early growth of the public library movement in America. As designed by Alexander Saeltzer (1814–1883), the book room of the Astor Library (1849–1854) merged the linear alcove and hall library forms (see 4-002). This space was encircled with alcoves subdivided by galleries into four eleven-foot-high tiers of shelving. At the same time that Astor's monumental reference room was rising in New York, George Ticknor (1791–1871) and Edward Everett (1794–1865) began to formulate a more radical vision for a free lending library in Boston. As conceived by its architect, Charles Kirk Kirby (1826–1910), and the library board, a large hall designed to accommodate a noncirculating reference collection of 200,000 volumes occupied the upper stories of a new edifice on Boylston Street, which was begun in 1855 (see 4-003–4-007). This monumental room was flanked on each of its long sides with ten alcoves that were divided into three tiers of galleries accessed by circular iron staircases. At ground level, a free lending library composed of 40,000 more popular books—one of the first of its kind in the country—was shelved in a smaller book hall that was located adjacent to a delivery area and several public reading rooms, including one reserved for women. With dedicated spaces for book storage and distribution, administration, and reading, the differentiation of functions exhibited in its plan placed this edifice firmly in the vanguard of modern public library design.[15]

While Ticknor's notion that a public library should include a free circulating collection would eventually have the greatest impact on the American library movement, it was the influence of the monumental book halls in Boston and New York that had the most immediate and striking effect on American library design. During the decade following the Civil War, almost all larger public libraries in this country, such as those in Brookline (1866–1869) and Springfield (1866–1871), Massachusetts, Cincinnati (1868–1874), Detroit (1874–1877), and Baltimore (1875–1878), constructed book rooms similar in form to these earlier models (see 4-010–4-014, 4-018, 5-005–5-006).

This widespread adaptation of the book hall was reinforced by the earliest literature on library planning available in this country. In 1853, for example, *Norton's Literary Gazette and Publishers' Circular* suggested that the "most suitable form" for a book room "seems to be a long and wide salon, well lighted from above or both sides." This space could be outfitted with bookshelves attached to the walls or arranged with alcoves and was to be joined to "some other smaller apartments" for administration and other library work. It was also recommended that a separate reading room should be included in the plan, so that patrons would "not be interrupted constantly by the noise of comers and goers."[16] Nathaniel B. Shurtleff in *A Decimal System for the Arrangement and Administration of Libraries* (Boston, 1856) and William Rhees in his *Manual of Public Libraries, Institutions, and Societies in the United States and British Provinces of North America* (Philadelphia, 1859) also advocated for a hall form of book storage. Rhees, as he acknowledged, borrowed many of his ideas from Edward Edwards's (1812–1836) even more influential and comprehensive publication *Memoirs of Libraries* (London, 1859). This two-volume work included descriptions, plans, and views of many of the most prominent library buildings on both sides of the Atlantic, including the Bodleian Library (1610 and 1613) and Radcliffe Camera (1737–1749) at Oxford, the Bibliothèque Ste.-Geneviève in Paris (1844–1850; IN-006), the Munich State Library (1832–1840), and the British Museum Reading Room in London (1854–1856; IN-002). Edwards also presented detailed descriptions of the new libraries in New York and Boston, and he included an additional chapter that made available in English a synopsis of other European literature on library design and administration.[17]

Encouraged by Ticknor and Everett's experiment in Boston, and made possible through state legislation modeled on an 1849 New Hampshire law that enabled individual municipalities to support libraries through taxation, the public library soon began to establish itself as a prominent fixture in the American landscape. While a handful of communities, such as South Danvers, Massachusetts (now Peabody; 1853–1854), and Oswego, New York (1855–1857), were able to erect dedicated library structures before the Civil War (see 5-001–5-004), it was after this conflict that a true building boom ensued. This boom was fueled by the rise of local philanthropy to fund the creation of ever more impressive library buildings, many of which (as in Peabody and Oswego) were dedicated as memorials to their benefactors or their families, typically with great fanfare. This surge in library construction created an opportunity for architects to propose a wide variety of architectural styles and arrangements to accommodate these institutions.[18]

## A NEW TYPOLOGY

Early experiments in library planning first coalesced into a recognizable library form, or typology, in the four public libraries designed by the Boston architect Henry Hobson Richardson (1838–1886) in Woburn, North Easton, Quincy, and Malden, Massachusetts, between 1876 and 1885 (see 5-018–5-027). In all of these buildings Richardson placed the collections in two-story, alcoved book rooms similar in disposition to that at Gore Hall, Harvard (see 2-011), where he had been a student. Critics then and now seem to agree that the most succinct of these monuments—where the architect achieved his greatest focus and clarity—is the Thomas Crane Public Library in Quincy. Here, a yawning entry arch and stair tower repose beneath an offset gable in almost perfect stasis (see 5-000). A prominent book wing to the left and a reading room on the right flank this central mass, completing the composition and architectural iconography of the building. Richardson's use of round arches, asymmetrical picturesque massing, and rock-face masonry, which loosely derived from the southern French Romanesque style of the eleventh and twelfth centuries, inspired a Romanesque revival during the last quarter of the nineteenth century. In honor of the power of this invention, this style is also often referred to as Richardsonian Romanesque. During the last decades of the nineteenth century, Richardson's new typology—iconographically and stylistically—would have a profound impact on the American architectural profession, with dozens of variations on his buildings appearing all across the United States.[19]

As a consequence of the formation of the American Library Association in 1876 and the appearance of its professional organ, the *Library Journal*, librarians also began to emerge during this period as significant critics of library planning—especially of the traditional type of interior arrangement that Richardson's two-story, alcoved book rooms represented. One of the earliest and sharpest of these detractors was Justin Winsor (1811–1897), who, as superintendent of the Boston Public Library from 1868 to 1877, had ample opportunity to observe first-hand the drawbacks of multistory book halls. He was joined by William Frederick Poole (1821–1894) in a series of articles that appeared in the *Library Journal* between 1876 and 1885, where he even more vociferously condemned their inefficient use of space, the damage caused to volumes by overheating in the upper alcoves, and the inconvenience they posed to library staff, who had to retrieve from these vertiginous galleries books for their patrons at a time when collections were still closed to the public. In place of the hall library, Poole advocated the employment of freestanding wooden bookcases set in high, single-story rooms, an arrangement similar to that at the University of Leiden (IN-008), which he presented in a model plan for a small public library building that was published in the *Library Journal* in 1885 (see 5-041). As an alternative to book halls and monumental reading rooms in larger institutions, Poole also proposed a subject-oriented arrangement of the collections,

a scheme he introduced at the Newberry Library in Chicago (1890–1893). Here, specialized departmental reference rooms, each with its related volumes shelved in freestanding bookcases and overseen by its specialized librarian, were distributed throughout the building.[20]

While Winsor advocated a similar form of freestanding shelving for smaller libraries, he also promoted more compact storage for larger libraries, similar to the stack systems that had appeared earlier in Europe at the British Museum in London (IN-004) and the Bibliothèque Nationale in Paris (1860–1867). "The first principle of architecture," he argued, should consist of "the primary adaptation of the building to its uses," not the creation of impressive public spaces. This meant that the form and location of the book storage system should be as practical as possible, or, as Winsor put it in 1876, "compact storage to save space, and short distances to save time."[21] Winsor's first opportunity to demonstrate these principles occurred in an addition that he devised in collaboration with the Boston architects William Robert Ware (1832–1915) and Henry Van Brunt (1832–1903) for Gore Hall at Harvard, where between 1875 and 1877 they created the first freestanding iron bookstack in the United States (see 2-031–2-033). This system consisted of six tiers of metal bookshelves hung from "iron skeleton uprights" that extended the full height of the building, and also supported an iron and terracotta roof and skylight.[22]

Although Richardson's impressive, yet generally impractical, book rooms often served as lightning rods for librarians' more general criticisms of contemporary architectural practice, it was—more than anything else, perhaps—the extended construction and debate surrounding the planning of the Library of Congress that served as the most significant catalyst for the profession's growing concern with library planning during the last quarter of the century. This debate began shortly after John L. Smithmeyer (1832–1908) and Paul J. Pelz (1841–1918) won the 1873 competition for a new library building to replace the cramped quarters it then occupied in the Capitol, and the debate did not die down until well after the Library of Congress opened in its new monumental building in 1897 (see 3-038–3-063). While this edifice incorporated a modern steel-and-iron stack designed by Bernard R. Green (1843–1914) to accommodate two million volumes, many librarians still vociferously condemned its extravagant lobbies and monumental reading room—which was modeled after the reading room in the British Museum Library in London—as an extravagant waste of space and money (see 3-041).[23]

The diversity of designs offered by other architects for the new Library of Congress building, in competition with Smithmeyer & Pelz, during the 1870s and 1880s reflect the growing eclecticism of American architectural taste during the last half of the nineteenth century. This eclecticism was represented by the revival of a wide variety of classical and medieval paradigms. Winning architects Smithmeyer & Pelz, for example, in an effort to placate an indecisive Congress, tendered proposals for the structure in the Renaissance Revival style (see 3-016) and in a more ornate "German" version of the same Renaissance genre (see 3-026). The former took the form of a monumental fifteenth-century Italian palace with round arches and classical columns. Smithmeyer & Pelz also submitted several Gothic Revival schemes, with pointed arches and a profusion of towers and turrets derived from European medieval buildings of the twelfth through the fifteenth centuries, as well as a variation on this style that employed colorful—or polychromatic—horizontal bands of brick and stone masonry of the type that the English critic John Ruskin (1891–1900) had promoted. Hence the latter was often referred to as Ruskinian or Victorian Gothic.

As collections expanded in America's larger libraries, the metal stack became the preferred method of book storage, while freestanding bookcases and modestly scaled stacks proved more practical for smaller collections, especially after the introduction of the first "open shelf" policies in these institutions in the 1890s. The new freedom enjoyed by library patrons in the country's smaller public libraries also encouraged librarians to endorse more open planning so that they could observe visitors from a single vantage point. This often took the form of a centrally located delivery or circulation desk. Progressive librarians at the end of the century also began to lobby for areas devoted to the needs of younger readers and eventually for dedicated children's reading rooms, often with their own separate entryways.

All of these late-nineteenth and early-twentieth-century innovations were touted in a growing corpus of literature on library planning and administration that was produced by library professionals during this era. While no exact consensus emerged on specific building arrangements or systems of book storage, the pioneering work of Poole and Winsor, along with that of other prominent librarians such as Melvil Dewey (1851–1931), William Fletcher (1844–1917), William Eastman (1835–1925), Arthur Bostwick (1860–1942), and John Cotton Dana (1856–1929), or the Boston book dealer Charles C. Soule (1832–1913), helped to place principles of utility and economy high on the agenda for new library buildings. Bostwick summarized this discussion in his aphorism "the Modern Library Idea," which he described in his 1910 book *American Public Library*.[24]

Much of the specialized furniture associated with these reforms, including complete shelving systems and bookcases, librarians' desks, card catalog cabinets and preprinted cards, even child-size chairs and reading tables, could be purchased through the Library Bureau, a librarians' cooperative founded by Melvil Dewey in 1888. Other firms, such as Snead and Company or the Fenton Metallic Manufacturing Company, also began to focus on the design and manufacture of library equipment. As the historian Abigail Van Slyck has demonstrated, the widespread impact of the more than $40 million expended by Andrew Carnegie (1835–1919) on library buildings between 1886 and 1917 helped to stimulate this new industry and facilitated the popularization of progressive planning ideals—especially as they applied to the design of smaller public libraries.[25]

# THE ROLE OF ANDREW CARNEGIE

Carnegie began his ambitious philanthropic project with the gift of a public library to Allegheny City (now part of Pittsburgh), Pennsylvania, in 1886 (see 6-003). Several others followed in communities in which this wealthy industrialist had personal interests. These emulated the Allegheny City building in general form and plan, often with the inclusion of large auditoriums, art galleries, swimming pools, gymnasiums, and even bowling alleys and pool halls (see 6-016). By the end of the century, the philanthropist expanded his giving (but for combined library and auditorium facilities only) to any community willing to provide a suitable site for a building and able to demonstrate that it had established a permanent means to contribute annual support for the purchase of books and the administration and maintenance of the institution. If his personal secretary, James Bertram (1872–1934), approved the plans, the philanthropist agreed to erect a structure valued at ten times this guaranteed local appropriation. By 1917, Carnegie and the Carnegie Foundation, which he established in 1911, had endowed 1,679 library buildings in the United States. While Carnegie agreed to finance the erection of a number of large urban libraries during the early years of his campaign, he quickly turned his full attention to the construction of smaller libraries in the country's hinterlands and branch libraries in its larger cities.

In the midst of Carnegie's campaign, Bertram, in collaboration with the architect Edward L. Tilton (1861–1933)—who promoted himself as a specialist in library planning—developed a set of design principles intended to streamline the review process for grant applications and to guide their prospective recipients. These "Notes on the Erection of Library Bildings [sic]" incorporated and disseminated to a wide audience many of the most important programming innovations that had been evolved by librarians and architects during the previous decades. Bertram's guidelines also illustrated half a dozen schematic plans for small library buildings (see 6-057). Following the lead of progressive librarians, these placed a strong emphasis on open planning so that, as Bertram stressed, "one librarian can oversee the entire library from a central point," the circulation or charging desk.[26]

In 1912, Tilton pushed this concept to its logical conclusion in his design for the second Springfield, Massachusetts, Public Library building; he developed the scheme in partnership with the library's director, John Cotton Dana (see 6-030–6-032). Here they all but eliminated interior walls on the main floor, utilizing low bookcases and glass partitions to demarcate the divisions of the library to either side of the central circulation desk. More frequently used books were shelved on this level—some in radiating bookcases—while less commonly requested volumes were stored in stacks in the basement. Building on this experience in Springfield, Tilton would further develop the open plan in schemes for public libraries such as those in Manchester, New Hampshire (1869–1871), Somerville, Massachusetts (1912–1913), and Wilmington, Delaware (1921–1922), as well as elsewhere during the post-Carnegie era.[27] The entrance of the United States into World War I brought a close to the Carnegie library campaign—as well as to most other building construction in this country—but Tilton continued to adapt the open plan in more than sixty army camp libraries that he designed in 1918–1919 as part of the Library War Service, an effort sponsored by the American Library Association and the Carnegie Corporation to supply books to American troops during the war (see 6-079–6-082).[28]

# CHANGING STYLES IN THE TWENTIETH CENTURY

Closely associated with the rise of the City Beautiful movement, the monumental classicism exhibited by so many Carnegie libraries was influenced by the rise in this country of a Beaux-Arts architectural educational system that was based on classical principles of design, as well as the impact of such popular events as the Columbian Exposition of 1893. The widely heralded appearance of McKim, Mead & White's and Carrère and Hastings's new public libraries in Boston and New York also contributed to this taste in library design, which began to displace Richardson's Romanesque Revival style as early as the 1890s (see 5-018–5-027). By the 1920s, schools of architecture and the profession in the United States expanded this Greco-Roman ideal to accommodate a multiplicity of Eurocentric interpretations of American history and destiny. These included the revival of a wide variety of early styles of architecture derived from the medieval and Renaissance eras of European, as well as American colonial, history.

Boston and New York also set the standard for America's larger urban and academic buildings. Following the example of McKim, Mead & White's Boston Public Library (see 4-024–4-032), which was itself heavily indebted to Henri Labrouste's design for the Bibliothèque Ste.-Geneviève, many of these later institutions disposed monumental reading rooms behind broad arcades of windows and arrayed the names of prominent authors across their facades. As in New York, and earlier at the Library of Congress, entryways were often aggrandized with broad flights of stairs, triumphal arches, and classical pediments (see 4-041–4-050). Elaborate ceremonial entry sequences, intended to impress patrons with the high-minded mission of these institutions, conducted them through the buildings and upward to massive card catalogs, centrally situated delivery areas, and immense public reading rooms.[29]

Improvements in electrical lighting and ventilating systems before and after the turn of the twentieth century facilitated the erection of ever-larger structures, with additional rooms for children's, periodical, and newspaper departments, special collections, and offices and workspaces for librarians, as well as greatly expanded book-storage systems. In New York, the main reading room, which encompassed a quarter acre of space, was oriented across the rear of the building atop a seven-story steel bookstack that supported seventy-five miles of shelving intended to accommodate eight million books (see 4-045–4-046). More commonly, these storage systems extended from the rear of the library. Whether behind, adjacent to, or below the reading rooms, these purely utilitarian storerooms were equipped with mechanical trams, conveyors, lifts, and other devices modeled on those first introduced at the Library of Congress (see 3-057–3-063) and in Boston during the late nineteenth century and designed to efficiently transport books from the closed stacks to public delivery desks.

While characteristically smaller in scale than their public counterparts, America's larger college and university libraries often followed the Boston model during the first half of the twentieth century, with impressive second-story reading rooms set in front of rearward-extending stacks. In style, these academic institutions typically adopted the fashion of other buildings on campus, which was often classical but could reflect the revival of many past European styles of architecture. Not surprisingly, the major exceptions in scale occurred at institutions such as Harvard and Yale. Widener Library at Harvard (1913), by Horace Trumbauer (1869–1938), was designed to house more than two million books (see 2-052–2-055). By the early 1930s, the Sterling Memorial Library (1927–1931) in New Haven would dramatically demonstrate the magnitude of its five-million-volume collection in sixteen tiers of shelving encased in a fourteen-story tower (see 2-070). At many universities, smaller, subject-oriented libraries were commonly located elsewhere on campus in their own library buildings or were housed with their associated departments or schools. Occasionally, wealthy alumni or patrons, such as Arthur A. Houghton Jr. (1906–1990) at Harvard, John Nicholas Brown (1861–1900) at Brown University, or William L. Clements (1861–1936) at the University of Michigan, endowed impressive memorial buildings—often modeled on the Morgan Library—to showcase rare book and special collections (see 1-019–1-025).

A limited number of subject-oriented departments, such as those devoted to business, history, or art and architecture, also could be found in large public institutions, where specialized reference librarians could assist patrons with these collections. William Poole had introduced this concept at the Newberry Library in the 1890s, but it was not until the construction of the Cleveland Public Library (1916–1925) that another major American institution fully embraced his scheme, now combined with modern compact storage (see 4-063–4-066). Here, the librarian William H. Brett (1846–1918), working with the architectural firm of Walker and Weeks, formulated a program in which books were arranged by topic in multistory stacks set around an open central court. Subject-oriented reading rooms, which were located adjacent to their associated collections, encircled these stacks around the exterior of the building in order to take full advantage of natural light and ventilation.[30]

Several years later, Bertram Grosvenor Goodhue (1869–1924) and librarian Everett R. Perry (1876–1933) embraced a similar scheme for the Los Angeles Public Library (1922–1926), one that placed a cruciform public service area in the center of the building, flanked by four stack towers (see 4-067–4-071). Related tiers of books opened into six departmental reading rooms and the reference department, which were located around the periphery of the building, again to allow a maximum of light and air to enter these spaces. In contrast to the classical articulation and massing of the Cleveland edifice, the varying functions of the Los Angeles library were freely articulated in its exterior massing and fenestration, while Goodhue's broad abstract surfaces were intended to communicate the progressive nature of the building's ferroconcrete construction. This was enriched with an elaborate sculptural program conceived by Goodhue and the poet and philosopher Hartley Burr Alexander (1873–1939) and realized by the sculptor Lee Oskar Lawrie (1877–1963).[31]

## OPEN PLANNING AND THE DEMOCRATIZATION OF LIBRARIES

By the 1930s, both the open-plan and subject-oriented library began to merge in programs such as that devised for the Enoch Pratt Library in Baltimore (1933) by its director, Joseph L. Wheeler (1884–1970; see 4-072–4-078). Working with Edward Tilton and his partner, Alfred M. Githens (1876–1973), who acted as consulting architects, Wheeler drew upon the modern department store as the model for his main service floor. Placed at sidewalk level behind prominent storefront windows (see 4-073), nine specialized collections separated only by low bookcases flanked a central circulation department. Each of these areas had its own staff and was tied to additional storage space in the basement by stairs and automated book lifts.[32]

While library construction abated somewhat during the Great Depression, public librarians continued their efforts to democratize this institution by offering library services to new constituencies through the introduction of bookmobiles and in makeshift quarters set up in migratory labor and refugee camps. Roosevelt's New Deal programs also sponsored the construction of a variety of public buildings, including libraries. These ranged from the monumental University of Texas Library (1931–1937) of Paul Cret (1876–1945), (see 2-072–2-073), to the new

IN-009. William J. Clinton Presidential Library, Little Rock, Arkansas. Polshek Partnership, architects; Ralph Appelbaum Associates, associated architects, 2000–2004. Carol M. Highsmith, photographer [between 1980 and 2006]. P&P,CMHA,LC-DIG-highsm-15677.

annex for the Library of Congress (Pierson and Wilson, 1935–1939; see 3-067–3-069). Toward the end of the Depression, Franklin Delano Roosevelt had a small presidential library (1939–1940; see 3-078–3-079) constructed in his hometown of Hyde Park, New York, in the Dutch Colonial style to reflect the seventeenth- and eighteenth-century architecture of the first Dutch settlers in the Hudson River Valley, where Hyde Park is located. This established a precedent for the proliferation of presidential libraries after the war, such as the William J. Clinton Presidential Library in Little Rock, Arkansas (2000–2004), which is housed in a 420-foot-long aluminum-and-glass box with 90-foot cantilevers at each end (IN-009).

The prewar culmination of open-library planning occurred in Brooklyn, where Alfred Githens and Francis Keally (1889–1978) employed this scheme on a grand scale in the new Central Library (1937–1941; see 4-085–4-093).[33] The structure was designed in the Art Moderne style, which mediated between the more austere functionalism of the increasingly popular Modern movement during the middle of the twentieth century and earlier revivals of past styles. Githens and Keally accomplished this by minimizing and abstracting historically derived ornament and sculpture and introducing into the design large expanses of flat, undecorated wall surfaces and dynamic, streamlined curves.

Detailed plans and descriptions of the Brooklyn Public Library, along with scores of others, were prominently featured in Githens and Wheeler's seminal publication, *The American Public Library Building: Its Planning and Design with Special Reference to Its Administration and Service* (1941). In this study the authors summarized more than a half-century of library planning theory and established standards for the design of these kinds of institutions for at least the next three decades. Keyes D. Metcalf (1889–1983) further reinforced Wheeler and Githens's ideas after the war in his equally significant book, *Planning Academic & Research Library Buildings* (1965). Here, and through his work as a library-building consultant after his retirement as Librarian of Harvard College in 1955, Metcalf championed the use of a modular system of construction with fixed interior columns placed to create the optimum flexibility in the arrangement of freestanding metal bookcases, reading tables, movable partition walls, and study carrels in broad horizontal rooms illuminated with fluorescent lighting (see 2-085–2-086). An early prototype for this new paradigm, the Lamont Library at Harvard (1947–1949), is well documented in the Prints and Photographs Division of the Library of Congress in the Gottscho-Schleisner Collection. Henry R. Shepley (1887–1962) of Coolidge, Shepley, Bulfinch, and Abott designed this undergraduate facility using a program devised by Metcalf (see 2-081–2-084).[34]

The prosperity of the 1950s, along with the thousands of veterans returned to school under the GI Bill, brought about a spectacular expansion of the nation's public colleges and universities. With a shifting curriculum placing more emphasis on research, hundreds of new academic libraries were constructed on these campuses, including many new undergraduate facilities. As returning veterans bought homes in the suburbs, the need for new public schools and libraries—or the expansion of older facilities—to serve them and their families grew as well. While the funding for these institutions and the erection of new buildings to house them fluctuated along with the economy, libraries during the latter half of the twentieth century were erected in record numbers and were often supplemented with new and expanded collections of books in the public schools.

While new technologies and shifting tastes in style have continued to alter the form and function of both academic and public libraries, the many innovations in library planning pioneered in the first half of the twentieth century continue to dominate the design of libraries to the present day. Ultimately these institutions (especially the public library) still serve as the most democratic of community spaces in America, serving all members of society as unique repositories of culture and knowledge accessible to all.

*Notes*

1. See Paula Young Lee, "Standing on the Shoulders of Giants: Boullée's 'Atlas' Facade for the Bibliothèque du Roi," *Journal of the Society of Architectural Historians* 57 (December 1998): 404–31; Jorge Luis Borges, *The Library of Babel*, trans. Andrew Hurley (Boston: David R. Godine, 2000); Umberto Eco, *The Name of the Rose*, trans. William Weaver (San Diego: Harcourt Brace Jovanovich, 1983); Alberto Manguel, *The Library at Night* (New Haven: Yale University Press, 2008).

2. P. R. Harris, *The Reading Room: The British Library* (London: The British Library, 1979), 11–17, The main reading room measured 140 feet in diameter and was set between iron bookstacks, which supported 25 miles of shelves.

3. Neil Levine, "The Romantic Idea of Architectural Legibility: Henri Labrouste and the Neo-Grec," in *The Architecture of the École des Beaux-Arts*, Arthur Drexler, ed. (New York, 1977), 351; and Henri Labrouste, "The Public Library at the Dawn of the New Library Science: Henri Labrouste's Two Major Works and Their Typological Underpinnings." Corinne Bélier, Barry Bergdoll, and Marc Le Coeur, *Henri Labrouste: Structure Brought to Light* (New York: The Museum of Modern Art, 2012) 164–79; and "A. M. le Directeur de la Revue d'Architecture," *Revue générale de l'architecture et des travaux publics* 10 (1852), col. 383.

4. Manguel, "Introduction," *The Library at Night* (New Haven: Yale University Press, 2008) 4–5.

5. Library of Congress, "Fascinating Facts," https://www. loc.gov/about/fascinating-facts/ (accessed April 21, 2016).

6. United States Bureau of Education, *Public, Society, and School Libraries*, Bulletin 1915, No. 25, Whole Number 278 (Washington, DC: Government Printing Office, 1901): 923; and "Number of Libraries in the United States," ALA Library Fact Sheet 1, http://www.ala.org/tools/libfactsheets/alalibrary-factsheet01 (accessed April 21, 2016).

7. Antoinette Downing and Vincent Scully, *The Architectural Heritage of Newport, Rhode Island: 1640–1915* (New York: American Legacy Press, 1951), 80–83.

8. Good sources on the early history of library archi-tecture are John W. Clark, *The Care of Books: An Essay on the Development of Libraries and Their Fittings, from the Earliest Times to the End of the Eighteenth Century* (Cambridge: Cambridge University Press, 1909); James W. P. Campbell. *The Library: A World History* (Chicago: University of Chicago Press, 2013), 91–151; and Nikolaus Pevsner, *A History of Building Types* (Princeton, NJ: Princeton University Press, 1976), 91–110.

9. Harry Clemons, *The University of Virginia Library, 1825–1950* (Boston: Gregg Press, 1972).

10. John M. Bryan, *America's First Architect: Robert Mills* (New York: Princeton Architectural Press, 2001), 268–72.

11. This is reproduced from a glass slide owned by Herbert Putnam, Librarian of Congress, which he presumably used to illustrate lectures on library planning and design. The source is unidentified but is similar to ideas concerning library plan-ning that were emerging during the first half of the nine-teenth century. See, for example, Leopold Constantin August, *Hesse's Bibliothéconomie; ou, Nouveau manuel complet pour l'ar-rangement, la conservation, et l'administration des bibliothèques*, new ed. (Paris: Roret, 1841); and Campbell, *The Library*, 91–151.

12. John Boll, "Library Architecture 1800–1875: A Comparison of Theory and Buildings with an Emphasis on New England College Libraries" (PhD diss., University of Illinois, 1961), 126–48; *Gore Hall: The Library of Harvard College, 1838–1913* (Cambridge, MA: Harvard University Press, 1917).

13. James Conaway, *America's Library: The Story of the Library of Congress, 1800–2000* (New Haven: Yale University Press in association with the Library of Congress, 2000), 46–48; Boll, "Library Architecture," 358–66; "The Boston Athenaeum," *Norton's Literary Gazette and Publishers' Circular* 2 (May 15, 1852); Boston Athenaeum, *Change and Continuity: A Pictorial History of the Boston Athenaeum* (Boston: Boston Athenaeum, 1976).

14. David A. Brenneman, "Innovations in American Library Design," in *Thomas Alexander Tefft: American Architecture in Transition, 1845–1860* (Providence, RI: Department of Art, Brown University, 1988), 61–67.

15. Harry Lydenberg, *History of the New York Public Library* (New York: New York Public Library, 1923), 1–25; Walter Muir Whitehill, *Boston Public Library: A Centennial History*

(Cambridge, MA: Harvard University Press, 1956), 34–47. For the early history of the public library movement in the United States, see Jesse H. Shera, *Foundations of the Public Library* (Chicago: University of Chicago Press, 1949); Sidney Ditzion, *Arsenals of a Democratic Culture: A Social History of the American Library Movement in New England and the Middle States, 1850–1900* (Chicago: American Library Association, 1947); Samuel S. Green, *The Public Library Movement in the United States, 1852–1893* (Boston: Boston Book, 1913); Rosemary Ruhig Dumont, *Reform and Reaction: The Big City Public Library in American Life* (Westport, CT: Greenwood Press, 1977).

16. "Hints upon Library Buildings," *Norton's Literary Gazette and Publishers' Circular* 3 (January 15, 1853): 1.

17. Nathaniel B. Shurtleff, *A Decimal System for the Arrangement and Administration of Libraries* (Boston: privately printed, 1856); and Edward Edwards, *Memoirs of Libraries, Including a Handbook of Library Economy*, 2 vols. (London: Trübner, 1859).

18. Kenneth A. Breisch, *Henry Hobson Richardson and the Small Public Library in America: A Study in Typology* (Cambridge, MA: MIT Press, 1987), 6–14.

19. Ibid.

20. Ibid., 221–27, 256–61; Kenneth A. Breisch, "William Frederick Poole and Modern Library Architecture," in *Modern Architecture in America: Visions and Revisions*, eds. R. G. Wilson and S. K. Robinson (Ames: Iowa State University Press, 1991), 52–72; William Landram Williamson, *William Frederick Poole and the Modern Library Movement* (New York: Columbia University Press, 1963).

21. Justin Winsor, "Library Building," in *Public Libraries in the United States of America: Their History, Condition and Management*, U. S. Department of Interior, Bureau of Education, Special Report, Part 1 (Washington, DC: U.S. Government Printing Office, 1876), 466.

22. William H. Jordy, *American Buildings and Their Architects: Progressive and Academic Ideals at the Turn of the Century* (New York: Doubleday, 1972), 326–27.

23. Helen-Anne Hilker, *Ten First Street, Southeast: Congress Builds a Library, 1886–1897* (Washington, DC: Library of Congress, 1980).

24. Abigail A. Van Slyck, *Free to All: Carnegie Libraries and American Culture, 1890–1920* (Chicago: University of Chicago Press, 1995), 25–43; Abigail A. Van Slyck, " 'The Utmost Amount of Effectiv [sic] Accommodation': Andrew Carnegie and the Reform of the American Library" *Journal of the Society of Architectural Historians* 50 (1991): 359–83.

25. Van Slyck, *Free to All*, 47–54

26. Ibid., 35–40.

27. Donald Oehlerts, "The Development of American Public Library Architecture from 1850 to 1940" (PhD diss., Indiana University, 1975), 117–21, 165–68.

28. Alfred M. Githens, "The Army Libraries and Liberty Theaters," *Architectural Forum* 29 (July 1918): 15–19.

29. Jordy, *American Buildings and Their Architects*, 314–75; Phyllis Dain, *The New York Public Library: A Universe of Knowledge* (New York: New York Public Library, 2000), 13–24; Samiran Chanchani, "Architecture and Central Public Libraries in America, 1887–1925: A Study of Conflicting Institutions and Mediated Designs" (PhD diss., Georgia Institute of Technology, 2002), 112–235.

30. Wheeler and Githens, *The American Public Library Building*, 317–19.

31. Kenneth A. Breisch, " 'A Source of Sure Authority': Library Building in Los Angeles during the Twentieth Century," in *The World from Here: Treasures from the Great Libraries of Los Angeles*, eds. Cynthia Burlingham and Bruce Whiteman (Los Angeles: UCLA Grunwald Center for the Graphic Arts and the Armand Hammer Museum of Art, 2002), 43–47; Wheeler and Githens, *The American Public Library Building*, 314–16.

32. Oehlerts, "The Development of American Public Library Architecture," 156–60.

33. Wheeler and Githens, *The American Public Library Building*, 332–34.

34. Keyes D Metcalf, *Planning Academic & Research Library Buildings* (New York: McGraw-Hill, 1965).

# 1 PRIVATE COLLECTIONS

During the eighteenth century, wealthy merchants and landowners privately accumulated many of America's earliest important book collections. While James Logan erected a small wooden building to house his library, others more typically placed theirs in a hall or room in their own residence. Whether for show or personal erudition, the intimate form of the personal, or "gentleman's," library has enjoyed an extended popularity in the homes of the wealthy, as well as in the guise of "domesticated" reading or rare book rooms in both private and public institutions. As America's prosperity expanded, individual exhibitions of culture and wealth grew in size and opulence, culminating in the lavish collections and monuments endowed by men such as J. P. Morgan, Henry E. Huntington, and Henry Clay Folger.

In parallel with the establishment of personal libraries, groups of individuals began to pool their resources to form collections through subscriptions and dues. After the Civil War, the proprietary associations began to be eclipsed by public libraries. In many instances, these earlier proprietary groups disbanded—especially women's library societies—and donated their books to the new, more democratic, American institution.

Opposite: 1-007, p. 36.

# RESIDENTIAL, OR "GENTLEMAN'S," LIBRARIES

The desire to own and collect books, and the nature of personal libraries that resulted from this urge, have changed little over time. Whether as working or professional libraries, or as a reflection of their owners' station in society, walls of books have supplied a degree of prestige and authority to their owners. For the less fortunate, a few worn volumes might represent some of one's most precious possessions.

1-001. Roy Takeno's desk, Manzanar Relocation Center, near Independence, California. Ansel Adams, photographer, 1943. P&P,Manzanar War Relocation Center Photographs,LC-DIG-ppprs-00277.

Roy Takeno was editor of the *Manzanar Free Press*, which was published by and for the inmates of this Japanese American internment camp from April 1942 until January 1, 1945. Takeno was born in Fresno in 1913 and had studied journalism at the University of Southern California. His library was a small but no doubt precious possession.

1-002. Central hall and library bookcases, Sabine Hall, Warsaw vicinity, Richmond County, Virginia.Landon Carter, 1730. Unidentified photographer, no date. P&P,HABS,VA,80-WAR.V,2-20.

Many country gentlemen during the colonial era of the country amassed relatively sizable libraries, which they often placed in the central passage of their rural estates in order to exhibit their wealth as well as erudition. Sabine Hall was the home of Landon Carter, one of the wealthiest men in the English colonies. At the time of Carter's death in 1779 his library numbered some five hundred volumes, which he stored in three mahogany bookcases that can be seen in situ in these HABS images, in the central passage of his house. What remained of this collection was removed and donated to the University of Virginia in 1979.

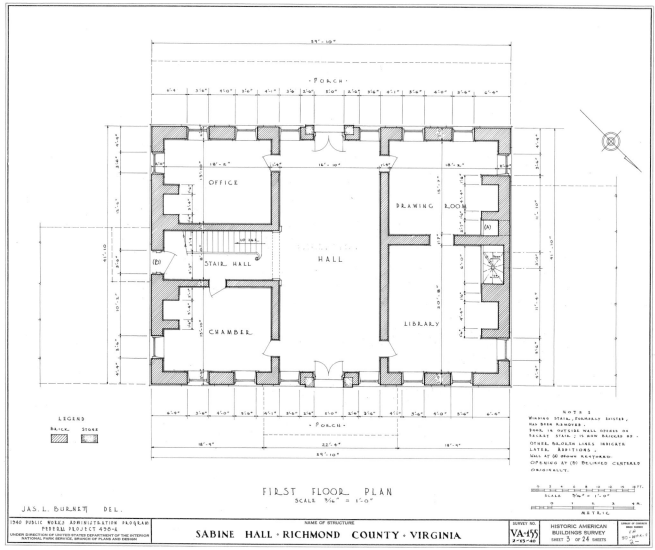

1-003. First floor plan, Sabine Hall, Warsaw vicinity,
Richmond County, Virginia. Landon Carter, ca. 1730.
Jas. L. Burnett, delineator, 1940. P&P,HABS,VA,80-
WAR.V,2-,sheet no. 3.

1-004. Monticello, Virginia. Thomas Jefferson, 1796–1809. Theodor Horydczak, photographer, ca. 1920–1950. P&P,HORY,LC-H814-M09-001.

By 1814, Thomas Jefferson amassed a personal library of between six and seven thousand books that he housed in the east wing of his home at Monticello, a villa that, like its ancient Roman predecessors, was intended as a place of retreat, entertainment, and study. In 1815 the books were sold to the federal government to become the foundation for the new Library of Congress, which had been destroyed when the British burned the Capitol building the previous year. A second fire in 1851 destroyed two-thirds of Jefferson's volumes.

1-005. Northeast wall, Library, Hayes Manor, Edenton vic., Chowan County, North Carolina. William Nichols, 1814–1817. C. O. Greene, photographer, 1940. P&P,HABS,NC,21-EDET.V,1-13.

The library at Hayes Manor is located in a small pavilion located to the left of the main plantation house erected by James Cathcart Johnston, who inherited an extensive library from his father, Samuel Johnston, the governor of North Carolina from 1787 to 1789. Despite the Palladian character of the plantation house as a whole, the octagonal room that he had built to display this collection represents a very early American example of the Gothic Revival style. What remain of the libraries of father and son are now housed in a replica of this room at the University of North Carolina.

1-006. Study of Ralph Waldo Emerson showing shelves of books, fireplace, and desk, Concord, Massachusetts. Copyright by Benjamin F. Mills, Boston, 1888. P&P,LC-USZ62-92337.

1-007. Library, Edwin John Beinecke residence, Greenwich, Connecticut. Gottscho-Schleisner, Inc., September 1942. P&P,GSC,LC-DIG-gsc-5a09045.

During his life, Edwin John Beinecke accumulated the largest collection of books, manuscripts, and works relating to Robert Louis Stevenson. He and his brother Frederick William Beinecke, who amassed one of the great private collections of Western Americana, donated their books to Yale University, along with an endowment to erect a building to house them. The Beinecke Library, which was designed in 1961 by Gordon Bunshaft of Skidmore, Owings and Merrill, is considered one of the great architectural masterpieces of the twentieth century (see AF-004).

1-008. Stevensonia, library, Edwin John Beinecke residence, Greenwich, Connecticut. Gottscho-Schleisner, Inc., December 1945. P&P,GSC,LC-DIG-gsc-5a12435.

1-009. Library, Paul Mellon residence, Upperville, Virginia. H. Page Cross, ca. 1945. Gottscho-Schleisner, Inc., June 1947. P&P,GSC,LC-G612-DIG-gsc-5a14000.

In 1966 Paul Mellon established the Yale Center for British Art, which houses his extensive collection of paintings and works on paper as well as the Paul Mellon Centre for Studies in British Art, in which his library now resides.

1-010. Library of the law firm Nemeroff, Jelline, Danzig & Paley, Empire State Building, New York, New York. Hans Weiss, designer, ca. 1944. Gottscho-Schleisner, Inc., 1945. P&P,GSC,LC-DIG-gsc-5a11652.

1-011. Model home library, Grand Central Palace Exhibit, New York, New York. Morris Lapidus, 1951. Gottscho-Schleisner, Inc., 1951. P&P,GSC,LC-DIG-gsc-5a17165.

This exhibit by the New York architect Morris Lapidus, like the Tillett library below, reflects the modest post–World War II counterparts to the great collections of previous eras shown on previous pages. Their prominent display reflects the fact that books still played a significant role in American family life.

1-012. D. David and Leslie Tillett residence, 170 East 80th St., New York, New York. Gottscho-Schleisner, Inc., 1951. P&P,GSC,LC-DIG-gsc-5a29493.

# FREESTANDING PRIVATE LIBRARIES

1-013. Loganian Library, Philadelphia, Pennsylvania. James Logan, 1745. In United States Department of Interior, Bureau of Education, *Public Libraries in the United States of America: Their History, Condition, and Management* (Washington, DC, 1876), pt. 1, pp. 7–8. GEN COLL, LC-DIG-ppmsca-15553.

By the mid-eighteenth century, James Logan, through his close association with the Penn family and his involvement in the early fur trade, had become one of the wealthiest men in the colonies and owner of one of its largest collections of books, which by the time he died in 1751 numbered some 2,600 volumes. He designed and endowed this small wooden building—the first freestanding library edifice in North America—so that his books could be made available to the public. The books and assets of the Loganian Library were merged into the Library Company of Philadelphia in 1792 (see 1-043–1-048).

LOGANIAN LIBRARY, 1745-'50.

1-014. General view from southwest, Stone Library, Adams Mansion, Quincy, Massachusetts. Edward C. Cabot, 1870. Cervin Robinson, photographer, 1962. P&P, HABS, MASS, 11-QUI, 5D-1.

Following instructions in the will of President John Quincy Adams that a fireproof building be constructed to house his library, his son, Charles Francis Adams, erected this two-story building in 1870. Here, he and his illustrious sons Henry and Brooks spent many hours working on their numerous publications.

1-015. General view of interior, from east, Stone Library, Adams Mansion, Quincy, Massachusetts. Edward C. Cabot, 1870. Cervin Robinson, photographer, 1962. P&P, HABS, MASS, 11-QUI, 5D-4.

Originally designed to house and exhibit the books of European royalty and religious institutions, the two-story book hall library, lined with impressive walls of books and encircled with a gallery, had by the nineteenth century become the province of the wealthy American gentleman. It would reach its apogee in the private libraries of men such as J. Pierpont Morgan, Henry Clay Folger, and Henry Huntington (see 1-019–1-024).

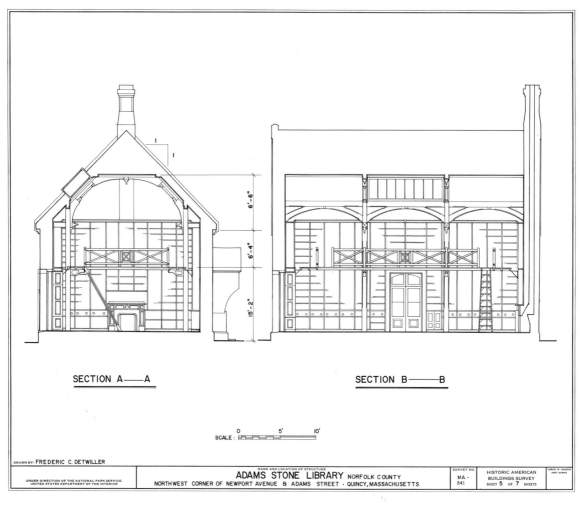

SECTION A——A

SECTION B———B

SCALE : 0 5' 10'

DRAWN BY: FREDERIC C. DETWILLER

| UNDER DIRECTION OF THE NATIONAL PARK SERVICE, UNITED STATES DEPARTMENT OF THE INTERIOR | NAME AND LOCATION OF STRUCTURE ADAMS STONE LIBRARY NORFOLK COUNTY NORTHWEST CORNER OF NEWPORT AVENUE & ADAMS STREET · QUINCY, MASSACHUSETTS | SURVEY NO. MA.- 841 | HISTORIC AMERICAN BUILDINGS SURVEY SHEET 5 OF 7 SHEETS | LIBRARY OF CONGRESS INDEX NUMBER |

1-016. Sections, Stone Library, Adams Mansion, Quincy, Massachusetts. Edward C. Cabot, 1870. Frederic C. Detwiller, delineator. P&P,HABS,MASS,11-QUI,5D-,sheet no. 5.

1-017. Library exterior, side view, Horace Howard Furness Estate Library, Lindenshade, Wallingford, Pennsylvania. Frank Furness, 1903. Ned Goode, photographer, 1962. P&P,HABS,PA,23-WALF,2A-1.

1-018. Horace Howard Furness seated at his library desk, Lindenshade, Wallingford, Pennsylvania. Frank Furness, 1903. Photocopy of photograph, early 1900s (in possession of Jayne family as of September 1962). P&P,HABS,PA,23-WALF,2A-5.

The noted Shakespearean scholar Horace Howard Furness is shown seated in his summer house library. His son Horace Howard Furness Jr. donated the Furness Shakespearean library to the University of Pennsylvania in 1933; there, it was housed in the library that was named for him, an edifice that had been designed by his brother Frank Furness (see 2-038–2-043).

# PRIVATE TREASURE HOUSES

A number of major collectors left their collections in trust, along with bequests or gifts of grand monuments intended to house and display them intact in elegant and impressive quarters. Often modeled on small Renaissance "casinos," these spaces explicitly invoke their earlier aristocratic roots, implicitly presenting their founders to the public in the guise of Renaissance patrons.

1-019. Morgan Library, New York, New York. McKim, Mead & White, 1902–1906. Detroit Publishing Co. 1908–1915. P&P,DETR,LC-DIG-det-4a22876.

The American banker J. Pierpont Morgan began collecting in earnest during the 1890s, eventually accumulating a vast collection of early printed books, illuminated and historical manuscripts, art objects, old master prints, drawings, and paintings. In 1902, he commissioned Charles McKim to design this well-known Renaissance Revival palace, which was constructed behind the Morgan brownstone on East 36th Street. In 1924, eleven years after his death, Morgan's son Jack established the library and building as a private, nonprofit institution and opened it to the public. The original building was enlarged with an annex four years later. In 1988 the house of J. P. Morgan Jr. became part of the museum section of the complex, and a garden courtyard was added three years later. With the completion of an addition by Renzo Piano in 2006, the library added new galleries, storage facilities, a restaurant, and an auditorium.

1-020. Main room, from entrance door, Morgan Library, New York, New York. McKim, Mead & White, 1902–1906. Samuel H. Gottscho, photographer, 1963. P&P,GSC,LC-DIG-gsc-5a29820.

1-021. Mr. Morgan's room, Morgan Library, New York, New York. McKim, Mead & White, 1902–1906. Samuel H. Gottscho, photographer, 1963. P&P,GSC,LC-DIG-gsc-5a29817.

1-022. Folger Shakespeare Library, Washington, D.C. Paul Philippe Cret, 1928–1932. Theodor Horydczak, photographer, ca. 1920–1950. P&P,HORY,LC-DIG-thc-5a47999.

The Folger Shakespeare Library opened in 1932 to house the Henry Clay and Emily Jordan Folger collection of Shakespeareana and other material relating to English history and literature of the sixteenth and seventeenth centuries. Henry Folger accumulated his wealth as president, and then chairman of the board, of Standard Oil. The building is located near the Library of Congress on property set aside for this purpose through a congressional resolution enacted in 1928. Paul Philippe Cret designed the white marble exterior in the Art Deco style, with aluminum door grilles and windows. Nine bas-relief scenes from Shakespeare's plays by the sculptor John Gregory and a freestanding statue of Puck by Brenda Putnam ornament the facade. Henry Clay Folger died in 1930 shortly after the cornerstone was laid for this building, but his wife, Emily Jordan Folger, lived to see it to completion. The Folger Library was opened in 1932 on April 23, Shakespeare's birthday.

1-023. View from the balcony at the west end, Folger Shakespeare Library, Washington, D.C. Paul Philippe Cret, 1928–1932. Theodor Horydczak, photographer, ca. 1920–1950. P&P,HORY,LC-DIG-thc-5a38380.

Cret's Elizabethian interior, with its lavishly carved ornament and medieval-style wood-beam ceiling, forms a strong contrast to the more modern Art Moderne classicism of the library's facade.

1-024. Aerial view of the Henry E. Huntington estate with the library to the right, San Marino, California. Myron Hunt, 1919–1925. Unidentified photographer, 1937. P&P,US GEOG,LC-DIG-ppmsca-15423.

By 1919, the year in which Henry E. Huntington—the developer of the Pacific Electric Railway Company and largest landowner in Southern California— signed the deed of trust in which he declared his intention to make his collection available as a research institution, it numbered more than 600,000 books and 2.5 million manuscripts. Huntington had the building that was designed to house and display this library constructed on his private estate, which, along with the gardens and house (seen in the lower left in this photograph), is now open to the public.

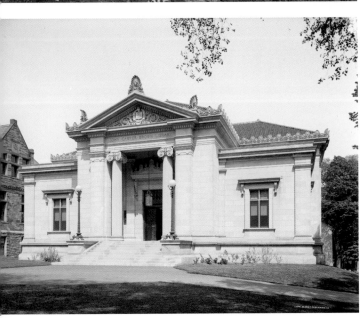

1-025. John Carter Brown Library, Brown University, Providence, Rhode Island. Shepley, Rutan, and Coolidge, 1904. Detroit Publishing Co., 1906. P&P,DETR,LC-D4-19700.

Along with buildings erected to display impressive individual collections on private estates or in the city, a number of donors erected small monuments, often loosely modeled on the Morgan Library, on America's university campuses to serve as repositories for their treasures and research centers for their faculties and graduate students (see also AF-004). Situated on the main yard of Brown University, this small Beaux-Arts temple was erected to house the extensive collection of Americana amassed by John Carter Brown and his son John Nicholas Brown.

# PROPRIETARY AND SOCIAL LIBRARIES

Following the model of Benjamin Franklin's Library Company of Philadelphia, which was established in 1731, merchants, women, mechanics, and workers across the colonies and in the new republic banded together to create a variety of athenaeums and lyceums; private literary, social, and circulating societies and clubs (often organized by women); and mechanics' and mercantile institutes. The smaller of these organizations commonly leased rooms or reused older buildings to house their collections and create spaces for reading. Before the Civil War, however, a handful of these institutions were able to erect their own buildings. The first of these was the Redwood Library in Newport, Rhode Island.

1-026. Photograph of a drawing by Pierre du Simitière of the Redwood Library in Newport, Rhode Island, in 1768. Peter Harrison, 1748–1750. P&P,HABS,RI,3-NEWP,15-1.

Gentleman-architect Peter Harrison designed the Redwood Library as a kind of diminutive Palladian temple, perhaps modeled on the Italian master's church of San Giorgio Maggiore in Venice (1565). Wooden Doric columns support a simple pedimented entryway.

1-027. View of exterior from west, Redwood Library, Newport, Rhode Island. Peter Harrison, 1748–1750. Cervin Robinson, photographer, 1970. P&P,HABS,RI,3-NEWP,15-3.

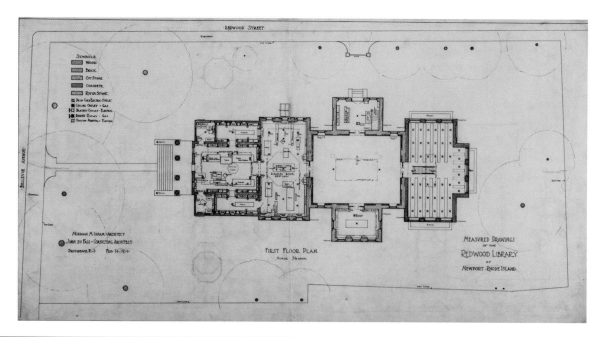

1-028. Photocopy of first floor plan drawn by Norman M. Isham, February 14, 1914, Redwood Library, Newport, Rhode Island. Peter Harrison, 1748–1750; George Snell, 1858; and George Champlin Mason, 1875. P&P,HABS,RI,3-NEWP,15-17.

1-029. Reference room, Redwood Library, Newport, Rhode Island. Peter Harrison, 1748–1750; Norman M. Isham, 1915. Arthur W. LeBoeuf, photographer, 1937. P&P,HABS,RI,3-NEWP,15-7.

The first reading room of the Redwood Library, shown here, measured just 37 by 25 feet. It housed the original collection of about 1,200 volumes on shelves attached to its walls. This room was restored to what was thought to be its original appearance by Providence architect and antiquarian Norman Morrison Isham in 1915. Two flanking wings, each only 12 feet square, enclosed a meeting room and additional reading space.

1-030. Library and Surgeons Hall, Fifth Street, Philadelphia, Pennsylvania. Dr. William Thornton, 1789–1791. Hand-colored engraving by William Birch and Son, 1800. P&P,LC-USZC4-559.

Benjamin Franklin founded the Library Company of Philadelphia in 1731—the first of its kind in the American colonies—when he convinced fifty subscribers to invest forty shillings each in this new endeavor. Sixty years later, the institution moved into this red-brick, Palladian edifice, which was

ornamented with white pilasters and a statue of Franklin set in a central niche. The Society remained in this building until 1880, when the collection was split between the Ridgway Library and a second building designed by Frank Furness on Locust Street (see 1-043–1-048).

1-031. The first New York Society Library building, Nassau Street, New York, New York, ca. 1795. Samuel Hollyer, engraver, 1909. P&P,LC-USZ62-92773.

The New York Society Library was established by subscribing members in 1754 and moved into its first building, which is pictured above, some four decades later. It was moved to a new Greek Revival building designed by Frederick Diaper in 1839 and then to its building on University Place a decade and a half later (see 1-037–1-038). In 1937, the institution was transferred to its present quarters on East 79th Street.

1-032. Front elevation, Boston Library, Franklin Place, Boston, Massachusetts. Charles Bulfinch, delineator, ca. 1793–1794. P&P,LC-USZC4-311.

This pavilion formed the centerpiece of Charles Bulfinch's Tontine Crescent, a residential complex of sixteen brick row houses that flanked it to form a great arc. The Boston Library Society, which was founded in 1792, occupied a large room behind the central Palladian window, with the Massachusetts Historical Society in the attic above it.

Front of Boston Library, Franklin place.

1-033. Athenaeum, Portsmouth, New Hampshire. Bradbury Johnson, 1805. Detroit Publishing Co., 1907. P&P,DETR,LC-DIG-det-4a13764.

This building was originally erected by the New Hampshire Fire and Marine Insurance Company. When the company went out of business in 1823, it transferred the property to the Portsmouth Athenaeum. During the 1860s, the center of the third floor was cut open to form a two-story library with an encircling mezzanine, which, along with the Athenaeum itself, survives to this day.

1-034. Providence Athenaeum, Providence, Rhode Island. William Strickland, 1831. Unidentified photographer, ca. 1900. P&P,LOT 8908,LC-DIG-ppmsca-15386.

With its monumental scale and two *in antis* Doric columns marking the entry, this building is a fine example of the Greek Revival style that came into vogue in the United States during the second decade of the nineteenth century. While the exterior remains largely intact, the interior was altered in 1868 and then again several times around the end of the nineteenth century. In 1906, Norman Morrison Isham added a rear wing to the edifice.

1-035. Northwest elevation, St. Francis Xavier Cathedral Library, Vincennes, Indiana. 1840. The Shores Studio, 1934. P&P,HABS,IND,42-VINC,1B-1.

The Reverend Benedict Joseph Flaget organized the oldest library in Indiana, the St. Francis Xavier Cathedral Library, in 1794. In addition to his books, this library continued to receive volumes from many well-known missionaries, priests, and others who were visitors to or residents of Vincennes. The small Greek Revival structure pictured here was erected in 1840 by Bishop Célestin de la Hailandière.

1-036. Perspective view from the northwest, Philadelphia Athenaeum, Philadelphia, Pennsylvania. John Notman, 1845–1847. Jack E. Boucher, photographer, 1972. P&P,HABS,PA,51-PHILA,116-1.

The Philadelphia Athenaeum was modeled on the London gentlemen's clubs designed by the British architect Sir Charles Barry, which themselves were intended to reflect the great palaces of early Italian patrons of the arts. This building is widely recognized as the first example of Renaissance Revival architecture in the United States. As such, it set an important precedent for other private library buildings and gentlemen's clubs in this country, such as the third New York Society building and the Boston Athenaeum (see 1-038–1-041).

1-037. New York Society Library building, University Place, New York, New York. E. Thomas and Son, 1856. E. P. McFarland, photographer, 1934. P&P,HABS,NY,31-NEYO,15-1.

This prominent New York subscription library, whose first building was erected in the late eighteenth century (see 1-031), occupied this building on University Place from 1856 until it was moved to its present location on East 79th Street in 1937. Books were arranged in three stories of alcoves (the main floor and two mezzanines) opening off of the longitudinal reading room that was located on the second story of the building.

1-038. Second floor reading room (looking south), New York Society Library building, University Place, New York, New York. E. Thomas and Son, 1856. E. P. McFarland, photographer, 1934. P&P,HABS,NY,31-NEYO,15-3.

1-039. Library of the American Antiquarian Society, Worcester, Massachusetts. Thomas Tefft, 1853. Unidentified photographer, ca. 1905. P&P,LOT 8908,LC-USZ62-104269.

1-040. Boston Athenaeum, Boston, Massachusetts. Edward C. Cabot and George M. Dexter, 1847–1859. Detroit Publishing Co., 1906. P&P,DETR,LC-DIG-det-4a13538.

The most lavish proprietary library erected in the United States up to this date, the program for this building called for galleries in which to display the Athenaeum's collections of painting and sculpture, with the principal library rooms located on the second floor. These consisted of a spacious hall that extended 114 feet along the rear of the building and two smaller rooms in front. One half of the large hall, which was bisected by a central diaphragm arch, displayed books and periodicals in glass wall cases, while the other was arranged in a series of wide alcoves set to either side of a central aisle. With an estimated capacity of fifty thousand books, this space was surrounded with an iron gallery that could be reached by any of five spiral iron staircases.

1-041. Book room, Boston Athenaeum, Boston, Massachusetts. Edward C. Cabot and George M. Dexter, 1847–1859. Charles Henry Currier, photographer, ca. 1908. P&P,LOT 1137-9,LC-DIG-ppmsca-15327.

1-042. Exterior, southwest elevation, Burlington Library, Burlington, New Jersey. 1864. Nathaniel R. Ewan, photographer, 1937. P&P,HABS,NJ,3-BURL,17-1.

The oldest library in continuous use in New Jersey, the Library Company of Burlington was chartered in 1757. This Greek Revival building was constructed in 1864, while the Library Company was still a subscription library. It is now operated in a newer building as a public library by the City of Burlington.

1-043. Library Company of Philadelphia, Ridgway Branch, Philadelphia, Pennsylvania. Addison Hutton, 1876. Detroit Publishing Co., 1900. P&P,DETR,LC-DIG-det-4a08434.

The Ridgway Library resulted from a large bequest for a new building made to the Library Company of Philadelphia by Dr. James Rush in 1869. Named for his wife and heir, Phoebe Ann Ridgway Rush, the central pavilion of this building was modeled on the Parthenon. Because of its location in south Philadelphia (which came about through the insistence of the donor's family), it was primarily used for storage, while a second building designed by Frank Furness on Locust Street became the more active reading room and lending library for the Society after it opened in 1880 (see 1-047–1-048).

1-044. General view of library interior, main room, from gallery, looking north, Ridgway Branch, Philadelphia, Pennsylvania. Addison Hutton, 1876. Jack E. Boucher, photographer, 1962. P&P,HABS,PA,51-PHILA,350-11.

1-045. General view of book room, looking east, Ridgway Branch, Philadelphia, Pennsylvania. Addison Hutton, 1876. Jack E. Boucher, photographer, 1962. P&P,HABS,PA,51-PHILA,350-14.

The books at the Ridgway were stored in multistory iron stacks, with a central light well.

1-046. Staircase and bridge detail, book room, second floor, Ridgway Branch, Philadelphia, Pennsylvania. Addison Hutton, 1876. Jack E. Boucher, photographer, 1962. P&P,HABS,PA,51-PHILA,350-17.

1-047. Library Company of Philadelphia, Locust Street, Philadelphia, Pennsylvania. Frank Furness, 1879–1880. Unidentified photographer, 1880–1890. P&P,LOT 8908,LC-DIG-ppmsca-15348.

Frank Furness's design for this building was chosen in an 1879 competition because it recalled the earlier William Thornton building on Fifth Street (see 1-030). It was demolished in 1940.

1-048. Library Company of Philadelphia, Locust Street, Philadelphia, Pennsylvania. Frank Furness, 1879–1880. Unidentified photographer, 1900–1905. P&P,LOT 8908,LC-DIG-ppmsca-15420.

1-049. Portland Library Association, Portland, Oregon. Chamberlain and Whidden, 1890–1893. Unidentified photographer, ca. 1893. P&P, LOT 8908 LC-DIG-ds-06550.

This subscription library was constructed with moneys from a $130,000 bequest to the Association by Miss Ella M. Smith. It bears strong resemblance to McKim, Mead & White's Boston Public Library (see 4-025), which was then under construction in the city where Chamberlain and Whidden had their office.

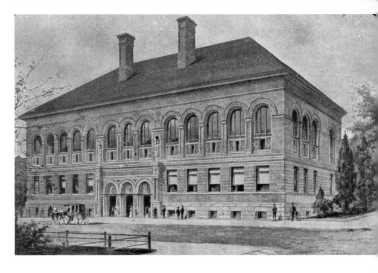

# COMMERCIAL LIBRARIES, BOOKSTORES, AND BOOK DEALERS

Besides providing materials for private collectors and libraries, bookstores have long served as community gathering places for book lovers, as well as centers of political and social action. During the eighteenth and nineteenth centuries, many book dealers also established commercial circulating libraries.

1-050. "The first circulating library in Boston was established by John Main in November, 1765." In calendar, 1939. P&P,LC-USZ62-99619.

John Main, a bookseller from Edinburgh, opened a bookstore and commercial circulating library in 1765 in Boston on King (now State) Street. He advertised his offerings in a catalog that listed some 1,200 books in literature, science, and the arts. This store closed in 1769 when Main, who supported British colonial policy, was attacked by an angry mob and returned to Great Britain. This depiction of Main amid his books appeared in 1939 in a calendar blotter used as an advertisement for the First National Bank of Boston.

1-051. Bookshop window, Chicago, llinois. John Vachon, photographer, 1940. P&P,FSA,LC-USF33-001961-M3.

Photographs of bookshop windows record a bygone era in book retailing that has been all but eliminated by new e-commerce enterprises such as Amazon, or the move of rare and commercial book dealers from physical spaces to the Internet. They were once a common sight on America's main streets

1-052. Dover Book Shop, business at 2672 Broadway, New York, New York. Gottscho-Schleisner, Inc., 1945. P&P,GSC,LC-DIG-gsc-5a11728.

# 2 ACADEMIC LIBRARIES

Because they possessed many of the country's largest collections of books, colleges and universities pioneered many innovations in American library design. The University of Virginia, Williams, Union, Princeton, and Brown all experimented with some form of centralized, or panoptic, arrangement, typically with a central desk or area from which librarians could observe the surrounding space, while Harvard introduced a metal stack system at Gore Hall (see 2-031–2-033). By the early twentieth century, universities were forced to erect new buildings capable of housing several million volumes along with a multitude of other university functions.

Before the middle of the nineteenth century, however, only a handful of institutions were of a size that warranted the construction of an independent building. At Harvard College even the most expansive of eighteenth-century American collections was housed after the rebuilding of Harvard Hall in 1766 in a 30- by 45-foot room set over the chapel. As reconstructed by library historian John Boll, the arrangement of this room followed earlier European precedents, with volumes shelved in tall, two-sided cases arranged in alcoves, five to either side of a central corridor (see IN-007). Libraries at Yale, Brown, and elsewhere appear to have been similarly configured.

Opposite: 2-014, p. 63.

# EARLY ACADEMIC LIBRARIES

Because the curriculum of America's colleges was primarily limited to the liberal arts and religion before the middle of the nineteenth century, most schools possessed only small collections of books, and access to them was often restricted to no more than a few hours per week. They thus required relatively little dedicated space for storage and reading.

2-001. "The prospect of the colledges [*sic*] in Cambridge in New England," The Burgis Engraving, Cambridge, Massachusetts. William Burgis, engraver, 1726. Re-engraved by Sidney L. Smith, 1906. P&P,LC-USZ62-86631.

Before it was destroyed by fire in 1764, the first library at Harvard, which included some 400 books left to the college by John Harvard at his death in 1638, was located in a small room on the second story of Harvard Hall. This is the building on the left in the Burgis Engraving. Its first printed catalog of 1723 lists a holding of some 3,500 volumes. It was moved to the new Harvard Hall (the central building in the print) when it was completed in 1766. By 1825, the collection, the largest in the country at the time, numbered some 25,000 books and pamphlets. In 1841 it was transferred to Gore Hall, which was designed to shelve 100,000 volumes (see 2-010–2-011).

2-002. Front elevation, University Hall, Brown University, Providence, Rhode Island. Attributed to Joseph Brown, 1770. Arthur W. LeBoeuf, photographer, 1937. P&P,HABS,RI,4-PROV,81A-1.

The Brown library was first housed in a single room in University Hall but was then moved to the first floor of Manning Hall in 1834, where it was situated beneath the chapel until 1878, when it was transferred to Robinson Hall (see 2-006, 2-028–2-030).

2-003. Panoramic view, University of Virginia, Charlottesville, Virginia. Thomas Jefferson, 1817–1826. Haines Photo Company, 1909. P&P,LC-USZ62-124513.

Not until 1825, when Thomas Jefferson's Rotunda was completed at the University of Virginia, did an American college or university possess a freestanding, purpose-built library. Even here, the bottom two stories were given over to other activities. The classical form of this edifice, which was derived from the Roman Pantheon, and its central position in the layout of the campus, seem to have been suggested to Jefferson by his colleague Benjamin Henry Latrobe. The Rotunda can be seen in this view at the far end of what Jefferson called his "academical village," which was composed of ten pavilions set to either side of a broad green. Its freestanding form and prominent location mark the library as a new secular focal point of the university in this Age of Enlightenment.

2-004. Rotunda (library), University of Virginia, Charlottesville, Virginia. Thomas Jefferson, 1817–1826. Unidentified photographer, after 1933. P&P,HABS,VA,2-CHAR,1A-1.

2-005. Rotunda (library), University of Virginia, Charlottesville, Virginia. Thomas Jefferson, 1817–1826. Unidentified photographer, ca. 1898. P&P,LC-DIG-ds-06610.

In 1895, Jefferson's Rotunda was gutted by fire and then rebuilt by Stanford White of McKim, Mead & White between 1896 and 1898; this is the interior shown in this view. The library was restored to Jefferson's original design between 1973 and 1976.

2-006. Front view, Manning Hall, Brown University, Providence, Rhode Island. Russell Warren, Tallman, and Bucklin, 1834. Arthur W. LeBoeuf, photographer, 1937. P&P,HABS,RI,4-PROV,81B-1.

# LINEAR ALCOVE LIBRARIES

The first linear alcove library in this country appears to have been suggested by Benjamin Henry Latrobe in one of his designs for the United States Capitol, a scheme that was later realized by his successor, Charles Bulfinch (see 3-003–3-006). The continued popularity of multistory alcove libraries in the United States may have been further stimulated by the appearance of two early European manuals on library management, both of which advocated this type of arrangement: Leopold August Constantin Hesse's *Bibliothéconomie* (Paris, 1841) and J. A. F. Schmidt's *Handbuch der Bibliothekwissenschaft* (Weimer, 1840).

2-007. South and west views (front), looking northeast, Library, University of South Carolina, Columbia, South Carolina. Attributed to Robert Mills, 1836–1840. M. B. Paine, photographer, 1934. P&P,HABS,SC,40-COLUM,2A-1.

2-008. Main reading room looking east, Library, University of South Carolina, Columbia, South Carolina. Attributed to Robert Mills, 1836–1840. M. B. Paine, photographer, 1934. P&P,HABS,SC,40-COLUM,2A-4.

The design for this two-story alcove library room for South Carolina College (now the University of South Carolina), which is attributed to Robert Mills, appears to have been based on Charles Bulfinch's library for the United States Capitol. Since a fire destroyed the Bulfinch room in 1851, the arrangement of the South Carolina library offers some idea of the appearance of the original Congressional Library (see 3-005–3-006). The library is illuminated with a series of round skylights that hover over the central hall and windows at the mezzanine level.

2-009. View from north gallery, Library, University of South Carolina, Columbia, South Carolina. Attributed to Robert Mills, 1836–1840. C. O. Greene, photographer, 1940. P&P,HABS,SC,40-COLUM,2A-8.

2-010. Gore Hall, Harvard College, Cambridge, Massachusetts. Richard Bond, 1837–1841. Unidentified photographer, ca. 1905. P&P,LC-DIG-ppmsca-15344.

Resembling a medieval Gothic chapel, Harvard's first purpose-built library was planned in the form of an elongated cross, with a 140-foot nave bisected by somewhat shorter transepts. Books were shelved in two-story alcoves that opened off of the central reading area. Ware and Van Brunt's metal stack addition of 1875–1877 (see 2-031–2-033) can be seen to the right of the earlier structure.

2-011. Gore Hall, Harvard University, Cambridge, Massachusetts. Richard Bond, 1837–1841. Unidentified photographer, between 1890 and 1910. In Scrapbook HS M2 in the AIA/AAF Collection, p. 41. P&P,LC-DIG-ds-06525.

2-012. East front, facing campus, Dwight Hall, Yale University, New Haven, Connecticut. Henry Austin, 1842. Ned Goode, photographer, 1964. P&P,HABS,CONN,5-NEWHA,6B-1.

2-013. Engraving of the east facade and floor plan, Dwight Hall, Yale University, New Haven, Connecticut. Henry Austin, 1842. D. C. Hinman, delineator. From *The New Englander* I, no. III (July 1843), between pp. 304 and 307. Photocopy from Yale Memorabilia, Yale University Sterling Memorial Library. P&P,HABS,CONN,5-NEWHA,6B-12.

The plan for the Yale College Library called for a series of five parallel rooms. The central hall had two-story alcoves, which echoed the scheme of Gore Hall at Harvard. This building was converted into Dwight Memorial Chapel in 1931, an appropriate new use given its Gothic Revival style, which, as at Harvard, is said to have been derived from King's College Chapel in Cambridge, England.

2-014. Interior of nave facing east, prior to 1931, Dwight Hall, Yale University, New Haven, Connecticut. Henry Austin, 1842. Photocopy, Yale University, Art Library, Art and Architecture Building. P&P,HABS,CONN,5-NEWHA,6B-5.

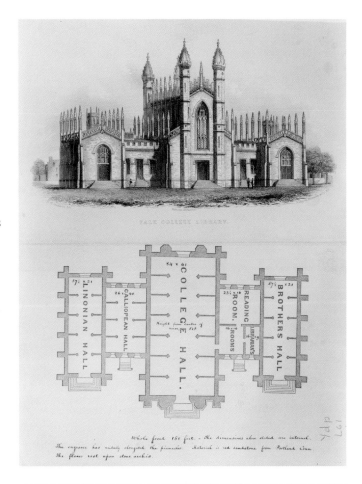

2-015. Facade (east) and south view, Gardiner A. Sage Library, New Brunswick Theological Seminary, New Brunswick, New Jersey. Detlef Lienau, 1875. Jack E. Boucher, photographer, December 1959. P&P,HABS,NJ,12-NEBRU,8-1.

Appropriately for a theological seminary, the design of the Gardiner A. Sage Library is said to be in the form of a fourth-century, early Christian basilica, with a high central nave illuminated with clerestory windows. The books were stored in two-story alcoves set in what would have been the side aisles of a church.

2-016. View of interior, facing northwest, Gardiner A. Sage Library, New Brunswick Theological Seminary, New Brunswick, New Jersey. Detlef Lienau, 1875. Jack E. Boucher, photographer, December 1959. P&P,HABS,NJ,12-NEBRU,8-5.

2-017. Billings Memorial Library, University of Vermont, Burlington, Vermont. Henry Hobson Richardson, 1883–1886. Detroit Publishing Co., 1902. P&P,DETR,LC-D4-16111.

The exterior elevation of this building is closely related to that of the architect's first public library at Woburn, Massachusetts (see 5-018), which its donor, Frederick Billings, specifically requested Richardson to emulate.

2-018. Book room, Billings Memorial Library, University of Vermont, Burlington, Vermont. Henry Hobson Richardson, 1883–1886. Unidentified photographer, ca. 1886. P&P, LOT 8908, LC-DIG-ppmsca-15376.

In addition to Richardson's trademark linear alcove book room, which echoes similar spaces in his earlier public libraries (see 5-019), the Billings Library also enclosed a polygonal reading room with two stories of shallow, radiating alcoves. This space was intended to house some 12,000 volumes, which Frederick Billings had purchased for the university from the estate of George Perkins Marsh.

2-019. Reading room, Billings Memorial Library, University of Vermont, Burlington, Vermont. Henry Hobson Richardson, 1883–1886. Unidentified photographer, ca. 1886. P&P, LC-DIG-ppmsca-15375.

2-020. Wilson Library, Dartmouth College, Hanover, New Hampshire. Samuel Thayer, 1884–1886. Detroit Publishing Co., ca. 1900. P&P,DETR,LC-DIG-det-4a08331.

The strong influence of the work of Henry Hobson Richardson at the end of the nineteenth century can be seen in the campus libraries at Dartmouth, Ohio State University, and the University of Kansas. His impact on the design of the small American public library was even more profound (see 5-018–5-027).

2-021. Orton Memorial Library of Geology and the Orton Geological Museum, Ohio State University, Columbus, Ohio. Detroit Publishing Co., 1900–1906. P&P,DETR,LC-DIG-det-4a11659.

Befitting the character of its collection, this Richardsonian Romanesque building was constructed using forty types of Ohio stone arranged like the geological strata of the state, with earlier geological specimens forming the lower parts of the structure and more recent specimens above.

2-022. Spooner Hall, University of Kansas, Lawrence, Kansas. Van Brunt & Howe, 1893–1894. Unidentified photographer [between 1894 and 1910?]. In Scrapbook HS M2 in the AIA/AAF Collection, p. 51. P&P,LC-DIG-ds-06527.

Spooner Hall, which was designed by the Kansas City firm of Van Brunt & Howe, was financed with a bequest of $91,000 from the Boston merchant William B. Spooner. Henry Van Brunt, who was a strong proponent of the Romanesque Revival at the end of the nineteenth century, had previously been in partnership in Boston with William Ware. Van Brunt and Ware had earlier designed the extension and metal stack system at Harvard (see 2-057–2-059), and the library at the University of Michigan (see 2-031–2-037).

# THE PANOPTIC PLAN

Although preceded by Thomas Jefferson's centralized library room for the University of Virginia, the panoptic plan was touted as a means of enlarging the Royal Library in Paris (now the Bibliothèque Nationale) by Benjamin Delessert in his book *Mémoire sur la Bibliothèque Royale* (Paris, 1835). The opening of the British Museum Reading Room in 1856 (see IN-002) further popularized this form and also had a profound effect on designs submitted to the competition for a new building for the Library of Congress in 1873 (see 3-013–3-028). According to an article that appeared in *Norton's Literary Gazette and Publishers' Circular* in 1853, Thomas Tefft developed the first panoptic library plan for Lawrence Hall at Williams College "under the direction of Prof. C. C. Jewett," who was then the college's librarian. When completed in 1847, it represented the first comprehensive attempt to incorporate modern library planning theory into the arrangement of an American library building. According to Jewett, it was "one of the few" libraries "in the planning of which the *internal conveniences* have been primarily consulted."

2-023. Nott Memorial Library, Union College, Schenectady, New York. Edward Tuckerman Potter, 1858–1876. Unidentified photographer, no date. P&P,HABS,NY,47-SCHE,9C-2.

Edward Tuckerman Potter's memorial sits on the site where the campus's original designer, French architect Joseph-Jacques Ramée, had intended to construct a classical rotunda, which was probably to be used as a chapel.

2-024. Nott Memorial Library, Union College, Schenectady, New York. Edward Tuckerman Potter, 1858–1876. Unidentified photographer, no date. P&P,HABS,NY,47-SCHE,9C-7.

2-025. Chancellor Green Library, Princeton University, Princeton, New Jersey. William Appleton Potter, 1873. Jack E. Boucher, photographer, 1964. P&P,HABS,NJ,11-PRINT,4D-1.

2-026. Reading room and plan, Chancellor Green Library, Princeton University, Princeton, New Jersey. William Appleton Potter, 1873. From *Library Journal*, vol. 2, no. 2 (October 1877), opposite p. 54. GEN COLL,LC-DIG-ppmsca-15574.

In the Ruskinian Gothic style, like his older brother's Nott Memorial Library at Union College, William Appleton Potter's Princeton configuration is an excellent example of the classic panoptic library. Because double-sided bookcases radiate from the central desk, the staff could easily observe all of the library's users.

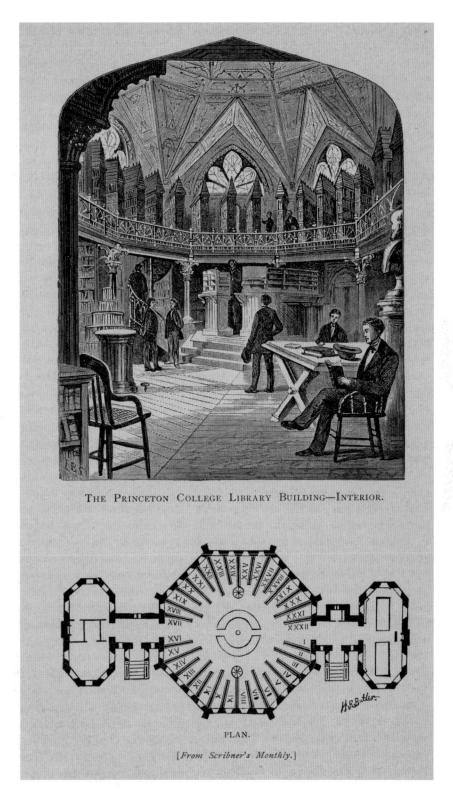

THE PRINCETON COLLEGE LIBRARY BUILDING—INTERIOR.

PLAN.

[*From Scribner's Monthly.*]

2-027. Reading room, Chancellor Green Library, Princeton University, Princeton, New Jersey. William Appleton Potter, 1873. Unidentified photographer, ca. 1905. P&P, LC-USZ62-104266.

2-028. South (front) view, Robinson Hall, Brown University, Providence, Rhode Island. Walker and Gould, 1875–1878. Laurence E. Tilley, photographer, 1958. P&P, HABS,RI,4-PROV,81C-1.

The design for this building, which followed an 1875 competition, was put forward at the time as one of the most progressive academic library arrangements in the country. Because the building was erected to accommodate a continually expanding collection that was expected to support a growing and diversifying curriculum, books were arranged by subject matter throughout the galleries and wings of the edifice, which were open to students and faculty alike.

2-029. North and west views, Robinson Hall, Brown University, Providence, Rhode Island. Walker and Gould, 1875–1878. Laurence E. Tilley, photographer, 1958. P&P,HABS,RI,4-PROV,81C-3.

2-030. Robinson Hall, reading room, Brown University, Providence, Rhode Island. Walker and Gould, 1875–1878. Unidentified photographer, ca. 1900. P&P,LC-DIG-ppmsca-15407.

# THE METAL STACK SYSTEM

Introduced in America at Gore Hall as an addition to the earlier alcove library, the freestanding iron and glass shelving system at Harvard was modeled on earlier stacks that had been constructed at the British Museum Reading Room in London (see IN-004) and the Bibliothèque Nationale in Paris. As book collections grew at ever-increasing rates during the late nineteenth and twentieth centuries, many of the larger academic and public libraries in the United States began to incorporate similar iron and glass shelving systems into their programs.

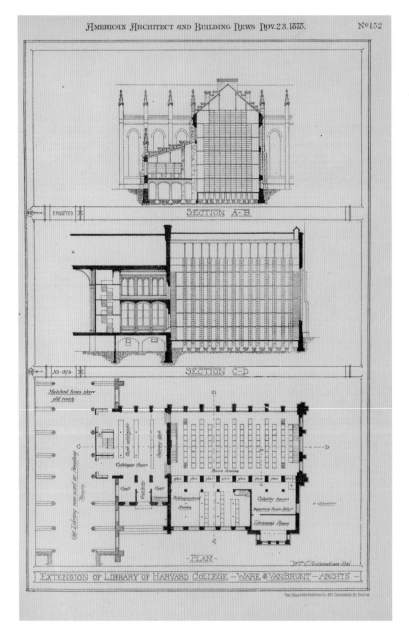

2-031. Extension of Library of Harvard College, Cambridge, Massachusetts. Ware and Van Brunt, 1875–1877. In *American Architect and Building News*, vol. 4, no. 152, November 23, 1878, opp. p. 173. GEN COLL,LC-DIG-ppmsca-15582.

At the third annual conference of the American Library Association in 1879, Henry Van Brunt proudly announced that "in this structure no sacrifice of convenience or economy has been made for the sake of any architectural pretense. The external aspects of the building are a legitimate growth from necessity, and have been adjusted so as to secure a proper and decent harmony of proportions and just significance of detail, no more, and no less."

2-032. Gore Hall, extension of the library, Harvard College, Cambridge, Massachusetts. Ware and Van Brunt, 1875–1877. In *American Architect and Building News*, vol. 4, no. 152, November 23, 1878, opp. p. 172. GEN COLL, LC-DIG-ppmsca-15581.

2-033. Original Gore Hall bookstack, Harvard University, Cambridge, Massachusetts. Ware and Van Brunt, 1875–1877. In Snead & Company Iron Works, *Library planning, bookstacks and shelving, with contributions from the architects' and librarians' points of view.* Jersey City, NJ, 1915, fig. 1. GEN COLL, LC-DIG-ppmsca-15558.

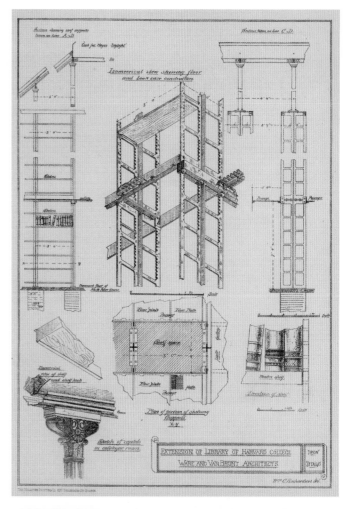

# THE MODERN UNIVERSITY LIBRARY

As collections and student bodies expanded toward the end of the nineteenth century, and as American academic institutions began to adopt the German university system, which stressed both teaching and scholarship, it became necessary to expand their library facilities as well. In addition to new undergraduate reading rooms and specialized seminar rooms, metal stack shelving became a common feature of these college and university libraries. Larger academic institutions by and large adopted the metal stack as the most efficient means of accommodating ever-increasing collections. These were typically appended onto large reading rooms and combined with a variety of specialized seminar rooms and workspaces for the staff.

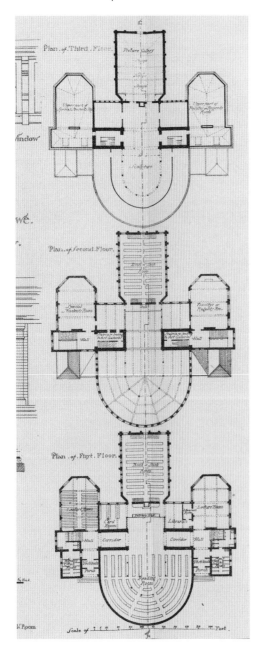

2-034. Main library, University of Michigan, Ann Arbor, Michigan. Ware and Van Brunt, 1883. Detroit Publishing Co., 1900–1910. P&P,DETR,LC-DIG-det-4a07511.

At Michigan, Ware and Van Brunt combined new spaces for work and study with a metal stack system of the type they had introduced at Harvard a few years earlier. In 1898, the stack was expanded to increase its capacity to 200,000 volumes.

2-035. Plans for the first and second floors, main library, University of Michigan, Ann Arbor, Michigan. Ware and Van Brunt, 1883. *American Architect and Building News*, no. 501 (August 1, 1885). P&P,LC-DIG-ds-06852.

2-036. Main library bookstack, University of Michigan, Ann Arbor, Michigan. Ware and Van Brunt, 1883. In Snead & Company Iron Works, *Library planning, bookstacks and shelving, with contributions from the architects' and librarians' points of view*, Jersey City, NJ, 1915, fig. 110. GEN COLL,LC-DIG-ppmsca-15559.

2-037. Main library reading room, University of Michigan, Ann Arbor, Michigan. Ware and Van Brunt, 1883. Detroit Publishing Co., 1900. P&P,DETR,LC-DIG-det-4a08608.

2-038. Library (Furness Building), University of Pennsylvania, Philadelphia, Pennsylvania. Frank Furness, 1888–1890. Detroit Publishing Co., 1900. P&P,DETR,LC-DIG-det-4a08444.

The program for this building, similar in plan to the University of Michigan library, was devised by Frank Furness's brother Horace Howard Furness in consultation with Justin Winsor and Melvil Dewey. Books were housed in an expandable iron and glass stack, which was connected through a delivery room to an expansive, sky-lit reading room. In 1933, Horace Howard Furness's son donated his father's library of Shakespeareana to the university, which in turn named this building for him.

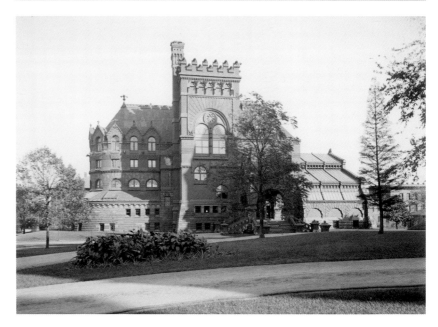

2-039. General view, Library (Furness Building), University of Pennsylvania, Philadelphia, Pennsylvania. Frank Furness, 1888–1890. Jack E. Boucher, photographer, 1964. P&P,HABS,PA,51-PHILA,566D-1.

2-040. Plan, Library (Furness Building), University of Pennsylvania, Philadelphia, Pennsylvania. Frank Furness, 1888–1890. In Talcott Williams, "Plans for the Library Building of the University of Pennsylvania," *Library Journal*, vol. 13, August 1888, p. 241. GEN COLL,LC-DIG-ppmsca-15575.

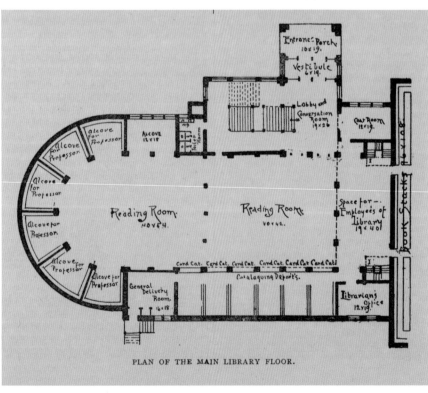

PLAN OF THE MAIN LIBRARY FLOOR.

2-041. Detail of spiral staircase, Library
(Furness Building), University of Pennsylvania,
Philadelphia, Pennsylvania. Frank Furness,
1888–1890. Jack E. Boucher, photographer, 1964.
P&P,HABS,PA,51-PHILA,566D-10.

2-042. Reading room, Library (Furness
Building), University of Pennsylvania,
Philadelphia, Pennsylvania. Frank Furness,
1888–1890. Unidentified photographer, ca. 1900.
P&P,LC-DIG-ppmsca-15371.

2-043. Library (Furness Building), University of
Pennsylvania, Philadelphia, Pennsylvania. Frank
Furness, 1888–1890. Jack E. Boucher, photographer,
1964. P&P,HABS,PA,51-PHILA,566D-9.

# RETURN TO CLASSICISM

Beginning in the 1890s, a new classical revival began to supplant the romance of Richardson's more picturesque Romanesque forms. It was inspired in part by principles of classical design espoused at the École des Beaux-Arts in Paris, which Americans began to attend in significant numbers toward the end of the nineteenth century. The Columbian Exposition of 1893 and the example of the Boston Public Library by McKim, Mead & White (see 4-025–4-032), who were major practitioners of the French-inspired mode of design, helped to spur this shift in taste. The regularity of plan and monumentality of form promoted by this aesthetic lent itself to the ever-increasing size of these institutions.

2-044. Gould Memorial Library, New York University, New York, New York. McKim, Mead & White, 1896–1903. Detroit Publishing Co., 1904. P&P,DETR,LC-DIG-det-4a11791.

Much as Jefferson had done three-quarters of a century earlier, McKim, Mead & White's plan for both New York and Columbia universities placed the library—in the form of a rotunda—as the centerpiece of the campus. Not coincidentally, Stanford White was responsible for the reconstruction of Jefferson's Rotunda after it was gutted by fire in 1895, as well as for this building (see 2-003–2-005).

2-045. Gould Memorial Library with School of Languages and Hall of Fame for Great Americans, New York University, New York, New York. McKim, Mead & White, 1896–1903. Detroit Publishing Co., ca. 1900–1910. P&P,DETR,LC-DIG-det-4a17427.

2-046. Panoramic view of Columbia University with the Low Memorial Library in the center, New York, New York. McKim, Mead & White, 1897–1898. Haines Photo Company, 1909. P&P, LC-USZ62-127401.

For the Low Library, Charles Follen McKim, following Jefferson's scheme at the University of Virginia, designed a domed rotunda, but with a central reading room flanked on four sides with bookstacks. Initially some of these spaces were given over to classrooms and administration, with the idea that the shelving would be expanded as the collection grew in size. This library replaced the library that had been erected on Columbia College's early midtown campus.

2-047. Low Memorial Library, Columbia University, New York, New York. McKim, Mead & White, 1897–1898. Unidentified photographer, between 1920 and 1950. P&P, LC-USZ62-118687.

2-048. The Library, Columbia College, Midtown Campus, Charles Coolidge Haight, 1884. Unidentified photographer [between 1882 and 1910?]. In Scrapbook HS M2 in the AIA/AAF Collection, p. 122. P&P, LC-DIG-ds-06536.

This was the library on the old Columbia College Campus, which was located in midtown Manhattan, before it was moved to its present location in Morningside Heights.

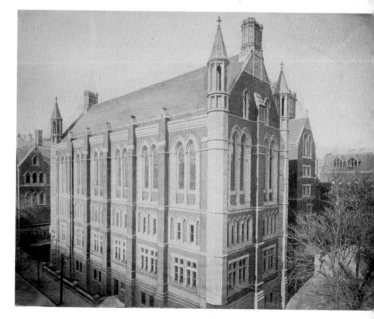

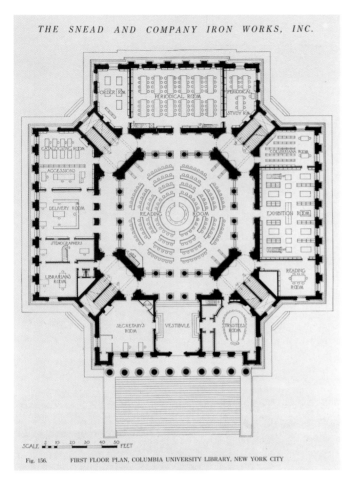

SCALE ... 5 10 20 30 40 50 FEET

Fig. 156.    FIRST FLOOR PLAN, COLUMBIA UNIVERSITY LIBRARY, NEW YORK CITY

2-049. First floor plan, Low Memorial Library, Columbia University, New York, New York. McKim, Mead & White, 1897–1898. In Snead & Company Iron Works, *Library planning, bookstacks and shelving, with contributions from the architects' and librarians' points of view*, 1915, fig. 156. GEN COLL,LC-DIG-ppmsca-15560.

2-050. Reading room, Low Memorial Library, Columbia University, New York, New York. McKim, Mead & White, 1897–1898. Detroit Publishing Co., ca. 1900–1910. P&P,DETR,LC-DIG-det-4a17284.

2-051. Snead Standard Stack in one of the third floor
seminar rooms, Low Memorial Library, Columbia
University, New York, New York. McKim, Mead &
White, 1897–1898. In Snead & Company Iron Works,
*Library planning, bookstacks and shelving, with contri-
butions from the architects' and librarians' points of view*,
1915, p. 149. GEN COLL,LC-DIG-ppmsca-15561.

2-052. Dedication of the Harry E. Widener Memorial Library on June 24, 1915, Harvard University, Cambridge, Massachusetts. Horace Trumbauer, 1913–1915. Unidentified photographer, 1915. P&P,LC-USZ62-83884.

The Harry Elkins Widener Memorial Library, which replaced Gore Hall (see 2-010–2-011, 2-031–2-033) when it opened, situated its central services in the middle of a large light court that was surrounded on three sides with Snead and Company metal stacks capable of storing 2,206,000 volumes in ten tiers of shelving. As at the Boston Public Library, which was also designed by McKim, Mead & White, a large reading room stretched across the upper stories of the building's facade (see 4-025). This became a standard scheme for many American academic libraries, such as the Ohio State University Library (1910–1913 or the Powell Library, University of California, Los Angeles (1929) (see 2-068).

2-053. Harry E. Widener Memorial Library, Harvard University, Cambridge, Massachusetts. Horace Trumbauer, 1913–1915. Detroit Publishing Co., ca. 1914–1920. DETR,LC-DIG-det-4a24856.

2-054. Second floor plan, Harry E. Widener Memorial Library, Harvard University, Cambridge, Massachusetts. Horace Trumbauer, 1913–1915. In Snead & Company Iron Works, *Library planning, bookstacks and shelving, with contributions from the architects' and librarians' points of view*, 1915, fig. 161. GEN COLL, LC-DIG-ppmsca-15562.

2-055. Catalog room, Harry E. Widener Memorial Library, Harvard University, Cambridge, Massachusetts. Horace Trumbauer, 1913–1915. Unidentified photographer, 1915. P&P, LC-DIG-ppmsca-15424.

As collections grew in size, dedicated card catalog rooms became the heart of the library. This was especially true in large academic libraries such as the Widener or large urban institutions, such as the New York Public Library, or the Library of Congress.

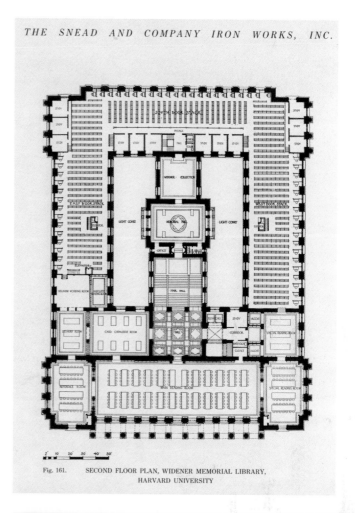

THE SNEAD AND COMPANY IRON WORKS, INC.

Fig. 161. SECOND FLOOR PLAN, WIDENER MEMORIAL LIBRARY, HARVARD UNIVERSITY

2-056. Thompson Library, Vassar College. Allen and Collins, 1905. Kadel Photo, Bain News Service, no date. P&P, LC-DIG-ggbain-50110.

Reflecting the growing academic eclecticism of the era, Allen and Collins, who would later design the Ohio State University Library in a classical idiom (see 2-058), turned to the English Perpendicular Gothic style for the Thompson Library at Vassar College. Mary Clark Thompson gave the building to the college as a memorial to her husband, Frederick Ferris Thompson, who had been a Vassar trustee and earlier benefactor of the library.

2-057. Thompson Library reading room, Vassar College. Allen and Collins, 1905. Unidentified photographer, ca. 1944. P&P, LC-DIG-ds-05705.

2-058. The Ohio State University Library, Columbus, Ohio. Allen and Collins, 1910–1913. Orr-Kiefer Co., photographer, 1915. P&P, LC-DIG-ds-06608.

The firm of Allen and Collins, as reflected in their designs for the Thompson Library at Vassar College, were primarily known for their work in the Gothic Revival style. At Ohio State University Library, however, they developed a Classical Revival building with, in the tradition of the Boston Public Library (see 4-025), a grand reading room on the second floor of the building.

2-059. Elevation sketch study, Library (Battle Hall), University of Texas, Austin, Texas. Cass Gilbert, ca. 1909. P&P,LC-USZ62-79446.

Cass Gilbert's sketch for this Renaissance Revival library reveals the clear influence of both the Boston Public Library (see 4-025) and the Bibliothèque Ste.-Geneviève (see IN-005). This formed the centerpiece of his 1909 campus plan, which would be supplanted by a new scheme developed by Paul Cret after 1930 (see 2-072).

2-060. Library (Battle Hall, University of Texas), Austin, Texas. Cass Gilbert, ca. 1909. Alfred T. Palmer, photographer, between 1940 and 1946. P&P,FSA,LC-USE6-D-000967.

Constructed of Texas limestone with terra-cotta ornament, this building was labeled as Spanish Renaissance in style, an allusion that was suggested by its broad hipped and red-tiled roof and wide, elaborately bracketed eaves.

2-061. West front, showing fountain and plaza, Stanford University Library (now Cecil H. Green Library), Stanford University, Palo Alto, California. Bakewell and Brown, 1913–1919. David G. De Vries, photographer, 1995. P&P,HABS,CAL,43-PALAL,8-1.

While planned before the war, the Cecil H. Green Library was not completed until just after the 1918 armistice. With its broad arcades and colonnades the Stanford University Library is a late example of the Romanesque Revival. It was designed by the San Francisco firm of Bakewell and Brown to reflect the earlier Richardsonian/Mission Revival style that Shepley, Rutan, and Coolidge had employed originally for their late-nineteenth-century campus plan.

2-062. South and east elevations, showing connection between the new library and the historic structure, Stanford University Library (now Cecil H. Green Library), Stanford University, Palo Alto, California. Bakewell and Brown, 1913–1919. David G. De Vries, photographer, 1995. P&P,HABS,CAL,43-PALAL,8-8.

This view shows the elevation of the seven-story stack wing.

2-063. Field room, overall view to east, Stanford University Library (now Cecil H. Green Library), Stanford University, Palo Alto, California. Bakewell and Brown, 1913–1919. David G. De Vries, photographer, 1995. P&P,HABS,CAL,43-PALAL,8-37.

As in many other large academic libraries of the era, the main (Field) reading room is located on the second floor and is illuminated with a broad band of windows. The circulation desk can be seen at the far end. These photographs were produced by the Historic American Building Survey to document the condition of the building before it underwent rehabilitation and seismic upgrading.

# ACADEMIC ECLECTICISM

Like architecture in the United States in general during the 1920s and 1930s, its college and university campuses and their libraries exhibited an eclectic assortment of styles, which ranged from the elegant Georgian revival features of the Founders Library at Howard University in Washington, D.C., to the Northern Italian Romanesque of the Powell Library at the University of California at Los Angeles. While often evoking historical and regional associations, the appropriation of earlier European building styles was also intended to confer a sense of age and venerability on these much newer American institutions.

2-064. Palmer Library, Connecticut College for Women, New London, Connecticut. Charles Adams Platt, 1923, with later wings by Shreve, Lamb & Harmon, 1941–1942. Gottscho-Schleisner, Inc., 1944. P&P,GSC,LC-DIG-gsc-5a19210.

2-065. Reading room, Palmer Library, Connecticut College for Women, New London, Connecticut. Shreve, Lamb & Harmon, 1941–1942. Gottscho-Schleisner, Inc., 1944. P&P,GSC,LC-DIG-gsc-5a10896.

2-066. Carrels in stack room, Palmer Library, Connecticut College for Women, New London, Connecticut. Shreve, Lamb & Harmon, 1941–1942. Gottscho-Schleisner, Inc., 1944. P&P,GSC,LC-DIG-gsc-5a10898.

2-067. Oliver Wendell Holmes Library, Phillips Academy, Andover, Massachusetts. William and Geoffrey Platt, 1931. Gottscho-Schleisner, Inc., 1937. P&P,GSC,LC-DIG-gsc-5a02883.

2-068. View of Powell Library from Dickson Plaza, facing southeast, Powell Library, University of California, Los Angeles, California. George W. Kelham and David Allison, 1929. Jonathan Farrar, photographer, 1994 or 1995. P&P,HABS,CA 2678-A-1.

In keeping with the climate of Southern California, Kelham and Allison's original scheme for the UCLA campus called for the employment of the Northern Italian Romanesque Revival, of which the Powell Library is an outstanding example. Its entrance is based on the facade of the Church of San Zeno in Verona, and the octagonal tower resembles that of the Church of San Sepolcro in Bologna, Italy. The library underwent an extensive rehabilitation and seismic upgrade after the Northridge earthquake of 1994.

2-069. Main Entryway, Sterling Memorial Library, Yale University, New Haven, Connecticut. James Gamble Rogers, 1927–1931. Carol M. Highsmith, photographer, 2011. P&P,CMHA,LC-DIG-highsm-19254.

In contrast to the modern Gothic style of its entryway, the Sterling Memorial Library incorporated a sixteen-tier metal stack at the rear, capable of accommodating five million volumes.

2-070. Sterling Memorial Library, Yale University,
New Haven, Connecticut. James Gamble Rogers,
1927–1931. Simonds Commercial Photography
Company, 1931. P&P,LC-USZ62-117464.

2-071. Cathedral of Learning, University of Pittsburgh, Pittsburgh, Pennsylvania. Charles Z. Klauder, 1926–1937. Theodor Horydczak, photographer, ca. 1920–1950. P&P, HORY, LC-DIG-thc-5a36301.

The Cathedral of Learning incorporated the university's library, classrooms, and administrative offices in a 42-story tower that reached a height of 535 feet.

2-072. Administration and library building, University of Texas, Austin, Texas. Paul P. Cret, 1931–1937. Unidentified photographer, between 1970 and 1975. P&P, LOT 11549, LC-DIG-ppmsca-15341.

Paul Philippe Cret was hired in 1930 as the university's supervising architect and commissioned to develop a new campus plan, which he completed three years later. This building faces the central plaza, on which Cass Gilbert's early library is also situated (see 2-059–2-060). Although Cret's structure was designed to house the university library, the administration and Board of Regents commandeered most of the space upon the building's completion. Cret intended the tower to accommodate the library stacks, but this never came to pass and the university eventually constructed a new library facility.

2-073. Administration and library building, University of Texas, Austin, Texas. Paul P. Cret, 1931–1937. Carol Highsmith, photographer, between 1980 and 2006. P&P, CMHA, LC-DIG-highsm-15113.

2-074. North (front) facade, Founders Library, Howard University, Washington, D.C. Louis E. Fry Sr. and the Office of Albert I. Cassell, 1934–1939. Dynecourt Mahon, photographer, 1979. P&P,HABS,DC,WASH,236-A-1.

Although the design for the Founders Library came from the office of Albert L. Cassell, who was the Superintendent of Buildings and Grounds of Howard University at the time it was produced, Louis E. Fry Sr. claimed credit for its actual execution. Inside and out the building exhibits the elegant classical ornament of the Georgian Revival style, with its distinctive combination of red brick walls and white wooden ornament. The Founders Library, in particular, is marked with a prominent central tower set over a Palladian window, a motif that is repeated behind the reference room desk. Intended to house some 20,000 volumes, it replaced an earlier Carnegie Library, which was erected in 1910.

2-075. Second floor, reference room looking west, Founders Library, Howard University, Washington, D.C. Louis E. Fry Sr. and the Office of Albert I. Cassell, 1934–1939. Dynecourt Mahon, photographer, 1979. P&P,HABS,DC,WASH, 236-A-25.

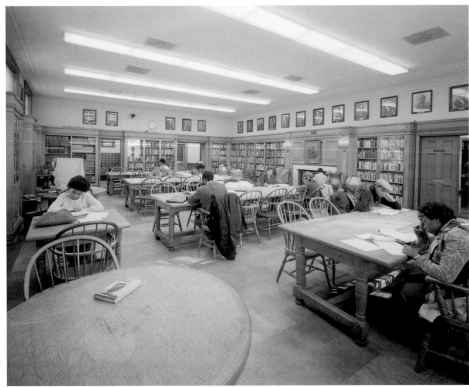

2-076. Second floor, reference room looking north, Founders Library, Howard University, Washington, D.C. Louis E. Fry Sr. and the Office of Albert I. Cassell, 1934–1939. Dynecourt Mahon, photographer, 1979. P&P,HABS,DC,WASH, 236-A-22.

2-077. First floor, Moorland-Spingarn room looking south, Founders Library, Howard University, Washington, D.C. Louis E. Fry Sr. and the Office of Albert I. Cassell, 1934–1939. Dynecourt Mahon, photographer, 1979. P&P,HABS,DC,WASH, 236-A-15.

# THE MODERN TRADITION

2-078. General view, looking northwest, E. T. Roux Library, Florida Southern College, Lakeland, Florida. Frank Lloyd Wright, 1941–1942. Walter Smalling Jr., photographer, 1979. P&P,HABS,FLA,53-LAKE,1D-1.

The Roux Library was sited as a pivotal element in Frank Lloyd Wright's 1938 master plan for Florida Southern College. For the library, he employed a semi-panoptic arrangement with terraces of reading tables encircling a central desk. The drama of his sweeping curves and interpenetrating spaces was enhanced with clerestory lighting. This structure, which now houses the Frank Lloyd Wright Visitor Center, was renamed the Thad Buckner Building in 1968.

2-079. Northwest side, E. T. Roux Library, Florida Southern College, Lakeland, Florida. Frank Lloyd Wright, 1941–1942. Walter Smalling Jr., photographer, 1979. P&P,HABS,FLA,53-LAKE,1D-4.

2-080. Library room, E. T. Roux Library, Florida Southern College, Lakeland, Florida. Frank Lloyd Wright, 1941–1942. Walter Smalling Jr., photographer, 1979. P&P,HABS,FLA,53-LAKE,1D-6.

2-081. West facade, Lamont Library, Harvard University, Cambridge, Massachusetts. Henry R. Shepley of Coolidge, Shepley, Bulfinch, and Abbott, 1947–1949. Gottscho-Schleisner, Inc., 1949. P&P,GSC,LC-DIG-gsc-5a15695.

The Lamont Library, the first independent undergraduate library building erected in the United States, appears first to have been proposed in 1938 by Keyes Metcalf, who would become a leading advocate of open planning, and was Librarian of Harvard College and director of the Harvard University Library between 1937 and 1955. Following World War II, he collaborated with Henry R. Shepley to create many of the innovations in modern library planning that he would later promote in his book *Planning Academic & Research Library Buildings* (1965). As ultimately demonstrated in the idealized modular plan, which appeared in this book, Metcalf suggested placing the stairwells outside the main building in order to maximize the flexibility of the floor space (see 2-085). He ultimately served as a consultant for more than 250 library buildings before his retirement in 1965.

2-082. Circulation Desk, Lamont Library, Harvard University, Cambridge, Massachusetts. Henry R. Shepley of Coolidge, Shepley, Bulfinch, and Abbott, 1947–1949. Gottscho-Schleisner, Inc., 1949. P&P,GSC,LC-DIG-gsc-5a15700.

The expansive circulation desk at the Lamont Library was designed for optimum efficiency of service.

2-083. First level reading room, Lamont Library, Harvard University, Cambridge, Massachusetts. Henry R. Shepley of Coolidge, Shepley, Bulfinch, and Abbott, 1947–1949. Gottscho-Schleisner, Inc., 1949. P&P,GSC,LC-DIG-gsc-5a15712.

The stacks at the Lamont Library were arranged as freestanding shelves, which opened directly off the reading room to provide easy access and to encourage browsing and research by the undergraduate students. Comfortable armchairs as well as desks were also provided for readers.

2-084. Long view, main corridor, third level, Lamont Library, Harvard University, Cambridge, Massachusetts. Henry R. Shepley of Coolidge, Shepley, Bulfinch, and Abbott, 1947–1949. Gottscho-Schleisner, Inc., 1949. P&P,GSC,LC-DIG-gsc-5a15718.

2-085. Secondary stairs outside main walls. From Keyes D. Metcalf, *Planning Academic & Research Library Buildings* (New York, 1965), fig. 1.1. GEN COLL,LC-DIG-ppmsca-15815.

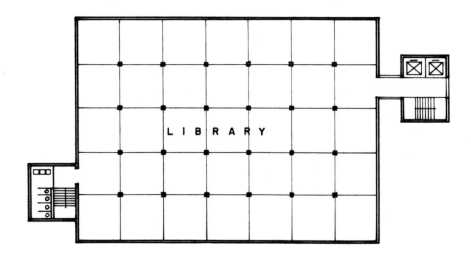

2-086. Freestanding bracket shelving. From Keyes D. Metcalf, *Planning Academic & Research Library Buildings* (New York, 1965), p. 138. GEN COLL,LC-DIG-ppmsca-15816.

According to Metcalf, bracket shelving offered "the best combination available of satisfactory performance with reasonable installation costs." This type of system was introduced at the Oberlin College Library in 1908. Following in the footsteps of the early library reformer William Frederick Poole, Metcalf argued that 7 1/2 feet was the optimum height for shelving. "Anything higher would require a stool. Anything lower would decrease the capacity by one-seventh or require 11-in. spacing of shelves, which would provide for only 79 percent of the books, instead of 90 percent which can go on shelves 12 in. on center."

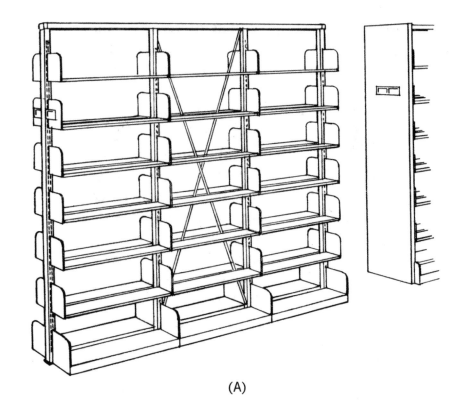

(A)

# 3 THE LIBRARY OF CONGRESS

The Library of Congress was established as a small reference collection for the use of Washington's legislators in 1800. Following that collection's destruction by the British army in 1814, Congress purchased the library of Thomas Jefferson, and Benjamin Henry Latrobe prepared plans to house it along the western facade of the resurrected Capitol building. Redesigned by Charles Bulfinch and opened in 1824, these quarters burned again in 1851 and were rebuilt by Thomas Ustick Walter. Following the passage of a new copyright law in 1870, which required the deposit of all copyrighted material in the Library of Congress, the collection rapidly outgrew the new quarters. The subsequent competition and design for, and construction of, a new building to house a greatly expanded Library of Congress stretched over almost three decades and became a focal point of debates on library design that began to take place during the same period. Designed by the architectural firm of Smithmeyer & Pelz, this new building was known originally as the Library of Congress, later as the Main Building. It was completed at a cost of $6,032,124.54, and opened to the public on November 1, 1897. It was renamed the Jefferson Building in 1980 in honor of the library's primary founder and early benefactor.

Opposite: 3-047, p. 130.

In 1939, the library was expanded to the east with the opening of the Annex Building. In 1980 this edifice was renamed the Adams Building, in honor of the second president of the United States, John Adams. A year later a third structure, the James Madison Building, was dedicated and opened to the public. Not surprisingly, the Prints and Photographs Division of the Library of Congress possesses a wealth of material related to the evolution and expansion of this institution, a small sample of which is included in this book.

3-001. Aerial view of Capitol Hill featuring the Madison, Jefferson, and Adams Buildings of the Library of Congress, Washington, D.C. Carol M. Highsmith, photographer, 2007. P&P,CMHA,LC-DIG-highsm-01903.

Pictured in the foreground in this aerial view of the Library of Congress complex is the Madison Building (1966–1981); immediately behind it is the Jefferson Building (1888–1897), with the dome. The Adams Building (1935–1939) is the structure behind the Madison Building to the right.

# THE FIRST CONGRESSIONAL LIBRARIES

3-002. Perspective from the northeast, United States Capitol, Washington, D.C. Benjamin Henry Latrobe, 1806. P&P,LC-DIG-ppmsca-09501.

Benjamin Henry Latrobe included a two-story library hall in his plan for the United States Capitol to house the congressional library that was established by Congress in 1800. Because the British burned the partially completed building in 1814, his library design was never realized.

3-003. Principal floor plan, United States Capitol, Washington, D.C. Benjamin Henry Latrobe, 1808. P&P,LC-DIG-ppmsca-40461.

Along with the chambers for the Senate and House of Representatives, the location of Latrobe's library can be seen in the upper-right-hand corner of his 1808 plan.

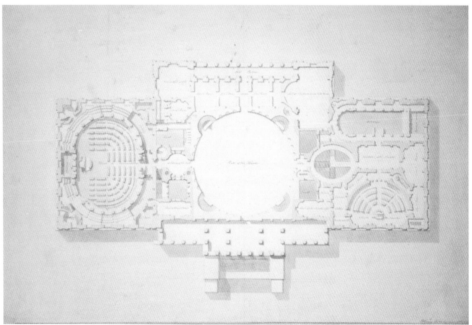

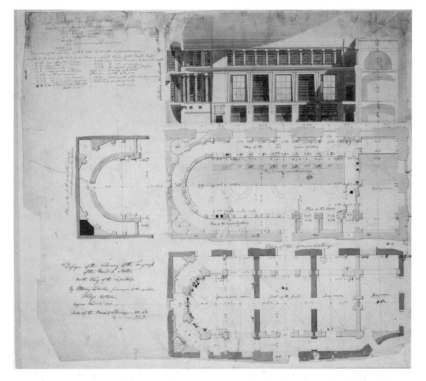

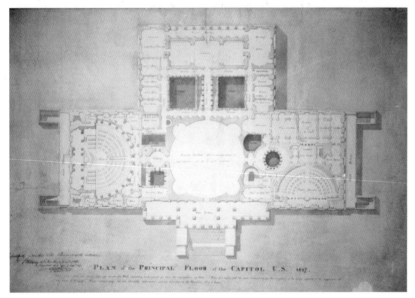

3-004. North wing, section and plans, Library of Congress, United States Capitol, Washington, D.C. Benjamin Henry Latrobe, 1808. P&P, LC-DIG-ppmsca-23928.

Inscriptions on the recto of this drawing read: "Defign of the Library of the Congrefs of the United States North Wing of the Capitol. By B. Henry Latrobe Surveyor of the public Bldgs U.States. begun Nov. 18. 1808.—"—"Section from South to North"—"Plan of the South end of the library lowest floor under the Gallery"—"Plan of the Ground story." On the verso, on the paper mount, is inscribed, "Egyptian design for LC of 1808 (Hamlin's *Benjamin H. Latrobe*, plate 25)." Latrobe planned to introduce book alcoves on the "floor level" of this room, depicted to the lower right in the middle plan.

3-005. Principal floor plan, United States Capitol, Washington, D.C. Benjamin Henry Latrobe, 1817. P&P, LC-DIG-ppmsca-23663.

In his 1817 plan for the rebuilding of the Capitol, Latrobe moved the congressional library to the center of the western side of the building and eliminated the book alcoves. This space was intended to house the library of Thomas Jefferson, which he sold to Congress in 1815 to replace the books destroyed by the British in 1814. Latrobe's design was eventually enlarged and redesigned by Charles Bulfinch with the alcove galleries that can be seen in Alexander Jackson Davis's plan (see 3-006). The library opened in 1824. Although this room was destroyed by fire in 1851, its form is thought to have been very similar to the 1836 arrangement for the University of South Carolina Library, which is attributed to Robert Mills (see 2-008–2-009).

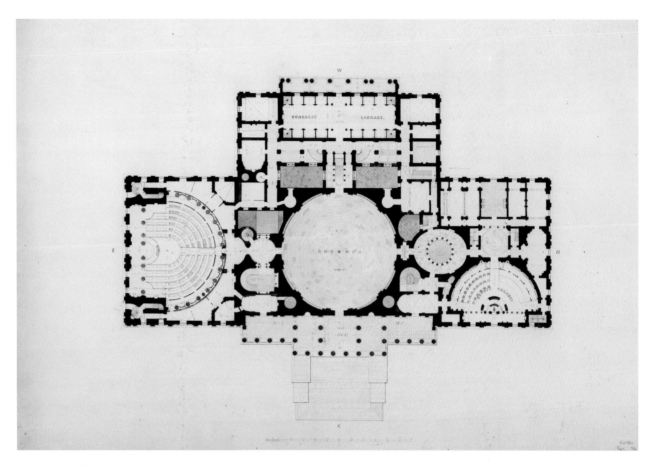

3-006. First floor with rotunda, Senate chamber, and library, United States Capitol, Washington, D.C. Alexander Jackson Davis, ca. 1832–1834. P&P,LC-USZ62-63158.

This drawing by Alexander Jackson Davis depicts the plan of the Capitol as completed by Charles Bulfinch in 1829.

3-007. The Library of Congress in the United States Capitol, Washington, D.C. Thomas Ustick Walter, 1851–1853. Unidentified artist, ca. 1853. P&P, LC-USZ62-1818.

This room replaced the earlier Bulfinch quarters, which were destroyed by fire on Christmas Eve, 1851, along with some 35,000 books. These included two-thirds of Thomas Jefferson's library. Walter designed a three-story reading area, flanked with alcove shelving of iron to prevent the recurrence of the earlier conflagrations.

3-008. "Scene in the old Congressional Library, Washington, D.C., showing present congested condition," United States Capitol, Washington, D.C. Thomas U. Walter, 1851–1853. W. Bengough, painter, 1897. P&P, LC-DIG-ppmsca-17588.

Depicted in the "Iron Room," with its overflow of books, is Ainsworth Rand Spofford, the sixth Librarian of Congress, who was appointed to the position by Abraham Lincoln in 1864. Under his leadership, the library grew from a congressional institution to the status of national library. Within years of passage of the new copyright law in 1870, the collection had outgrown these quarters, prompting the librarian to lobby for a new building—which would not be completed until 1897, the year this illustration was published.

3-009. East wall, Library, Tennessee State Capitol, Nashville, Tennessee. William Strickland, 1845–1859. Jack E. Boucher, photographer, 1970. P&P,HABS,TENN,19-NASH,1-8.

The library in the Tennessee State Capitol building was modeled on Thomas U. Walter's fireproof library in the federal Capitol, and thus gives us a good idea of its original form. This design and its extensive use of iron apparently came about after William Strickland's death in 1854 through the influence of Samuel D. Morgan, a prominent member of the building commission, which was composed of Nashville businessmen. The ornate interior was lit with gas jets and elaborate gas chandeliers manufactured by Cornelius and Company of Philadelphia. A second Philadelphia firm, Wood and Perrot, supplied the decorative ironwork.

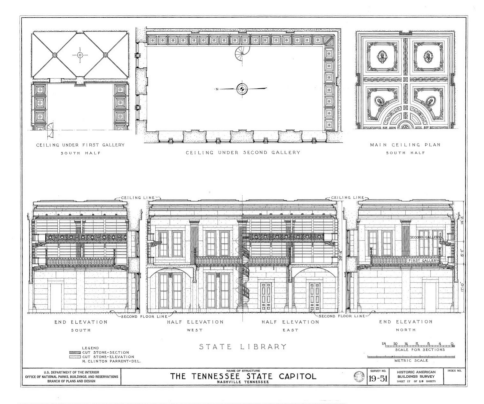

3-010. Longitudinal section, Library, Tennessee State Capitol, Nashville, Tennessee. William Strickland, 1845–1859. H. Clinton Parrent, delineator, 1934. P&P,HABS,TENN,19-NASH,1-(sheet 17 of 23).

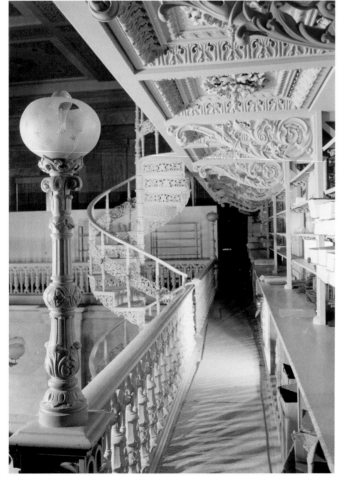

3-011. East wall, detail of balcony, Library, Tennessee State Capitol, Nashville, Tennessee. William Strickland, 1845–1859. Jack E. Boucher, photographer, 1970. P&P,HABS,TENN,19-NASH,1-9.

# LIBRARY OF CONGRESS: THE 1873 COMPETITION

Authorized by Congress in 1873, a competition for a new library building drew twenty-eight entries. The program for this institution called for a fireproof building of iron and stone with a central domed reading room inspired by the panoptic form of the British Museum Reading Room in London (see IN-002). The unprecedented size of this new building also encouraged experimentation with new types of compact book storage to hold the ever-increasing numbers of books in the collection. The competition was won by John L. Smithmeyer and Paul J. Pelz. Its Germanic Neoclassical character betrays Pelz's architectural training in Germany and with Detlef Lienau in New York. An alternate entry by the same architects seems to reflect the German *Rundbogenstil*, or round-arch style, a mode of design that was very popular in that country at mid-century. A proposal by the Swedish-born architect Adolph Emil Melander placed second. A selection of the entries by architects Leon Beaver and John Fraser further reflects the eclectic nature of American architecture at the time, as well as a variety of panoptic plans.

3-012. Winning design for a new building for the Library of Congress, perspective view, Washington, D.C. Smithmeyer & Pelz, 1873. P&P, LC-DIG-ppmsca-31513.

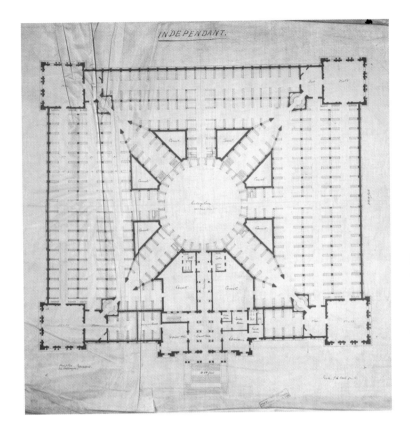

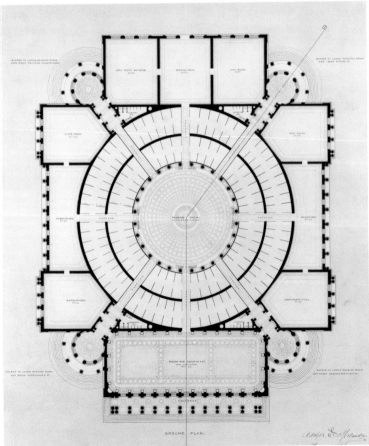

3-013. Floor plan for a new building for the Library of Congress, Washington, D. C. Smithmeyer & Pelz, 1873. P&P, LC-USZ62-63175.

3-014. Floor plan for a new building for the Library of Congress, Washington, D.C. Adolph E. Melander, 1873. P&P, LC-USZ62-59057.

3-015. Competition entry for a new building for the Library of Congress, perspective rendering, Washington, D.C. Adolph E. Melander, 1873. P&P, LC-DIG-ppmsca-31435.

3-016. Alternative competition entry for a new building for the Library of Congress, front, exterior elevation, Washington, D.C. Smithmeyer & Pelz, 1873. P&P, LC-USZC4-1301.

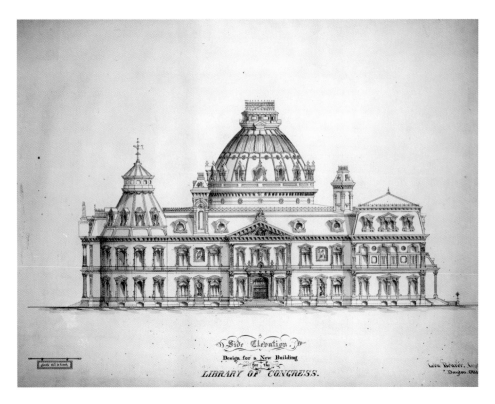

3-017. Design for a new building for the Library of Congress, front elevation, Washington, D.C. Leon Beaver, 1873. P&P, LC-USZ62-63236.

3-018. Design for a new building for the Library of Congress, perspective view, Washington, D.C. Leon Beaver, 1873. P&P, LC-DIG-ppmsca-31512.

3-019. Design for a new building for the Library of Congress, ground floor plan, Washington, D.C. Leon Beaver, 1873. P&P, LC-USZ62-59061.

3-020. Design for a new building for the Library of Congress, longitudinal section, Washington, D.C. Leon Beaver, 1873. P&P, LC-USZ62-63237.

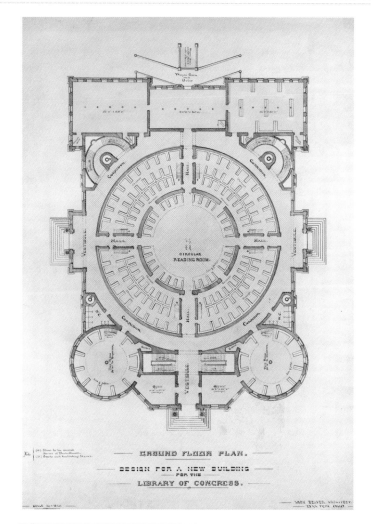

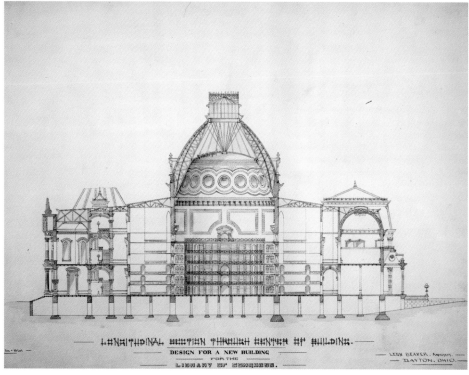

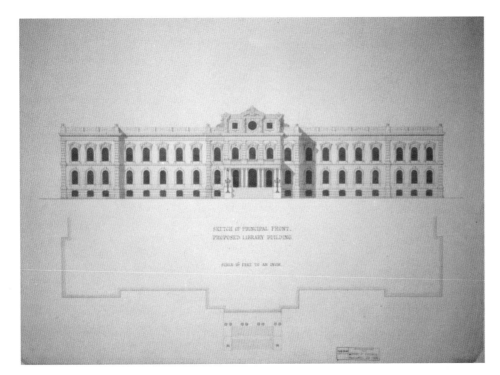

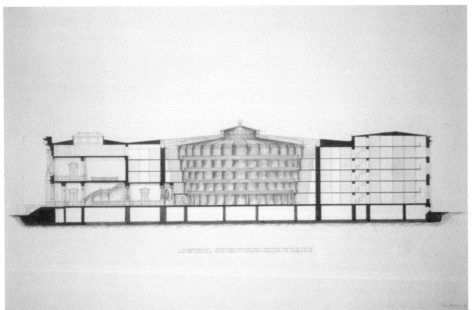

3-021. Design for a new building for the Library of Congress, sketch of principal front, Washington, D.C. John Fraser, 1873. P&P,LC-USZC4-1077.

3-022. Design for a new building for the Library of Congress, longitudinal section, Washington, D.C. John Fraser, 1873. P&P,LC-USZC4-1075.

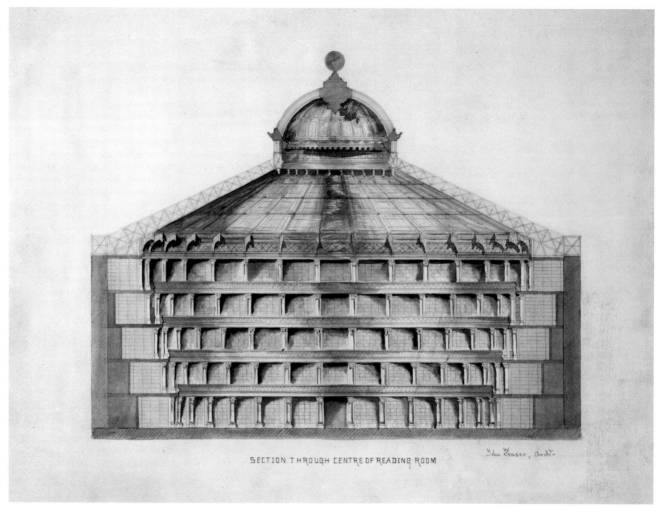

SECTION THROUGH CENTRE OF READING ROOM

John W. Fraser, Arch't.

3-023. Design for a new building for the Library of Congress, section through center of reading room, Washington, D.C. John Fraser, 1873. P&P,LC-USZ62-63223.

# EVOLUTION OF THE JEFFERSON BUILDING, 1874–1886

Between 1874 and 1886, John L. Smithmeyer and Paul J. Pelz, winners of the competition, were directed numerous times by congressional overseers to change the plan and style of their original design, as well as to consider a number of alternate locations for the building. In the meantime, the original competitors as well as new aspirants for this plum commission—such as Alexander R. Esty—submitted forty-one additional designs. Finally, in 1886, Congress passed a bill authorizing the construction of a Renaissance Revival version of Smithmeyer & Pelz's original submission on a site just to the east of the Capitol.

3-024. Design for a new building for the Library of Congress, perspective rendering, Washington, D.C. Alexander R. Esty, after ca. 1873. P&P, LC-DIG-ppmsca-31519.

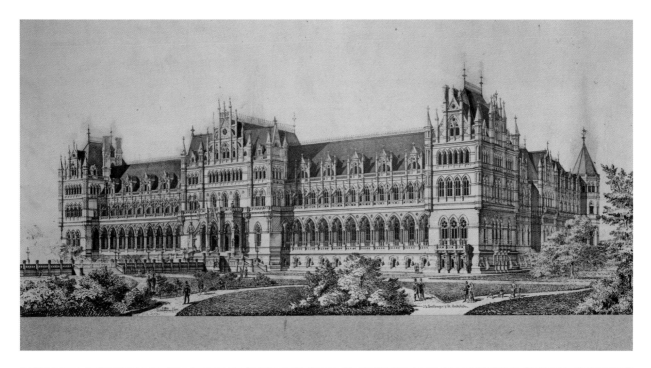

3-025. Modification for a "Victorian Gothic" design for the Library of Congress, perspective, Washington, D.C. Smithmeyer & Pelz, 1875–1879. P&P,LC-USZ62-63184.

3-026. Plan for the Proposed National Library, "German Renaissance" style, for the Judiciary Square site, Washington, D.C. Smithmeyer & Pelz, ca. 1875–1879. P&P,LC-DIG-ppmsca-31515

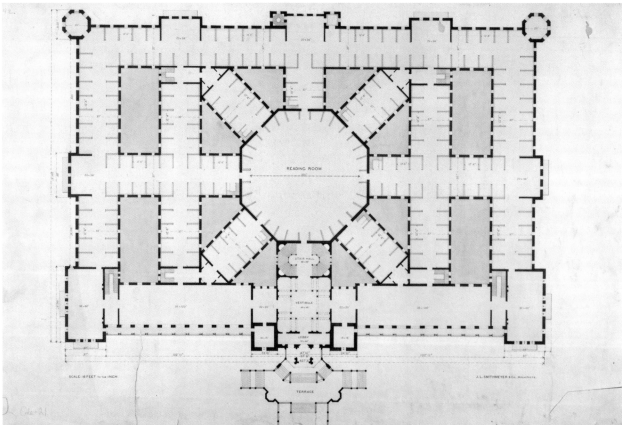

3-027. Perspective view of "Plan for the Extension of the Capitol (with introduction of turrets)," Washington, D.C. Smithmeyer & Pelz, 1880. P&P,LC-USZ62-46798.

3-028. First story plan for Library of Congress, Washington, D.C. Smithmeyer & Pelz, ca. 1875–1879. P&P,LC-USZ62-59054.

# DESIGNS BETWEEN 1886 AND 1888

Even after approval of Smithmeyer & Pelz's final Renaissance Revival scheme in 1886, controversy over the new building continued. As Congress vacillated over the budget, the architects continued to submit variations on their approved design. In response to the tension between Congress and the architects, and between the architects themselves, John Smithmeyer was dismissed in 1888. Paul Pelz was then appointed as Chief Architect, but placed under the supervision of Brig. Gen. Thomas Lincoln Casey, Chief of the Army Corps of Engineers, and the civil engineer, Bernard R. Green, who was named Superintendent of Construction. Work on the new building would finally begin in 1888, and the cornerstone was laid on November 25, 1889.

3-029. Perspective view of the "Design of the Congressional Library Building Adopted by Act of Congress, Approved April 18, 1886," Washington, D.C. Smithmeyer & Pelz, September 1888. P&P, LC-USZ62-116301.

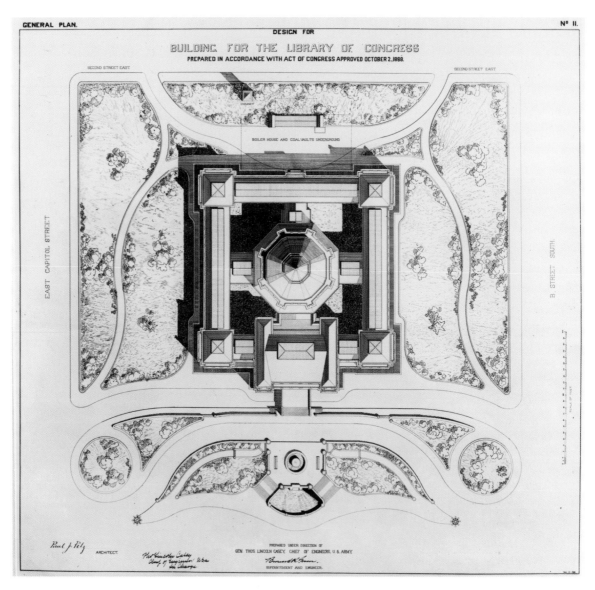

3-030. "Design for the Library of Congress, Washington, D.C., prepared in accordance with an Act of Congress approved October 2, 1888, prepared under the direction of Gen. Thomas Lincoln Casey." Paul J. Pelz, 1888. P&P, LC-USZ62-105955.

3-031. Perspective view of the "Building for the
Library of Congress, View from the South-West,"
Washington, D.C. Smithmeyer & Pelz, 1885.
P&P,LC-USZ62-59282.

3-032. Perspective view of the "Building of the Library
of Congress, View from Senate wing of Capitol,"
Washington, D.C. Attributed to Paul J. Pelz, ca. 1889–
1896. P&P,LC-USZ62-68138.

3-033. Laying the cornerstone of the northwest pavilion, Library of Congress (Jefferson Building), Washington, D.C. Smithmeyer & Pelz, 1888–1897. Unidentified photographer, November 25, 1889. P&P, LC-USZ62-73536.

3-034. Exterior walls of the north stack, looking toward the Capitol, Library of Congress (Jefferson Building), Washington, D.C. Smithmeyer & Pelz, 1888–1897. Unidentified photographer, December 4, 1891. P&P, LC-USZ62-59151.

3-035. View of the superstructure taking form
above the rotunda, Library of Congress (Jefferson
Building), Washington, D.C. Smithmeyer & Pelz,
1888–1897. Unidentified photographer, May 10, 1893.
P&P,LC-USZ62-73543.

3-036. The keystone placed in the southwest clerestory arch of the rotunda, Library of Congress (Jefferson Building), Washington, D.C. Smithmeyer & Pelz, 1888–1897. Unidentified photographer, June 1892. P&P, LC-USZ62-51462.

3-037. Iron framework of the dome's superstructure above the rotunda, Library of Congress (Jefferson Building), Washington, D.C. Smithmeyer & Pelz, 1888–1897. Unidentified photographer, 1893. P&P, LC-USZ62-73545.

# THE COMPLETED BUILDING

Despite many earlier controversies, the new building for the Library of Congress (now the Jefferson Building to distinguish it from two annexes designed and constructed during the 1930s and 1960s–70s) opened on November 1, 1897. It was restored at a cost of some $70 million during the 1980s–90s.

3-038. West front, Library of Congress (Jefferson Building), Washington, D.C. Smithmeyer & Pelz; and Edward Pearce Casey, 1888–1897. Jack E. Boucher, photographer, 1975. P&P,HABS,DC,WASH,461A-1.

3-039. Library of Congress (Jefferson Building), Washington, D.C. Smithmeyer & Pelz; and Edward Pearce Casey, 1888–1897. F. W. Brehm, photographer, 1906. P&P,PAN US GEOG-District of Columbia no. 6.

3-040. "Court of Neptune" fountain, Library of Congress (Jefferson Building), Washington, D.C. Roland Hinton Perry, 1897–1898. Carol M. Highsmith, photographer, 2007. P&P,CMHA,LC-DIG-highsm-09128.

Perry's Court of Neptune fountain served as the introduction to the rich allegorical program of sculptures, murals, and mosaics that was developed by Edward Casey, the son of Brig. Gen. Thomas Lincoln Casey, who was hired to oversee the decorative program for the building. In 1896 Superintendent of Construction Bernard R. Green reported that the total cost of these decorations came to some $364,000; the fountain cost $22,000.

3-041. Perspective view of the Great Hall, Library of Congress (Jefferson Building), Washington, D.C. Smithmeyer & Pelz and Edward Pearce Casey, 1888–1897. Paul J. Pelz, 1888. P&P,LC-USZ62-51463.

3-042. Great Hall, view from the second floor south corridor, Library of Congress (Jefferson Building), Washington, D.C. Smithmeyer & Pelz; and Edward Pearce Casey, 1888–1897. Carol M. Highsmith, photographer, 2007. P&P,CMHA,LC-DIG-highsm-01970.

The sculptor Philip Martiny executed the staircase figures. Elmer Ellsworth Garnsey was responsible for coordinating the exuberant mural decorations of the main hall.

3-043. Grand staircase from vestibule, Library of Congress (Jefferson Building), Washington, D.C. Smithmeyer & Pelz and Edward Pearce Casey, 1888–1897. Alfred S. Campbell,photographer, 1900. P&P,LC-USZ62-60744.

3-044. *Evolution of the Book, Oral Tradition*, east corridor of the Great Hall, Library of Congress Thomas Jefferson Building, Washington, D.C. John W. Alexander, 1896–1897. Carol M. Highsmith, photographer, 2007. P&P,CMHA,LC-DIG-highsm-02011.

3-045. *Evolution of the Book, the Printing Press*, east corridor of the Great Hall, Library of Congress Thomas Jefferson Building, Washington, D.C. John W. Alexander, 1896–1897. Carol M. Highsmith, photographer, 2007. P&P,CMHA,LC-DIG-highsm-02015.

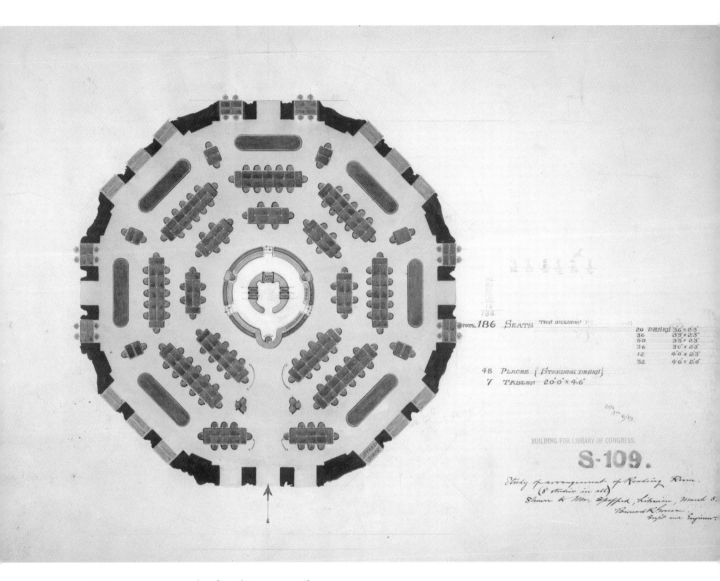

3-046. Arrangement study of reading room, Library of Congress (Jefferson Building), Washington, D.C. Smithmeyer & Pelz and Edward Pearce Casey, 1888–1897. P&P, LC-USZ62-63180.

This study depicts the panoptic arrangement of the readers' tables around a raised central librarians' desk, from which the staff could observe the behavior of their patrons. This scheme, as well as the great domed reading room, were based on the model of the British Museum Reading Room in London (see IN-002).

3-047. Interior, main reading room, looking east, Library of Congress (Jefferson Building), Washington, D.C. Smithmeyer & Pelz; and Edward Pearce Casey, 1888–1897. Jack E. Boucher, photographer, 1974. P&P,HABS,DC, WASH,461A-13.

3-048. View from above showing researcher desks, Main Reading Room of the Library of Congress Thomas Jefferson Building, Washington, D.C. Smithmeyer & Pelz; and Edward Pearce Casey, 1888–1897. Carol M. Highsmith, photographer, 2009. P&P,CMHA,LC-DIG-highsm-11604.

3-049. Interior, main reading room, looking east, Library of Congress (Jefferson Building), Washington, D.C. Smithmeyer & Pelz and Edward Pearce Casey, 1888–1897. Jack E. Boucher, photographer, 1974. P&P,HABS,DC, WASH,461A-15.

3-050. Students in the reading room of the Library of Congress with the Librarian of Congress, Herbert Putnam, watching, Library of Congress (Jefferson Building), Washington, D.C. Smithmeyer & Pelz and Edward Pearce Casey, 1888–1897. Frances Benjamin Johnston, photographer, ca. 1899. P&P,LC-USZ62-4541.

3-051. Interior of dome displaying half of the
Evolution of Civilizations mural in collar, Main
Reading Room of the Library of Congress
Thomas Jefferson Building, Washington, D.C.
Smithmeyer & Pelz; and Edward Pearce Casey,
1888–1897. Carol M. Highsmith, photographer, 2007.
P&P,CMHA,LC-DIG-highsm-02071.

3-052. *The Evolution of Civilization*, Library of
Congress (Jefferson Building), Washington,
D.C. Edwin Howland Blashfield, ca. 1896–1897.
P&P,LC-USZ62-104459.

In this segment of the murals that encircle the base
of the lantern above the main reading room, Edwin
Blashfield depicted allegorical figures representing
great civilizations of the world.

3-053. Allegorical figure of History, main reading room, Library of Congress (Jefferson Building), Washington, D.C. Daniel Chester French, ca. 1896–1897. Ann Day, photographer, 2001. P&P, LC-DIG-ppmsca-02987.

3-054. Manuscript division, Library of Congress (Jefferson Building), Washington, D.C. Smithmeyer & Pelz and Edward Pearce Casey, 1888–1897. Harris & Ewing, photographers, between ca. 1930 and ca. 1940. P&P, LC-USZ62-108263.

3-055. Catalog division, Library of Congress (Jefferson Building), Washington, D.C. Smithmeyer & Pelz and Edward Pearce Casey, 1888–1897. Harris & Ewing, photographers, ca. 1927. P&P, LC-USZ62-75117.

3-056. Woman at card catalog, Library of Congress (Jefferson Building), Washington, D.C. Smithmeyer & Pelz and Edward Pearce Casey, 1888–1897. Jack Delano, photographer, between 1930 and 1950. GEN COLL, LC-USZ62-100400.

3-057. Reproduction of drawing of bookstack, Library of Congress (Jefferson Building), Washington, D.C. Bernard R. Green, April 1890. Artist unknown, no date. P&P, LC-USZ62-105956.

Designed by Bernard R. Green, the Library of Congress stacks consisted of forty-three miles of shelving able to accommodate an unprecedented two million volumes. The contract for producing this system was awarded to Snead & Company Iron Works of Louisville, Kentucky, which went on to become a primary manufacturer of library storage systems in North America during the early twentieth century.

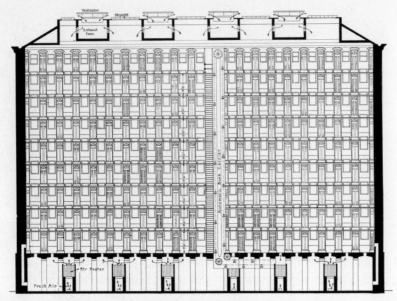

THE SNEAD AND COMPANY IRON WORKS, INC.

Fig. 4.    LONGITUDINAL SECTION OF NORTH STACK, LIBRARY OF CONGRESS,
WASHINGTON, D. C.

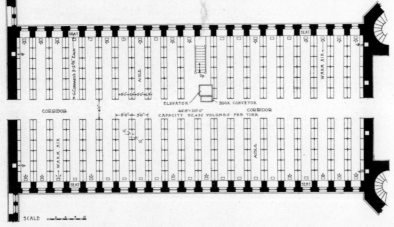

Fig. 5.    PLAN OF NORTH STACK, LIBRARY OF CONGRESS, WASHINGTON, D. C.

3-058. Longitudinal section and plan of the north stack, Library of Congress (Jefferson Building), Washington, D.C. Bernard R. Green, 1889–1896. From Snead & Company Iron Works, *Library planning, bookstacks and shelving, with contributions from the architects' and librarians' points of view*, Jersey City, NJ, ca. 1915, figs. 4 and 5. GEN COLL,LC-DIG-ppmsca-15563.

3-059. Interior of the bookstack, Library of Congress (Jefferson Building), Washington, D.C. Smithmeyer & Pelz; Edward Pearce Casey; and Bernard R. Green, 1888–1897. Harris & Ewing, photographers, ca. 1925. P&P,LC-USZ62-60735.

3-060. Congressional Library south book-stack, Library of Congress (Jefferson Building), Washington, D.C. Smithmeyer & Pelz; Edward Pearce Casey; and Bernard R. Green, 1888–1897. L.C. Handy Studio, ca. 1895–1897. P&P,LC-USZ62-90208.

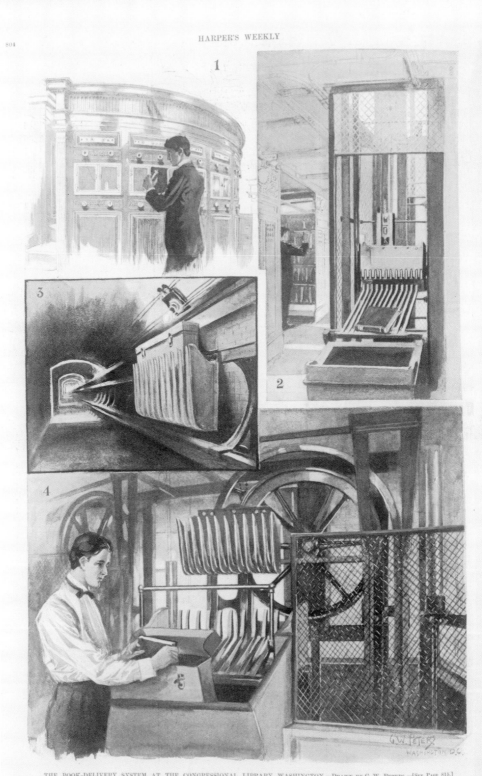

THE BOOK-DELIVERY SYSTEM AT THE CONGRESSIONAL LIBRARY, WASHINGTON.—Drawn by G. W. Peters.—[See Page 815.]

1. The Distributing Desk in the centre of the Rotunda; showing Telephones, Pneumatic and Speaking Tubes, communicating with the Book-Stacks and the Capitol.   2. Book-stack Elevator; with Rack for automatically removing the Books.   3. Under-ground Book-Trolley running from the Library to the Capitol.   4. Sending and Receiving Station to the under-ground Trolley.

3-061. The book-delivery system, Library of Congress (Jefferson Building), Washington, D.C. Smithmeyer & Pelz; Edward Pearce Casey; and Bernard R. Green, 1888–1897. From *Harper's Weekly* 41 (August 14, 1897), p. 804. P&P, LC-USZ62-118958.

Orders for books were transmitted from the delivery desk to the reading room via an elaborate system of conveyors and elevators.

3-062. Book conveyors, Library of Congress (Jefferson Building), Washington, D.C. Smithmeyer & Pelz; Edward Pearce Casey; and Bernard R. Green, 1888–1897. Levin C. Handy, photographer, ca. 1900. P&P, LC-USZ62-90221.

3-063. Book conveyors, Library of Congress (Jefferson Building), Washington, D.C. Smithmeyer & Pelz; Edward Pearce Casey; and Bernard R. Green, 1888–1897. Levin C. Handy, photographer, ca. 1900. P&P, LC-USZ62-90220.

# JOHN ADAMS BUILDING

The Library of Congress Annex was built at a cost of $8 million. When completed, it encompassed twenty acres of floor space with a capacity of nine million volumes, nearly twice that of the original Jefferson building. These were stored on shelves supported by concrete floors, encircled with reading rooms and workspaces. This simple and functional shelving system replaced the traditional metal stacks of the previous decades.

3-064. Library of Congress Annex (John Adams Building) with the Folger Library and Jefferson Building of the Library of Congress, Washington, D.C. Theodor Horydczak, photographer, ca. 1920–1950. P&P,HORY,LC-DIG-thc-5a38336

While the massing of the new Annex building, seen in the center of this photograph, responds to the Jefferson building to its west, its Art Moderne style, white Georgia marble, and North Carolina pink granite reflect Paul Cret's Folger Library, which can be seen to the left (see 1-022).

3-065. Perspective rendering, Library of Congress, John Adams Building, Washington, D.C. Pierson & Wilson, Alexander B. Trowbridge, 1935–1939. P&P,LC-USZ62-74738.

3-066. Aerial view showing construction of the east front extension of the Library of Congress Annex (John Adams Building), Washington, D.C. Pierson and Wilson, Alexander B. Trowbridge, 1935–1939. Unidentified photographer, 1933. P&P,LC-USZ62-73534.

3-067. Library of Congress Annex (John Adams Building), Washington, D.C. Pierson and Wilson, Alexander B. Trowbridge, 1935–1939. Theodor Horydczak, photographer, ca. 1920–1950. P&P,HORY,LC-DIG-thc-5a38333.

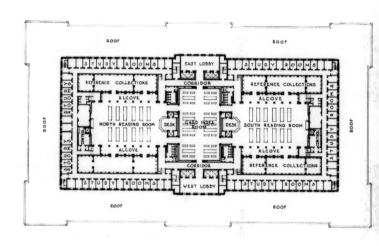

· READING · ROOM · (FIFTH) · FLOOR · PLAN ·
· ANNEX · BUILDING ·
· LIBRARY · OF · CONGRESS ·

3-068. Fifth floor plan with north and south reading rooms, Library of Congress Annex (John Adams Building), Washington, D.C. Pierson and Wilson, Alexander B. Trowbridge, 1935–1939. P&P,LC-USZ62-109559.

3-069. Reading room, Library of Congress Annex (John Adams Building), Washington, D.C. Pierson and Wilson, Alexander B. Trowbridge, 1935–1939. Theodore Horydczak, photographer, ca. 1920–1950. P&P,HORY,LC-DIG-thc-5a38342.

The catalog room and main reading rooms were located on the fifth floor over the library's bookstacks. The murals in the frieze by Ezra Winter depicted Chaucer's Canterbury pilgrims in the north reading room and scenes inspired by the writings of Thomas Jefferson in the south.

# JAMES MADISON BUILDING

Although erected after 1950, the James Madison Building forms one of the triad of structures designed to house the vast collections of the Library of Congress. Librarian of Congress L. Quincy Mumford began planning for this third building in 1957, but its construction was not authorized for another eight years. The cornerstone was laid in 1974 and the building opened in 1981, at a cost of nearly $131 million. This 400- by 500-foot marble box contains 2,100,000 square feet.

3-070. Exterior view from corner of Independence Ave. and 2nd St., Library of Congress James Madison Building. Carol M. Highsmith, photographer, 2007. P&P,CMHA,LC-DIG-highsm-03169.

While "modern" in its stripped-down severity, the Madison Building is articulated with thin piers intended to reference Washington's neoclassical heritage. Outrage over the original design and scale of the structure led the government to authorize a review by an American Institute of Architects committee in 1967, but the design seems to have been very little altered.

3-071. Perspective rendering, James Madison
Building, Library of Congress, Washington, D.C.
DeWitt, Poor, and Shelton, 1966–1981. Rendering by
Rudolph Associates, 1966. P&P,LC-USZ62-116855.

The watered-down classicism of DeWitt, Poor, and
Shelton's second annex for the Library of Congress
reflects their attempt to symbolically mediate between a modernist aesthetic and federal
Washington. Inside is an open plan with partition
walls forming double-loaded corridors that allow
for the creation of flexible study and storage rooms
to either side. Because of their anonymous character, these long, inhospitable passageways have been
color-coded in an attempt to orient visitors to the
building. Cast as neutral steel or concrete and glass
containers for their contents and functions, the cold
and impersonal severity of many libraries of this era
demonstrates—inside and out—the difficulty of
adapting the more functional principles of corporate
and industrial modernism to the design of cultural
institutions.

3-072. Exterior view. Main entrance and information kiosk (added later). Library of Congress James Madison Building, Washington, D.C. DeWitt, Poor, and Shelton, 1966–1981. Carol M. Highsmith, photographer, 2007. P&P,CMHA,LC-DIG-highsm-03178.

3-073. James Madison Building, Library of Congress, Washington, D.C. Perspective, lobby. DeWitt, Poor, and Shelton, 1966–1981. Unidentified artist, 1972. P&P,LC-USZ62-114233.

# OTHER GOVERNMENT LIBRARIES

In addition to the Library of Congress, there are hundreds of other reference collections maintained for the use of public servants and employees that fall under the jurisdiction of the federal government. During the early nineteenth century these were typically small, requiring relatively little in the way of specialized accommodation, but by the middle of the century many departments and agencies began to incorporate purposefully designed library quarters to house their growing collections of books and documents. Like the library in William Strickland's Tennessee State Capitol in Nashville (see 3-009–3-011), these early spaces often emulated the alcoved book room of the Library of Congress (see 3-007).

3-074. State Department Library, Executive Office Building, Washington, D.C. Alfred B. Mullett, architect, William McPherson, decorator, 1876. Unidentified photographer, 1860–1900. P&P,LC-USZ62-123616.

3-075. West wing/library, uppermost (fifth) stack level with shelves manufactured by Snead and Company Iron Works, view facing west, Army War College, Fort Lesley J. McNair, Washington, D.C. McKim, Mead & White, 1903–1907. Jet Lowe, photographer, 1995. P&P,HABS,DC,WASH,393-13.

The Army War College was established as a significant feature of the "New Army" created by President Theodore Roosevelt and Secretary of War Elihu Root, and the library served as central repository of information for the military command.

3-076. Snead book stacks, lower (first) stack level, view facing northwest, Army War College, Fort Lesley J. McNair, Washington, D.C. McKim, Mead & White, 1903–1907. Jet Lowe, photographer, 1995. P&P,HABS, DC,WASH,393-16.

3-077. U.S.S. *Brooklyn* library. Detroit Publishing Co., ca. 1896–1901. P&P,DETR,LC-DIG-det-4a14051.

# THE MODERN PRESIDENTIAL LIBRARY

Following the modest lead of Franklin Delano Roosevelt, who erected a small presidential library near his family home in Hyde Park, New York, presidential libraries have become ever more prominent monuments in the American landscape.

3-078. East facade, Franklin Delano Roosevelt Library, Hyde Park, New York. Louis Simon and Franklin Delano Roosevelt, 1939–1940. Gottscho-Schleisner, Inc., 1941. P&P,GSC,LC-DIG-gsc-5a07074.

In 1937, President Roosevelt produced an early sketch and plan for this library, which was influenced by the forms of traditional Dutch fieldstone farmhouses of the region. Although he subsequently worked with the architect, Louis Simon, Roosevelt himself closely supervised the construction of the building, which was erected on the grounds of his Hyde Park estate to house his papers. On July 4, 1940, the president turned the library over to the federal government under the jurisdiction of the National Archives, creating an important precedent for subsequent presidential libraries.

3-079. Exhibition Hall, Franklin Delano Roosevelt Library, Hyde Park, New York. Louis Simon and Franklin Delano Roosevelt, 1939–1940. Gottscho-Schleisner, Inc., 1941. P&P,GSC,LC-DIG-gsc-5a07083.

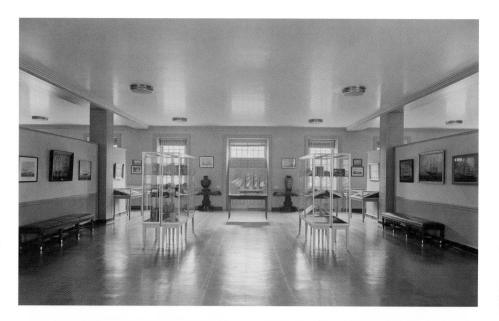

3-080. The Lyndon Baines Johnson Library and Museum, also known as the LBJ Presidential Library, Austin, Texas. Skidmore, Owings, and Merrill; and Brooks, Barr, Braeber, and White, 1967–1971. Carol M. Highsmith, photographer, 2014. P&P,CMHA,LC-DIG-highsm-27862.

This massive ten-story concrete and travertine building was designed by Gordon Bunshaft of Skidmore, Owings, and Merrill, who also designed the elegant Beinecke Rare Book and Manuscript Library at Yale University (see AF-004). Housed in the central hall of the building, the archives—not unlike the rare book collection at Yale—are visible behind a five-story glass curtain wall.

# 4 LARGE URBAN LIBRARIES

When John Jacob Astor died in 1848, he left $400,000 for the foundation and support of a free reference library in New York City. Because this institution served as a reference institution only, open for short periods of time at inconvenient hours, it attracted almost immediate criticism and its reputation grew increasingly conservative and elitist as the century progressed. Despite these mixed reviews, its presence in New York City marked it as a critical catalyst for the burgeoning public library movement in the United States. Not only were the first serious discussions concerning the founding of the Boston Public Library begun during the years it was rising, but the first American articles on library design began to appear in *Norton's Literary Gazette and Publishers' Circular*. Two plans, reproduced in this periodical in 1853, depicted a hall library and a hall with alcoves. These illustrations accompanied the earliest published discussion of library planning to appear in the United States. The article basically presented a synopsis of the architectural section of Leopold Constantin Hesse's *Bibliothéconomie* (Paris, 1841). Variations of these schemes—especially the employment of multistory alcoves—would dominate the design of large public libraries for the next three decades. In the midst of this growing

Opposite: 4-035, p. 173.

interest in libraries George Ticknor and Edward Everett began to formulate their vision for a free lending library in Boston.

Given the cost and complexity of their design, the construction of these buildings initially proceeded at a slower pace than that of their smaller cousins. By the end of the century, however, a number of larger cities, such as Cincinnati, Buffalo, Chicago, and New York, undertook the construction of grand new central buildings—Boston had already replaced its earlier structure with McKim, Mead & White's Italian Renaissance–inspired palace on Copley Square. All of this building activity encouraged experimentation with new types of compact book storage to hold the ever-increasing numbers of books in these collections. With this new democratization of reading came greatly enlarged reading rooms and delivery areas; children's, periodical, and newspaper departments; special collections; and workrooms for sorting, repairing, and cataloging books.

Following the end of World War II, and spurred by the economic prosperity of the 1920s, a number of major cities resumed library building campaigns, with new central libraries rising in Cleveland, Los Angeles, Philadelphia, Baltimore, and Brooklyn. The librarians at Cleveland, Los Angeles, and Baltimore experimented with subject-oriented departments, while Philadelphia maintained the type of monumental general reading room popularized at the Boston Public Library. While Alfred Githens introduced open planning at Brooklyn, he was ultimately constrained by existing foundations that had been laid for an earlier design for the building.

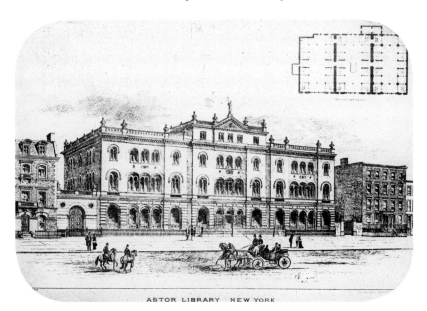

ASTOR LIBRARY   NEW YORK

4-001. Astor Library with plan, New York, New York. Alexander Saeltzer, 1849–1853; Griffith Thomas, 1859; and Thomas Stent, 1881. Unidentified artist, ca. 1890. P&P,LC-DIG-ds-06537.

Saeltzer's initial elevation for the south wing of the Astor Library was—as critic Montgomery Schuyler would note some four decades later—substantially indebted to Frederich von Gärtner's *Rundbogenstil*, or round-arched style, designs for the new State Library in Munich, a building that had opened in 1842. The Astor was expanded in the same style in 1859 with what was to become the central pavilion of this privately endowed reference library after a third (north) wing was added in 1881. In 1895 the Astor merged with the Lenox Library and the Tilden Trust to form the New York Public Library, and its collection moved to the newly completed New York Public Library central building at Fifth Avenue and 42nd Street in 1911.

# HALL LIBRARIES

Promoted by the examples of the Astor and Boston public libraries and the first published discussions of library management and planning at mid-century, which all advocated for this kind of space, the alcoved hall became the dominant form of book storage for larger American public libraries well into the 1880s. This plan often merged the earlier, more centralized form of the European book hall, or *Saal-bibliothek*, with an impressive multistory alcove system.

4-002. First book hall, Astor Library, New York. Alexander Saeltzer, 1849–1853; Griffith Thomas, 1859; and Thomas Stent, 1881. Wood engraving from *Gleason's Pictorial*, vol. 6 (1854), p. 124. P&P,LC-USZ62-83861.

Combining an alcove system with the height and breadth of a hall library, the Astor reading room formed one of the most impressive spaces in New York City when it opened in 1854. Its expansiveness was achieved through an extensive and innovative use of iron in the galleries and roof structure of the building. Following an admonition common among library theorists at the time, the iron was also intended to render the structure fireproof. The original book room is to the far right in the plan (upper right, 4-002), with the 1859 addition in the middle and the 1881 book room on the left.

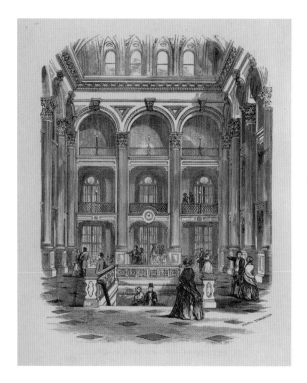

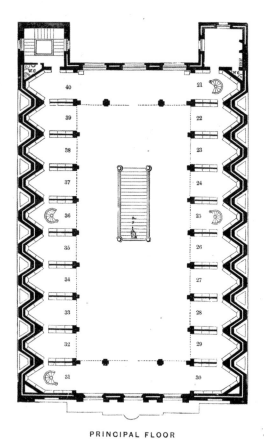

PRINCIPAL FLOOR

4-003. Main floor, Boston Public Library, Boston, Massachusetts. Charles Kirk Kirby, 1855–1859. Hammatt Billings, artist, and John Andrew, engraver. In *Proceedings at the dedication of the building for the Public Library of the City of Boston, January 1, 1858* (Boston, 1858). GEN COLL,LC-DIG-ppmsca-15580.

The second floor of the Boston Public Library was designed as a noncirculating reference room capable of holding an unprecedented 200,000 books in twenty three-story alcoves, ten to either side of a 52-foot-high hall. The acceptance of the book hall in the United States was reinforced by the literature on library design available during this period. In 1859, for example, William Rhees authored the *Manual of Public Libraries, Institutions, and Societies in the United States and British Provinces of North America*, the second American text on library management. While this book was largely devoted to administrative and cataloging matters, it included a short chapter on "The Construction and Furnishing of Library Buildings," which also advocated for the hall library form.

4-004. Exterior view, Boston Public Library, Boston, Massachusetts. Charles Kirk Kirby, 1855–1859. Unidentified artist. In *Proceedings at the dedication of the building for the Public Library of the City of Boston, January 1, 1858* (Boston, 1858). GEN COLL,LC-DIG-ppmsca-15601.

4-005. Principal floor, Boston Public Library, Boston, Massachusetts. Charles Kirk Kirby, 1855–1859. Unidentified artist. In *Proceedings at the dedication of the building for the Public Library of the City of Boston, January 1, 1858* (Boston, 1858). GEN COLL,LC-DIG-ppmsca-15578.

4-006. Transverse section, Boston Public Library, Boston, Massachusetts. Charles Kirk Kirby, 1855–1859. Unidentified artist. In *Proceedings at the dedication of the building for the Public Library of the City of Boston, January 1, 1858* (Boston, 1858). GEN COLL,LC-DIG-ppmsca-15577.

4-007. Plan, first floor lending library, Boston Public Library, Boston, Massachusetts. Charles Kirk Kirby, 1855–1859. Hammatt Billings, artist, and John Andrews, engraver. In *Proceedings at the dedication of the building for the Public Library of the City of Boston, January 1, 1858* (Boston, 1858). GEN COLL,LC-DIG-ppmsca-15579.

The lower level of the Boston Public Library was given over to the first modern lending library in America. This consisted of a "room for conversation and the delivery of books," which was located directly behind the entryway, where a grand staircase led up to the main book hall. A general reading room, capable of seating some two hundred readers, was situated to the right of this delivery area, which also opened into a smaller ladies' or "special" reading room. Extending across the back of the building was a book hall. This space was designed to hold approximately forty thousand volumes, which would be lent to the public at the long delivery counter, which acted—in the words of the librarian Justin Winsor—as the "one point of contact between the readers and officials."

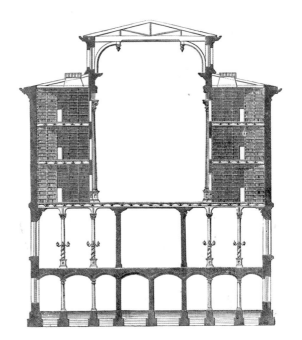

TRANSVERSE SECTION.

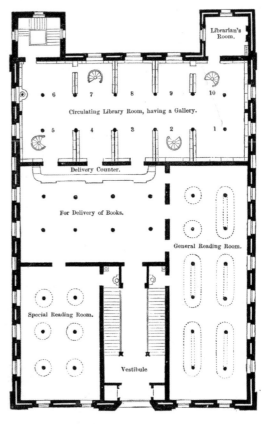

FIRST STORY

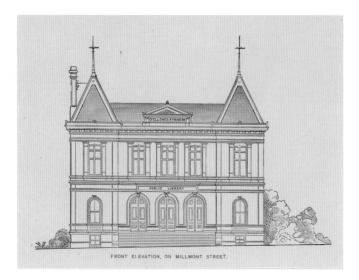

FRONT ELEVATION, ON MILLMONT STREET.

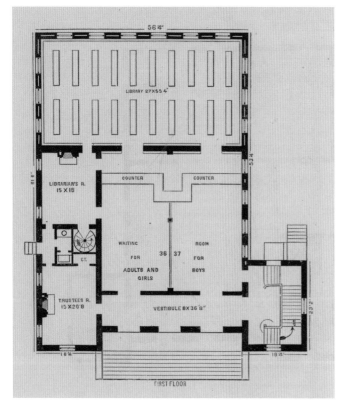

FIRST FLOOR

4-008. Roxbury Branch of the Boston Public Library, Boston, Massachusetts. Bradlee and Winslow, with Justin Winsor, 1872–1873. Unidentified artist. In *Dedication Services of the Fellowes Athenaeum and the Roxbury Branch of the Boston Public Library, July 9, 1873* (Boston, 1873). GEN COLL, LC-DIG-ppmsca-15572.

In his plan for one of the earliest branch libraries in the country, the librarian Justin Winsor borrowed from the general arrangement of the first-floor circulation department of the first Boston Public Library building, where he was serving as superintendent. Here, the first floor was given over almost entirely to the lending of books, while the upper story was relegated to reading. As in the main library, a separate book-storage room was isolated from the public along the back of the branch building, the books being retrieved by the librarians and handed to the public at the delivery counter.

4-009. First floor plan, Roxbury Branch of the Boston Public Library, Boston, Massachusetts. Bradlee and Winslow, with Justin Winslow, 1872–1873. Unidentified artist. In *Dedication Services of the Fellowes Athenaeum and the Roxbury Branch of the Boston Public Library, July 9, 1873* (Boston, 1873). GEN COLL, LC-DIG-ppmsca-15573.

4-010. Springfield City Library, Springfield,
Massachusetts. George Hathorne, 1866–1871.
Detroit Publishing Co., ca. 1900–1910.
P&P,DETR,LC-DIG-det-4a17491.

As opposed to the Renaissance Revival style of the
Boston Public Library, George Hathorne designed
this building in the Gothic mode, with pointed rather
than round arches, at a cost of $100,000.

4-011. Reading room, Springfield City Library, Springfield, Massachusetts. George Hathorne, 1866–1871. Unidentified photographer, ca. 1905. P&P,LC-USZ62-104271.

4-012. Public Library of Cincinnati, Cincinnati, Ohio. James H. McLaughlin, 1868–1874. In *Harper's Weekly*, March 21, 1874. P&P, LC-DIG-ds-06546.

The book hall at Cincinnati was appended to a remodeled opera house that had been purchased by the Board of Managers of the public library in 1868. It measured 105 by 75 feet and was 55 feet high. It is likely that William Frederick Poole's experience at this library, where he served as director from 1869 to 1873, contributed to his deep antipathy toward hall libraries. It was in spaces such as this, he noted in 1883 in the *Library Journal*, with its "immense hall, fifty or sixty feet high, surrounded with tiers, galleries where the bindings perish with heat, and to which attendants must climb for books which ought to be within reach on the working floors." Additionally, he would later write, a book hall arrangement was next to impossible to enlarge. "Shall it be extended heavenward," he asked sarcastically, "and more galleries be piled on these, with more wasted space in the nave, greater difficulty of access to books, and more extravagance in the heating? Shall the transepts and chancel be built, so that the plan will represent the true ecclesiastical cross? However pious these improvements and gratifying to the taste of the refined architect, they are expensive, they involve demolishing much that has already been constructed, and they will give but little additional room."

4-013. Peabody Institute, (now the George Peabody Library), Baltimore, Maryland. Edmund G. Lind, 1858–1878. William Henry Jackson, photographer, 1902. Detroit Publishing Co. P&P,DETR,LC-DIG-det-4a09471.

The library department of this institution, which opened to the public in 1868, was originally located on the second floor of the west (left) wing of the building. In 1878, Lind added a second wing to the right. It encloses the most impressive surviving multilevel iron book room in this country. It rises 61 feet to the skylight in the ceiling, with iron stacks fabricated by the Bartlett-Robbins Company of Baltimore.

4-014. Book hall, Peabody Institute (now the George Peabody Library), Baltimore, Maryland. Edmund G. Lind, 1858–1878. Carol M. Highsmith, photographer, 2012. P&P,CMHA,LC-DIG-highsm-18386.

4-015. Perspective rendering, Lenox Library, New York, New York. Richard Morris Hunt, 1871. P&P,AIA/AAF Collection,LC-USZC4-14969.

This original presentation rendering depicts the facade of the Lenox Library on Fifth Avenue and strongly reflects Richard Morris Hunt's years in Paris from 1846 to 1855. The style of the building is in the Neo-Grec mode that he would have been exposed to at the time, and the rich watercolor, ink, and graphite presentation shows his early training as a student at the École des Beaux-Arts.

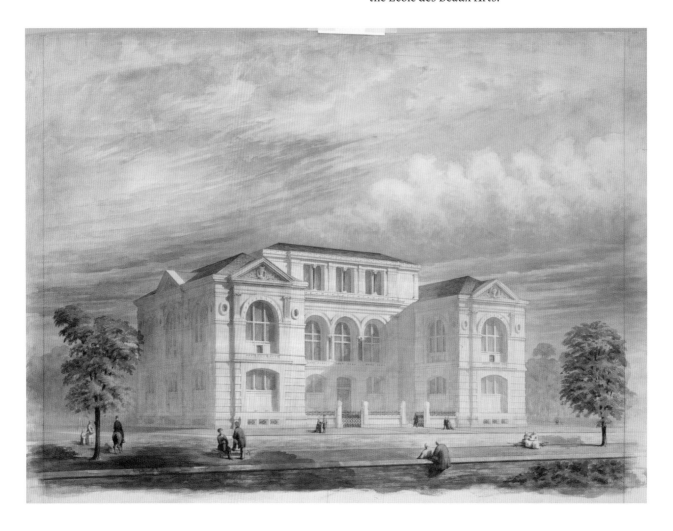

4-016. Lenox Library, New York, New York. Richard Morris Hunt, 1870–1877. Detroit Publishing Co., ca. 1900–1906. P&P, DETR, LC-D4-16369.

The Lenox Library was privately endowed by New York merchant and real estate tycoon James Lenox to house his collection of rare books, manuscripts, and Americana. While these collections were nominally available to scholars and others, like the Astor collection, the library was widely criticized for its elitist nature. It was merged into the New York Public Library in 1895 and moved to its new quarters in 1911.

4-017. Reading room, Lenox Library, New York, New York. Richard Morris Hunt, 1870–1877. Detroit Publishing Co., ca. 1900–1905. P&P, DETR, LC-DIG-ppmsca-15416.

4-018. Detroit Public Library, Detroit, Michigan. Brush and Smith, 1877. Detroit Publishing Co., 1906. P&P,DETR,LC-DIG-det-4a13463.

4-019. Indianapolis Public Library, Indianapolis, Indiana. Williams and Otter, 1891–1892. Detroit Publishing Co., ca. 1900–1906, P&P,DETR,LC-DIG-det-4a11596.

4-020. Los Angeles Public Library in the Los Angeles City Hall, Los Angeles, California. Unidentified photographer, ca. 1905. P&P,LOT 8908,LC-DIG-ppmsca-15408.

Like many public libraries in America, the Los Angeles Public Library led a perambulatory existence during its early years. Created by city ordinance in 1878, it was housed in the city hall from 1889 to 1906. After that, it was shuttled about the city, sharing space in several office and commercial buildings—including the Hamburger Department Store—before coming to rest in its current home in 1926 (see 4-067–4-071).

4-021. Minneapolis Public Library, Minneapolis, Minnesota. Long and Kees, 1888–1889. Detroit Publishing Co., ca. 1900–1906. P&P,DETR,LC-DIG-det-4a12298.

After the mid-1880s, many American libraries large and small began to reflect the fashion of the Romanesque Revival, or Richardsonian Romanesque, popularized by the great success of the work of Boston architect Henry Hobson Richardson. In contrast to the classical style, it was typically characterized by a strongly picturesque composition, round arches, and heavily rusticated stonework.

4-022. Forbes Library, Northampton, Massachusetts. William C. Brocklesby, 1891–1894. Detroit Publishing Co., ca. 1900–1906. P&P,DETR,LC-DIG-det-4a11986.

4-023. Cossit Library, Memphis, Tennessee. Lorenzo B. Wheeler, 1893. Detroit Publishing Co., 1906. P&P,DETR,LC-DIG-det-4a17925

# ESTABLISHING THE MODERN AMERICAN LIBRARY

Without question, the most significant achievements in the design and planning of the first large, modern library buildings in the United States occurred in Boston, Chicago, and New York during the late nineteenth and early twentieth centuries. While other large American cities also undertook the erection of new buildings for their public libraries, none had nearly as strong an impact on the form of the institution as these. Like the smaller public libraries erected in this country just before and after the turn of the last century, these large urban buildings reflect the gradual eclipse of Henry Hobson Richardson's Romanesque Revival vocabulary by a renewed interest in classicism. McKim, Mead & White's iconic "Palace for the People" on Copley Square in Boston (1887–1895) in particular established a new ideal for the American public library that would by the end of the nineteenth century impact the representation of libraries large and small all across the country. By the onset of World War I, the presence of the chaste white classical temple or palace clearly identified the presence of thousands of public libraries on Main Streets and public squares throughout the land.

4-024. Panoramic view of Copley Square with the
Boston Public Library, Boston, Massachusetts.
McKim, Mead & White, 1887–1895. Haines
Photo Company, 1910. P&P, PAN US GEOG-
Massachusetts, no. 68 (E size).

# THE SECOND BOSTON PUBLIC LIBRARY BUILDING

Designed to replace the aging and outdated building on Boylston Street, the second Boston Public Library was clothed in a Renaissance Revival style that both Charles Follen McKim and Stanford White would have become familiar with during their student years at the École des Beaux-Arts in Paris. The reading room arcade also evokes Henri Labrouste's great Bibliothèque Ste.-Geneviève (see IN-005) in that city, as well as the palaces of Italy's great fifteenth-century patrons of the arts. Here, the "Brahmins" who controlled the board of the library intended to create a palace for the people of Boston.

4-025. Boston Public Library, Boston, Massachusetts. McKim, Mead & White, 1887–1895. Detroit Publishing Co., ca. 1910–1920. P&P,DETR,LC-DIG-det-4a24493.

The facade of the Boston Public Library, with its broad arcade of windows and inscribed names of authors, was based on Henri Labrouste's earlier Bibliothèque Ste.-Geneviève in Paris. It would become one of the great models for library design in America during the first third of the twentieth century.

4-026. Entrance arches, Boston Public Library, Boston, Massachusetts. McKim, Mead & White, 1887–1895. Detroit Publishing Co., 1907. P&P,DETR,LC-DIG-det-4a13788.

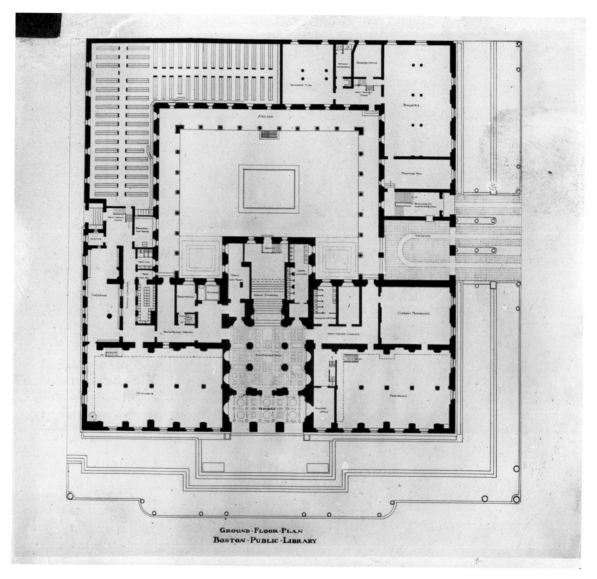

4-027. Ground floor plan, Boston Public Library, Boston, Massachusetts. McKim, Mead & White, 1887–1895. P&P,LC-DIG-ds-06553.

The library was arranged around a small Renaissance courtyard, with an atrium and grand staircase leading up to the second floor reading room. The closed stacks occupied one corner of the building on multiple floors.

4-028. Courtyard, Boston Public Library, Boston, Massachusetts. McKim, Mead & White, 1887–1895. Detroit Publishing Co., 1909. P&P,DETR,LC-DIG-det-4a23186.

The arcaded "cortile" of the library, which is based on similar courtyards found in fifteenth-century Italian Renaissance palaces in Florence, offers a welcome refuge from the noise and chaos of the city.

4-029. Grand staircase and Puvis de Chavannes murals, left section, Boston Public Library, Boston, Massachusetts. McKim, Mead & White, 1887–1895. Detroit Publishing Co., 1901. P&P,DETR,LC-DIG-det-4a23573.

The French painter Puvis de Chavannes was commissioned to produce a mural cycle for the grand stairway of the library in 1893. Entitled *The Muses of Inspiration: Hail the Spirit, The Harbinger of Light*, it depicts allegorical representations of Poetry, Philosophy, History, and Science. In the foreground of the photograph is one of two recumbent lions carved out of Siennese marble by Louis St. Gaudens, brother of the better-known American sculptor Augustus Saint-Gaudens.

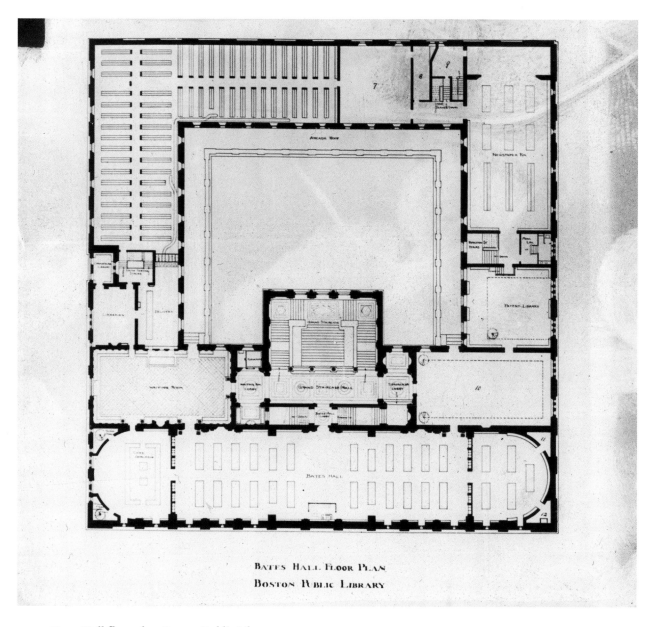

4-030. Bates Hall floor plan, Boston Public Library,
Boston, Massachusetts. McKim, Mead & White, 1887–
1895. P&P,LC-DIG-ds-06539.

4-031. Bates Hall, Boston Public Library, Boston, Massachusetts. McKim, Mead & White, 1887–1895. Ernest Peixotto, illustrator, 1896. P&P,CAI—Peixotto,no. 1 (B Size).

The impressive main reading room of the second Boston Public Library building is named for Joshua Bates, the first great benefactor of the public library. Like the library's courtyard, its coffered barrel vault looks back to the Italian Renaissance for inspiration.

4-032. Delivery room with Edward Austin Abbey murals, Boston Public Library, Boston, Massachusetts. McKim, Mead & White, 1887–1895. Curtis & Cameron, photographers, 1898. P&P, LC-USZ62-64865.

The encircling frieze of the delivery room, which was painted by Edward Austin Abbey and installed in 1895, depicts *The Quest and Achievement of the Holy Grail*.

# CHICAGO

Established after the great fire of 1871, the Chicago Public Library during the 1890s agreed to divide its responsibilities with the John Crerar and Newberry libraries, which were established as research institutions devoted to science and the humanities respectively. The new public library building on Michigan Avenue was constructed to house the popular circulating collections. The Crerar, which was established in 1897, contracted in the 1950s with the Illinois Institute of Technology to provide that school's library services and moved into a new building on the IIT campus in 1962 (see AF-001).

4-033. Plan for an ideal library. In William Frederick Poole, "The Construction of Library Buildings," *American Architect and Building News* 10 (September 17, 1881), fig. 4, p. 131. GEN COLL,LC-DIG-ppmsca-15584.

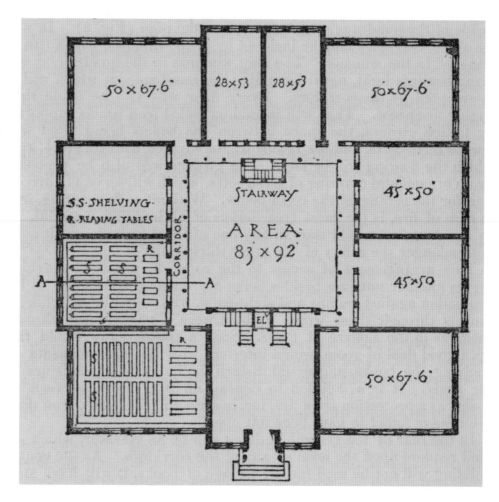

4-034. Newberry Library, Chicago, Illinois. Henry Ives Cobb, 1888–1893. Detroit Publishing Co., 1901. P&P,DETR,LC-DIG-det-4a08709.

As director of the Newberry Library from 1887 until 1894, William Frederick Poole, working with the Chicago architect Henry Ives Cobb, was able to partially realize his earlier proposal for an ideal reference library. In contrast to the great hall libraries of the previous decades, this would be composed of individual reading rooms each devoted to a specialized area of study. In Chicago this was to take the form of a four-story Romanesque Revival structure with subject-oriented rooms opening around a central courtyard. Each room would have its own attendant, and books would be stored in freestanding double-sided bookcases, which would occupy about two-thirds of the space. These shelves would be no more than eight feet high for easy access. Because of its inflexibility and extravagant waste of space, this system quickly proved impracticable, and only one wing of this building was completed.

4-035. Chicago Public Library, Chicago, Illinois. Shepley, Rutan, and Coolidge, 1891–1897. Cervin Robinson, photographer, 1963. P&P,HABS,ILL,16-CHIG,14-2.

Shepley, Rutan, and Coolidge, the successor firm to Henry Hobson Richardson, here adapted the classical idiom of Chicago's Columbian Exposition of 1893, as well as the facade of McKim, Mead & White's Boston Public Library. The building now serves as the Chicago Cultural Center.

4-036. Reading room, Chicago Public Library, Chicago, Illinois. Shepley, Rutan, and Coolidge, 1891–1897. Unidentified photographer, between 1900 and 1960. P&P,LC-DIG-ds-06543.

4-037. Interior, south staircase, Chicago Public Library, Chicago, Illinois. Shepley, Rutan, and Coolidge, 1891–1897. Cervin Robinson, photographer, 1963. P&P,HABS,ILL,16-CHIG,14-3.

In the tradition of many earlier public libraries, a Civil War Memorial Hall, dedicated to the Grand Army of the Republic, occupies the entire second story of this building. Rich mosaics and elaborate lighting fixtures by Louis Comfort Tiffany ornament the staircase that leads up to the second floor.

4-038. Grand Army of the Republic Room, Chicago Public Library, Chicago, Illinois. Shepley, Rutan, and Coolidge; and Louis Comfort Tiffany, 1891–1897. Cervin Robinson, photographer, 1963. P&P,HABS,ILL,16-CHIG,14-5.

# THE NEW YORK PUBLIC LIBRARY

As noted earlier, the New York Public Library was created in 1895 when the Astor and Lenox libraries merged with the Tilden Trust (see 4-001–4-002, 4-015–4-017). Because the library was established as a private, nonprofit corporation, in 1897 the city donated the site for the new building at the location of the former Croton Reservoir. This same year a competition for the design of the building, based upon a scheme developed by the institution's director, Dr. John Shaw Billings, was held. The entry of John Merven Carrère and Thomas Hastings was subsequently chosen from eighty-eight original entries.

4-039. Competitive Design for the New York Public Library, W. H. Symonds, 1897. In Scrapbook HS M2 in the AIA/AAF Collection, p. 69. LC-DIG-ds-06530.

4-040. Competitive Design for the New York Public Library, Brite and Bacon, 1897. Boston: Heliotype Printing Co., [1897?]. In Scrapbook HS M2 in the AIA/AAF Collection, p. 66. P&P, LC-DIG-ds-06528.

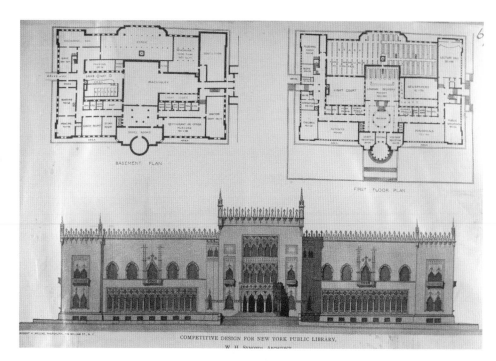

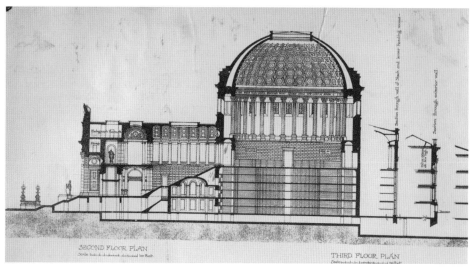

4-041. Central building, New York Public Library, New York, New York. Carrère and Hastings, 1897–1911. Detroit Publishing Co., 1908. P&P,DETR,LC-DIG-det-4a28067.

Architects Carrère and Hastings were both graduates of the École des Beaux-Arts in Paris and had worked as draftsmen in the office of McKim, Mead & White. Their impressive and monumental exteriors and interiors reflected the wishes of the library trustees as well as their own classical training. At the same time, they managed to merge this classical monumentality with the efficiency of Billings's plan to create one of the greatest institutions—and buildings—of its type in the world.

4-042. Entrance, New York Public Library, central building, New York, New York, Carrère and Hastings, 1897-1911, Detroit Publishing Co., between 1910 and 1920. P&P,DETR,LC-DIG-det-4a24389.

4-043. Rear stack view, central building, New York Public Library, New York, New York. Carrère and Hastings, 1897–1911. Detroit Publishing Co., ca. 1910–1920. P&P,DETR,LC-DIG-det-4a16380.

The library's director, Dr. John Shaw Billings, developed the plan of the library for maximum efficiency, with a monumental reading room set atop an equally impressive bookstack. The main reading room encompassed a quarter acre of space set atop a seven-story steel bookstack that supported seventy-five miles of shelving intended to accommodate eight million books. Librarians in the reading room communicated with runners in the stacks via pneumatic tubes. Volumes were then raised from the shelves to the central delivery desk by a system of book lifts.

4-044. Third floor plan, central building, New York Public Library, New York, New York. Carrère and Hastings, 1897–1911. In Snead & Company Iron Works, *Library planning, bookstacks and shelving, with contributions from the architects' and librarians' points of view* (Jersey City, NJ, 1915), fig. 149. GEN COLL,LC-DIG-ppmsca-15565.

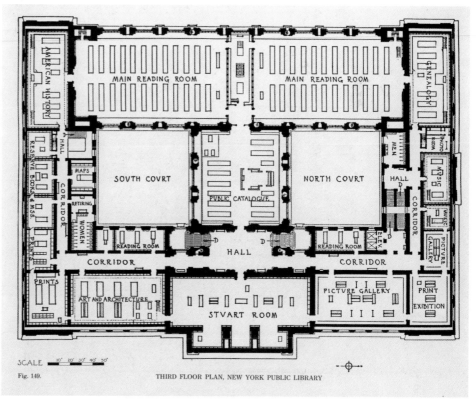

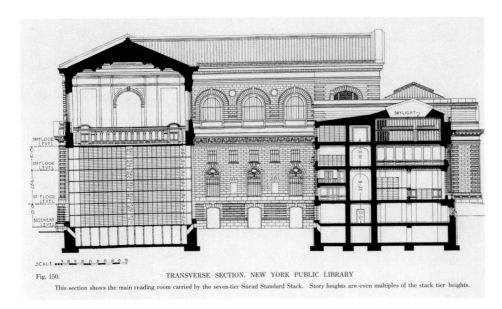

Fig. 150.    TRANSVERSE SECTION, NEW YORK PUBLIC LIBRARY

This section shows the main reading room carried by the seven-tier Snead Standard Stack.    Story heights are even multiples of the stack tier heights.

4-045. Transverse section, central building, New York Public Library, New York, New York. Carrère and Hastings, 1897–1911. In Snead & Company Iron Works, *Library planning, bookstacks and shelving, with contributions from the architects' and librarians' points of view* (Jersey City, NJ, 1915), fig. 150. GEN COLL,LC-DIG-ppmsca-15566.

4-046. Main stack room, central building, New York Public Library, New York, New York. Carrère and Hastings, 1897–1911. In Snead & Company Iron Works, *Library planning, bookstacks and shelving, with contributions from the architects' and librarians' points of view* (Jersey City, NJ, 1915), fig. 115. GEN COLL,LC-DIG-ppmsca-15567.

4-047. Main entrance hall, central building, New York Public Library, New York, New York. Carrère and Hastings, 1897–1911. Detroit Publishing Co., ca. 1910–1920. P&P,DETR,LC-DIG-det-4a24343.

4-048. Catalog room, central building, New York Public Library, New York, New York. Carrère and Hastings, 1897–1911. Detroit Publishing Co., ca. 1910–1920. P&P,DETR,LC-DIG-det-4a24341.

4-049. Main reading room, central building, New York Public Library, New York, New York. Carrère and Hastings, 1897–1911. Unidentified photographer, 1911. P&P,US GEOG,LC-DIG-ppmsca-15428.

The main reading room of the library is located atop the steel stacks. It stands 52 feet in height, covers a quarter of an acre, and can accommodate seven hundred readers.

4-050. Dr. Henry W. Berg Room, central building, New York Public Library, New York, New York. Eggers and Higgins, 1940. Gottscho-Schleisner, Inc., 1940. P&P,GSC,LC-DIG-gsc-5a05666.

Along with later acquisitions, this room was designed to house several thousand rare books and manuscripts in English and American literature given to the New York Public Library in 1940 by Albert A. Berg in memory of his brother Henry, who had died two years earlier. Berg also donated $250,000 for the construction of a special room to house the collection and for its maintenance on the upper floor of the central library building. With its classical detailing and fine woodwork, this space was clearly intended to evoke the aura of a private gentleman's library.

4-051. Milwaukee Public Library and Museum, Milwaukee, Wisconsin. Ferry and Clas, 1894–1898. Detroit Publishing Co., 1901. P&P,DETR,LC-DIG-ppmsca-13671.

This design by the Milwaukee firm of Ferry and Clas was chosen from seventy-four entries submitted to a competition for the building, which was judged by William Robert Ware. Like many of its contemporary institutions, which were being funded by Andrew Carnegie, the program included a library, museum, and auditorium.

4-052. Elevation, Public Library, Fall River, Massachusetts, Cram, Wentworth and Goodhue, 1896–1899. *The Architectural Review* 6 (January 1902), plate I. P&P,LC-DIG-ds-06522.

The Fall River Public Library was constructed at a cost of $252,000 and could house 400,000 books in two stacks set to either side of the main reading room.

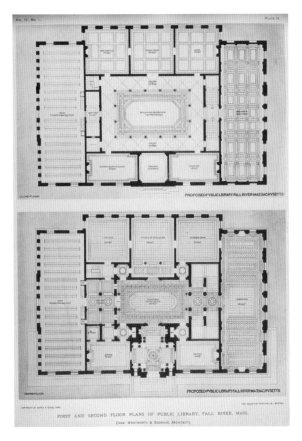

4-053. First and second floor plans, Public Library, Fall River, Massachusetts, Cram, Wentworth and Goodhue, 1896-1899. *The Architectural Review* 6 (January 1902), plate IV. P&P, LC-DIG-ds-06523.

4-054. Longitudinal section, Public Library, Fall River, Massachusetts, Cram, Wentworth and Goodhue, 1896-1899. *The Architectural Review* 6 (January 1902), plate II. P&P, LC-DIG-ds-06524.

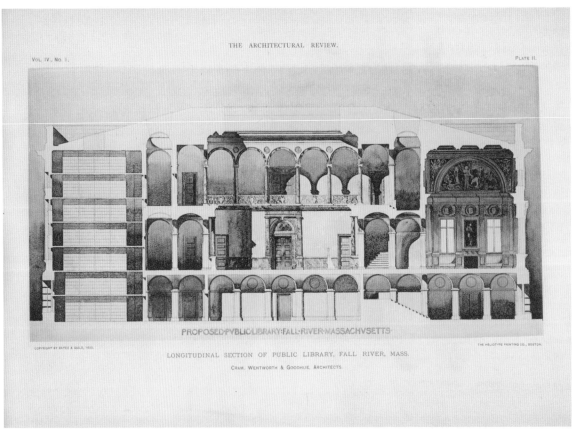

4-055. Deborah Cook Sayles Public Library, Pawtucket, Rhode Island. Cram, Goodhue, and Ferguson, 1899–1901. Unidentified photographer, ca. 1901. P&P, LOT 8908, LC-DIG-ppmsca-15394.

In 1898 Frederic Clark Sayles offered $150,000 to the city of Pawtucket, Rhode Island, for a public library to be dedicated as a memorial to his late wife Deborah Cook Sayles. The philanthropist was descended on both sides of his family from Roger Williams, the seventeenth-century founder of Providence Plantation (later the Colony of Rhode Island), and he and his brother were prominent local manufacturers and members of numerous Pawtucket boards and associations. Designed in the Greek Revival style with a monumental Ionic portico, and an estimated shelf capacity of 150,000 volumes, the library was dedicated on January 1, 1902, just a year before Frederic's death.

4-056. Deborah Cook Sayles Public Library, Pawtucket, Rhode Island. Cram, Goodhue, and Ferguson, 1899–1901. Unidentified photographer, between 1902 and 1910. P&P, LC-DIG-ds-06526.

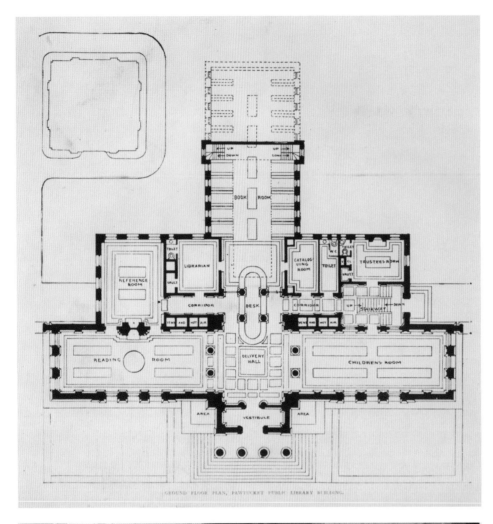

GROUND FLOOR PLAN, PAWTUCKET PUBLIC LIBRARY BUILDING.

4-057. Ground floor plan, Deborah Cook Sayles Public Library, Pawtucket, Rhode Island. Cram, Goodhue and Ferguson, 1899–1901. P&P, LOT 8908, LC-DIG-ppmsca-15404.

4-058. Rotunda and delivery desk, Carpenter Memorial Library, Manchester, New Hampshire. Edward L. Tilton, 1912–1914. In *The Carpenter Memorial Library, Dedication Exercises, November 18, 1914* (Concord, NH, 1916), opposite p. 33. GEN COLL, LC-DIG-ppmsca-15549.

While classical in style, the interior arrangement of the Carpenter Library exhibits the type of central circulation desk and open plan championed by Tilton and the library profession at the time.

4-059. Carpenter Memorial Library, Manchester, New Hampshire. Edward L. Tilton, 1912–1914. In *The Carpenter Memorial Library, Dedication Exercises, November 18, 1914* (Concord, NH, 1916), frontispiece. GEN COLL,LC-DIG-ppmsca-15548.

The Carpenter Memorial Library was given to Manchester by Frank P. Carpenter as a memorial to his wife, Eleanora Blood Carpenter. Designed in the style of a Renaissance Revival palace, this mode was chosen (the architect noted in his description of the building that appears in the dedication booklet) because "it expresses best the eclectic culture and and refinement that a modern library typifies."

4-060. General reading room showing oak bookstacks, Carpenter Memorial Library, Manchester, New Hampshire. Edward L. Tilton, 1912–1914. In *The Carpenter Memorial Library, Dedication Exercises, November 18, 1914* (Concord, NH, 1916), opposite p. 35. GEN COLL,LC-DIG-ppmsca-15550.

SOVTH ELEVATION ~ 1/16 SCALE

4-061. Central Library building, Indianapolis, Indiana, Paul Philippe Cret with Zantzinger, Borie and Medary, 1914–1917. P&P,LOT 4484,LC-DIG-ds-06616.

Designed by the French-trained Cret, and erected at a cost of $526,000, the chaste classical lines of this library are already moving towards the Art Deco form of his Folger Shakespeare Library of a decade later (see 1-022–1-023). As at that building, visitors enter directly into a grand hall flanked by two long ranks of reading rooms that extend along the sides of the building and embrace the stack area.

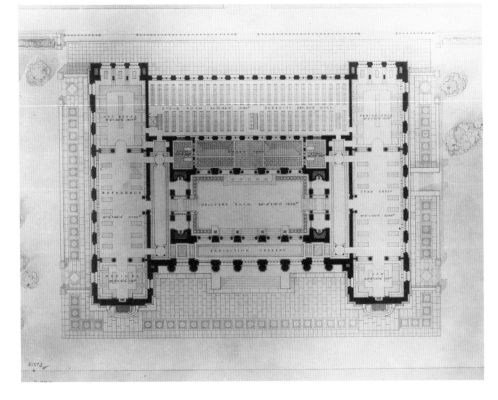

4-062. Central Library building, Indianapolis, Indiana, Paul Philippe Cret with Zantzinger, Borie and Medary, 1914-1917. P&P,LC-DIG-ds-06618.

# 1915 TO 1945

The widespread prosperity of the 1920s allowed larger municipalities that had not been able to raise large central libraries earlier to construct buildings and experiment with combinations of, or variations on, departmentalized programs and open planning, often through municipally allocated funds and special bond issues. They also continued to direct municipal funding to the construction of hundreds of branches intended to provide modern library facilities to the tens of thousands of immigrants and working-class residents who occupied their neighborhoods.

4-063. Cleveland Public Library, Cleveland, Ohio. Walker and Weeks, 1916–1925. Frances Kacala, photographer, 1968. P&P, Specific Subject File, LC-DIG-ds-06555.

The Cleveland library was sited opposite the Federal Building on the mall, which formed the central axis of Daniel H. Burnham's 1903 City Beautiful civic-center plan. Arranged according to a program developed by its director, William H. Brett, subject-oriented reading rooms occupied the periphery of the building. Each of these opened inward into publicly accessible, multistory stacks that ringed the central light well. Adjacent shelves housed the books most closely related to these specialized reading rooms.

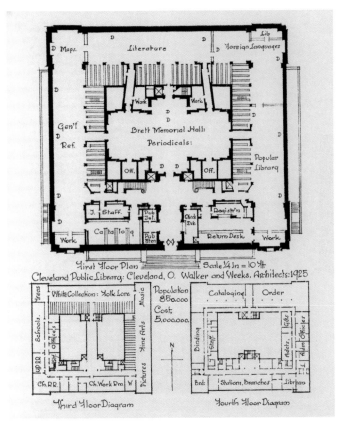

4-064. Plans, Cleveland Public Library, Cleveland, Ohio. Walker and Weeks, 1916–1925. In Alfred Morton Githens and Joseph Lewis Wheeler, *The American Public Library Building* (New York, 1941), p. 315. GEN COLL,LC-DIG-ppmsca-15823.

4-065. Transverse section, Cleveland Public Library, Cleveland, Ohio. Walker and Weeks, 1925. In Alfred Morton Githens and Joseph Lewis Wheeler, *The American Public Library Building* (New York, 1941), p. 316. GEN COLL,LC-DIG-ppmsca-15824.

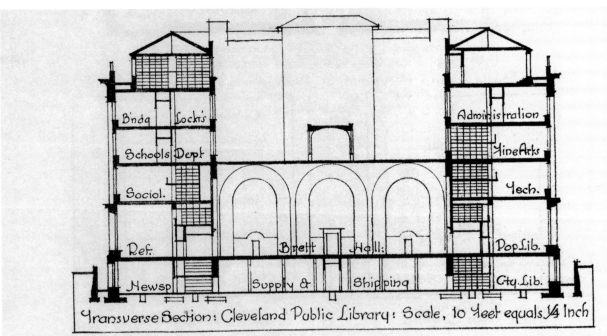

4-066. The John G. White Room, Cleveland Public Library, Cleveland, Ohio. Walker and Weeks, 1925. From Alfred Morton Githens and Joseph Lewis Wheeler, *The American Public Library Building* (New York, 1941), p. 116. GEN COLL,LC-DIG-ppmsca-15820.

4-067. Axial view, west elevation, Los Angeles Public Library, Los Angeles, California. Bertram G. Goodhue and Carlton M. Winslow Sr., 1922–1926. Marvin Rand, photographer, 1971. P&P,HABS,CAL,19-LOSAN,65-9.

Goodhue derived the style of the Los Angeles library from earlier designs that he and the sculptor Lee Oskar Lawrie had developed for the Nebraska State Capitol, where they introduced the geometric, abstract massing, integrated architectural sculpture, and high central tower seen here. In Nebraska as well, Goodhue and Lawrie began collaborating with the poet and philosopher Hartley Burr Alexander. In both monuments this collaboration produced complex iconographic and sculptural programs related to the differing functions and meanings of the two buildings.

4-068. General view, looking southeast from across Fifth Street, Los Angeles Public Library, Los Angeles, California. Bertram G. Goodhue and Carlton M. Winslow Sr., 1922–1926. Marvin Rand, photographer, 1971. P&P,HABS,CAL,19-LOSAN,65–5.

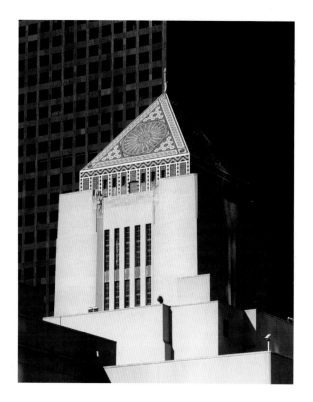

4-069. Tower of the Central Library, Los Angeles Public Library, Los Angeles, California. Bertram G. Goodhue and Carlton M. Winslow Sr., 1922–1926. Carol M. Highsmith photographer, 2013. P&P,CMHA,LC-DIG-highsm-24333.

At the apex of the central tower is a gilded hand holding a torch, which acts as the central symbol of the library's iconographic program developed by the philosopher Hartley Burr Alexander and based on the theme "the light of learning."

4-070. Second floor plan, Los Angeles Public Library, Los Angeles, California. Bertram G. Goodhue and Carlton M. Winslow Sr., 1922–1926. In Alfred Morton Githens and Joseph Lewis Wheeler, *The American Public Library Building* (New York, 1941), p. 319. GEN COLL,LC-DIG-ppmsca-15825.

At the core of Goodhue's plan was a great central rotunda, which was located on the second floor of the building and acted as a point of convergence for elevators, staircases, and corridors. These corridors in turn led to the subject-oriented reading rooms that encircled the building. Four stack towers, which were accessible from each of these rooms, housed the collection.

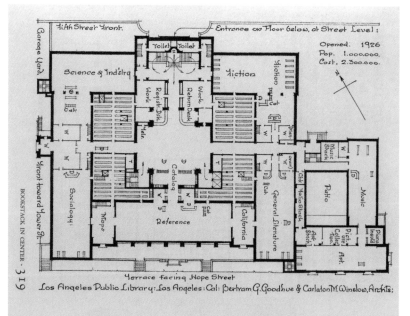

4-071. Interior, rotunda dome, Los Angeles Public Library, Los Angeles, California. Bertram G. Goodhue and Carlton M. Winslow Sr., 1922–1926. Marvin Rand, photographer, 1971. P&P,HABS, CAL,19-LOSAN,65-10.

A bronze chandelier, nine feet in diameter, hangs from the apex of the dome. This displays a blue glass globe surrounded by signs of the zodiac. Designed by Goodhue and modeled by Lee Lawrie, the chandelier weighs two thousand pounds. It was manufactured by the Thomas Day Company of Los Angeles and cost $40,000.

4-072. Enoch Pratt Free Library, Baltimore, Maryland. Clyde and Nelson Friz, architects; Edward Tilton and Alfred Githens, consulting architects, 1926–1933. Carol M. Highsmith, photographer, 2011. P&P,CMHA,LC-DIG-highsm-20527.

4-073. Library window, Enoch Pratt Free Library, Baltimore, Maryland. Clyde and Nelson Friz, architects; Edward Tilton and Alfred Githens, consulting architects, 1926–1933. In Alfred Morton Githens and Joseph Lewis Wheeler, *The American Public Library Building* (New York, 1941), p. 204. GEN COLL, LC-DIG-ppmsca-15821.

The ten-foot-tall exhibit windows built into the facade at street level were, like the showcase windows of a modern department store, intended to draw prospective patrons into the library.

4-074. Plan, Enoch Pratt Free Library, Baltimore, Maryland. Clyde and Nelson Friz, architects; Edward Tilton and Alfred Githens, consulting architects, 1926–1933. In Alfred Morton Githens and Joseph Lewis Wheeler, *The American Public Library Building* (New York, 1941), p. 204. GEN COLL,LC-DIG-ppmsca-15826.

Joseph L. Wheeler, director of the library at the time, worked closely with Tilton and Githens, whom he had appointed as consulting architects in 1928 to develop a modern open plan with subject-oriented departments set to either side of the centrally located catalog and circulation department on the first floor, at sidewalk level. The "live" (or most popular) books in the adult collection, about 150,000 reference and circulating volumes, were arranged by department on the first floor, which measured 140 by 300 feet. Departments were separated by seven-foot bookcases with walls placed only where necessary. The bulk of the Pratt Library's collection (more than one million volumes) was housed in three tiers of stacks in the basement below their respective specialized reading areas. This level also contained workrooms and a children's reading room, which had its own entryway.

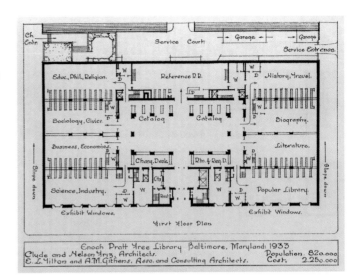

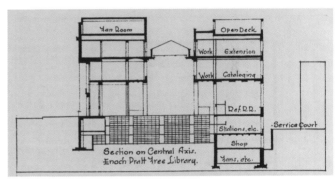

4-075. Section on central axis, Enoch Pratt Free Library, Baltimore, Maryland. Clyde and Nelson Friz, architects; Edward Tilton and Alfred Githens, consulting architects, 1926–1933. In Alfred Morton Githens and Joseph Lewis Wheeler, *The American Public Library Building* (New York, 1941), p. 326. GEN COLL,LC-DIG-ppmsca-15827.

4-076. Entryway, Enoch Pratt Free Library, Baltimore, Maryland. Clyde and Nelson Friz, architects; Edward Tilton and Alfred Githens, consulting architects, 1926–1933. Holmes I. Mettee, photographer, ca. 1933. P&P,LC-DIG-ds-06563.

4-077. Central hall, Enoch Pratt Free Library, Baltimore, Maryland. Clyde and Nelson Friz, architects; Edward Tilton and Alfred Githens, consulting architects, 1926–1933. Carol M. Highsmith photographer, 2011. P&P,CMHA,LC-DIG-highsm-20519.

4-078. Reading room and shelves, Enoch Pratt Free Library, Baltimore, Maryland. Clyde and Nelson Friz, architects; Edward Tilton and Alfred Githens, consulting architects, 1926–1933. Holmes I. Mettee, photographer, ca. 1933. P&P, Processing Reserve, LC-DIG-ds-06564.

4-079. Rendering of the facade, Free Library of Philadelphia, Central Library, Philadelphia, Pennsylvania, Horace Trumbauer and Julian Abele, ca. 1908. P&P, LOT 4484, LC-DIG-ds-06611.

While the early designs for this building date to 1908, construction did not begin until 1917. Trumbauer and Abele based their design on the twin Ministère de la Marine and Hôtel de Crillon buildings on the Place de la Concorde in Paris.

4-080. View of library in environmental context, looking northeast from the roof of the Franklin Institute Free Library of Philadelphia, Central Library, Philadelphia, Pennsylvania, Horace Trumbauer and Julian Abele, 1917–1927. Joseph Elliott, photographer, 2008. P&P,HABS,PA-6749-1.

The Free Library of Philadelphia was the first structure to be erected along Philadelphia's new City Beautiful parkway, which was inspired by the Champs Elysées in Paris to link City Hall to the Philadelphia Museum of Art and Fairmount Park. In *The American Public Library Building* (1941), Wheeler and Githens described the Free Library as a reversion to an older type of plan, which ignored subsequent innovations in efficiency. But the plan dates back to 1908, when many of its features were in vogue among architects of large public libraries. As in New York or Boston, a grand staircase forms the central core of the building and leads up to the principal floor of the institution. As in the New York Public Library, a large reading room—here devoted to art, architecture, and archaeology (now Pepper Hall)—sits over the bookstacks. As at Boston, the main reading room extends across the facade of the building.

4-081. Main stair hall, looking west from second floor, Free Library of Philadelphia, Central Library, Philadelphia, Pennsylvania, Horace Trumbauer and Julian Abele, 1917–1927. Joseph Elliott, photographer, 2008. P&P,HABS,PA-6749-20.

4-082. Main reading room, second floor, looking east, Free Library of Philadelphia, Central Library, Philadelphia, Pennsylvania, Horace Trumbauer and Julian Abele, 1917–1927. Joseph Elliott, photographer, 2008. P&P,HABS,PA-6749-32.

4-083. Pepper Hall, second floor, looking east, Free
Library of Philadelphia, Central Library, Philadelphia,
Pennsylvania, Horace Trumbauer and Julian Abele,
1917–1927. Joseph Elliott, photographer, 2008.
P&P,HABS,PA-6749-33.

4-084. Stacks, fourth level, Free Library of Philadelphia, Central Library, Philadelphia, Pennsylvania, Horace Trumbauer and Julian Abele, 1917–1927. Joseph Elliott, photographer, 2008. P&P, HABS, PA-6749-40.

4-085. Main facade, Central Library (Ingersoll Memorial), Brooklyn, New York. Githens and Keally, 1937–1941. Gottscho-Schleisner, Inc., 1941. P&P, GSC, LC-DIG-gsc-5a06136.

Although they were constrained by an awkward site and existing foundations that had been laid for the uncompleted 1906 design of Raymond F. Almirall, Alfred Githens and Francis Keally were able to create an Art Moderne monument that incorporated many of Githens's contemporary planning innovations, particularly in the formation of the triangular open plan that occupies the center of the building.

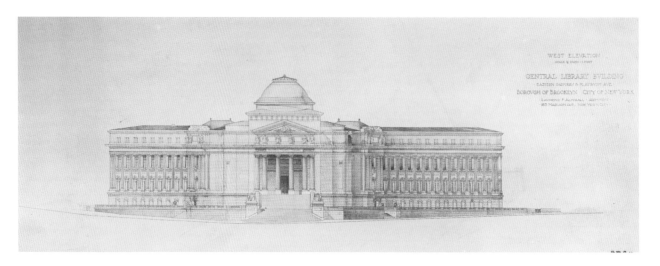

4-086. Proposed design, Central Library, Brooklyn, New York. Raymond F. Almirall, [1908]. P&P, LC-DIG-ds-06615.

4-087. Entry screens, Central Library (Ingersoll Memorial), Brooklyn, New York. Githens and Keally, 1937–1941. Gottscho-Schleisner, Inc., 1941. P&P,GSC,LC-DIG-gsc-5a06276.

Paul Jennewein sculpted the bas-reliefs and Thomas H. Jones created the screen over the entryway to the library. These gigantic doors measured fifty feet in height.

4-088. First floor plan, central portion, Central Library (Ingersoll Memorial), Brooklyn, New York. Githens and Keally, 1937–1941. In Alfred Morton Githens and Joseph Lewis Wheeler, *The American Public Library Building* (New York, 1941), p. 333. GEN COLL,LC-DIG-ppmsca-15828.

The Brooklyn library was arranged around a monumental central hall, which contained the card catalog and circulation department, with reading rooms and proposed future reading rooms arrayed around it. A long curving balcony provided circulation between the two primary wings.

4-089. Foyer, Central Library (Ingersoll Memorial), Brooklyn, New York. Githens and Keally, 1937–1941. Gottscho-Schleisner, Inc., 1941. P&P,GSC,LC-DIG-gsc-5a06269.

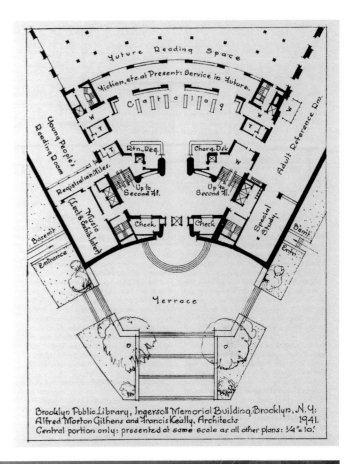

4-090. Librarian's desk, Central Library (Ingersoll Memorial), Brooklyn, New York. Githens and Keally, 1937–1941. Gottscho-Schleisner, Inc., 1941. P&P,GSC,LC-DIG-gsc-5a06264.

4-091. Card catalog, Central Library (Ingersoll Memorial), Brooklyn, New York. Githens and Keally, 1937–1941. Gottscho-Schleisner, Inc., 1941. P&P,GSC,LC-DIG-gsc-5a06190.

4-092. Balcony, Central
Library (Ingersoll
Memorial), Brooklyn,
New York. Githens
and Keally, 1937–1941.
Gottscho-Schleisner, Inc.,
1941. P&P,GSC,LC-DIG-
gsc-5a06194.

4-093. Children's read-
ing room, from balcony,
Central Library (Ingersoll
Memorial), Brooklyn,
New York. Githens
and Keally, 1937–1941.
Gottscho-Schleisner, Inc.,
1941. P&P,GSC,LC-DIG-
gsc-5a06265.

PUBLIC LIBRARY, (MEMORIAL HALL), NORTHAMPTON, MASS.

# 5 SMALL PUBLIC LIBRARIES

The first state legislation that allowed communities to establish municipal taxation for the support of libraries was enacted in New Hampshire in 1849. Within twenty-five years some five hundred free public libraries had been founded in the United States, more than half of these early institutions in New England. The vast majority had to make do with cramped quarters in the town hall or post office, or the basement or spare room in a local church or store; during this early period of library development, only three dozen towns managed to erect small, dedicated library buildings. About two-thirds of these were endowed through local philanthropy fed with the enormous profits accumulated by northern industrialists and merchants during and after the Civil War. The form of these small public buildings reflected the eclectic taste of the era, with styles ranging from Italianate to Romanesque, Gothic, and Classical Revival. The structures typically focused on a single book room, with the occasional addition of a reading room and perhaps a small office for the librarian.

By the end of the nineteenth century some 450 purpose-built structures marked the American countryside. More than 80 percent of these were erected by local philanthropists—a phenomenon that was eclipsed by the

Opposite: 5-009, p. 209.

remarkable largesse of Andrew Carnegie during the first decades of the twentieth century. With capacities of 30,000 and 100,000 volumes, the larger of these institutions experimented with a variety of alcove and book hall configurations to shelve their collections; they also incorporated a number of features introduced early on in the arrangement of the lending department at the Boston Public Library (see 4-007). These included book storage rooms separated from the public with delivery desks, public and women's reading rooms, and offices for staff. Many early public libraries also included auditoriums, art galleries, and natural history collections. The story of their evolution, like that of the department store or railway station, represents a study in the invention and development of a new and essentially modern building typology.

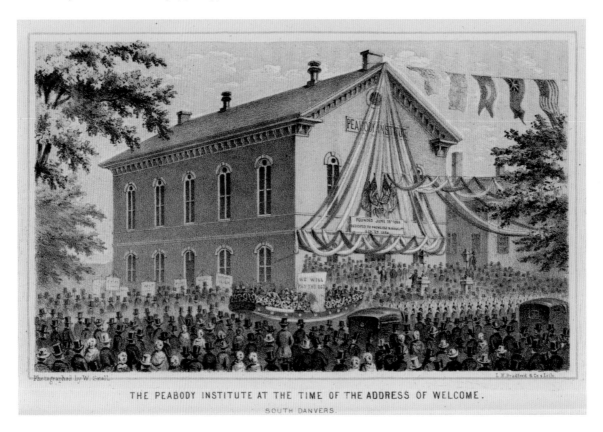

THE PEABODY INSTITUTE AT THE TIME OF THE ADDRESS OF WELCOME.
SOUTH DANVERS.

5-001. The Peabody Institute at the time of the address of welcome for George Peabody, South Danvers (now Peabody), Massachusetts. 1853–1854. Lithograph by L. H. Bradford and Company; photographed by W. Snell. In *Proceedings at the reception and dinner in honor of George Peabody, esq. of London, by the citizens of the old town of Danvers, October 9, 1856. To which is appended an historical sketch of the Peabody institute, with the exercises at the laying of the corner-stone and at the dedication* (Boston, 1856), opposite p. 5. GEN COLL,LC-DIG-ppmsca-15546.

In 1852, George Peabody, an American financier and expatriate living in London, offered to give $20,000 to his native village of South Danvers (renamed Peabody in 1868), Massachusetts, for the establishment of a lyceum that would include both an auditorium for free public lectures and a public library. As would often be repeated elsewhere during the nineteenth century, the institution opened with great fanfare in 1854 as a free lending library, perhaps the first such building in the country to be solely devoted to this purpose.

5-002. Arch erected by the Webster Club for the welcome of George Peabody, Main Street, South Danvers (now Peabody), Massachusetts. Lithograph by J. H. Bufford. In *Proceedings at the reception and dinner in honor of George Peabody, esq. of London, by the citizens of the old town of Danvers, October 9, 1856. To which is appended an historical sketch of the Peabody institute, with the exercises at the laying of the corner-stone and at the dedication* (Boston, 1856), opposite p. 47. GEN COLL,LC-DIG-ppmsca-15547.

George Peabody returned to his hometown in 1856, where he was greeted with celebrations and parades. His example—which was widely acclaimed—along with that of fellow London expatriate Joshua Bates, who in 1852 gave $50,000 to the Boston Public Library, did much to promote local library philanthropy in the nineteenth century.

5-003. East front, Oswego City Library, Oswego, New York. Hewes and Rose, 1854–1856. Paul L. and Sally L. Gordon, photographers, 1966–1967. P&P,HABS,NY,38-OSWE,3-1.

In 1853, exactly one year and a day after Peabody's offer to Danvers was made public, the radical abolitionist Gerritt Smith notified residents of Oswego, New York, that he intended to make available $25,000 for the establishment of a similar institution in that community.

5-004. Main library room, Oswego City Library, Oswego, New York. Hewes and Rose, 1855–1857. Paul L. and Sally L. Gordon, photographers, 1966–1967. P&P,HABS,NY,38-OSWE,3-5.

Books were shelved in alcoves that opened to either side of a central reading area.

5-005. Brookline Public Library, Brookline, Massachusetts. Louis Weissbein, 1866–1869. Unidentified photographer, ca. 1890. P&P,LOT 8908,LC-DIG-ppmsca-15380.

At Brookline, five two-story alcoves were set to either side of a single large hall that appears to have occupied the bulk of the original edifice, which is depicted with several later additions in this photograph. Constructed at a cost of $45,000, the library was expected to hold 44,000 volumes, with "arrangements possible" for 20,000 to 25,000 more if additional shelving was added.

5-006. Alcoves and gallery in the book room, Brookline Public Library, Brookline, Massachusetts. Louis Weissbein, 1866–1869. Unidentified photographer, ca. 1905. P&P,LC-DIG-ppmsca-15406.

5-007. Manchester City Library, Manchester, New Hampshire. George W. Stevens, 1869–1871. Detroit Publishing Co., ca. 1900–1920. P&P,DETR,LC-DIG-det-4a22633.

5-008. Free Public Library of Concord, Concord, Massachusetts. Snell and Gregerson, 1872–1873. Detroit Publishing Co., ca. 1900–1910. P&P,DETR,LC-DIG-det-4a22666.

Books in the Free Public Library of Concord were stored in a three-story-high alcove in a rotunda with an elongated octagonal footprint. This hall was divided into a reference and a lending library and had a projected capacity of 35,000 volumes (by 1890 discovered to be nearer to 20,000), all of which, according to its architects, Snell and Gregerson of Boston, could be "seen at a glance." While patrons were allowed access to this book hall, a railing and delivery desk segregated them from the collection. A separate reading room, librarian's office, and additional workspace for the library staff were arrayed along a central hallway, which led to the rotunda. The reading room, noted the architects on their plan, was also oriented so that its users would be "in view of the librarian's desk in the main Book Room."

5-009. Northampton Free Public Library and Memorial Hall, Northampton, Massachusetts. James H. McLaughlin, 1871–1874. Detroit Publishing Co., 1907. P&P,DETR,LC-DIG-det-4a13749.

In Northampton, the collection was shelved in seven-foot-high, double-faced bookcases placed in parallel rows in the center, or nave, of the book room. This extended from the rear of the main pavilion, which housed a Civil War memorial on its ground floor with a picture gallery and museum above.

5-010. Berkshire Athenaeum and Museum, Pittsfield, Massachusetts. William A. Potter, 1874–1875. Detroit Publishing Co., ca. 1900–1906. P&P,DETR,LC-DIG-det-4a13123.

Following the example of the first floor plan of the first Boston Public Library (see 4-007), the book room at Pittsfield was isolated from a delivery area and "conversation" room by a prominent delivery desk. Along with these spaces, a small consulting and reference library, reading room, librarian's office, and trustees' room were arrayed about a central atrium and staircase, which led up to a picture gallery and natural history cabinet on the second floor.

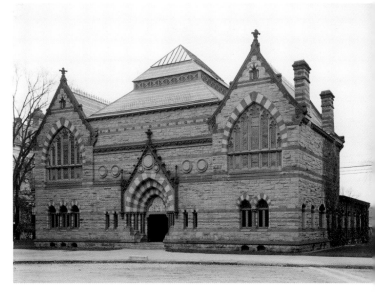

# ARCHITECTS, PATRONS, AND LIBRARIANS, 1875–1990

In addition to the centennial of the American Revolution, 1876 witnessed the publication of the land-mark government report *Public Libraries in the United States of America: Their History, Condition, and Management*, the founding of the American Library Association, and the inaugural publication of the *Library Journal*, the official organ of this new professional organization. The same year marked the birth of *American Architect and Building News*, a periodical that, along with the *Library Journal*, would publish the designs for dozens of libraries and articles on their planning over the next decades. Among the first of the designs to appear in the United States was a group of studio exercises produced by fourth-year architecture students at the Massachusetts Institute of Technology under the tutelage of William Ware using a program devised by the librarian Justin Winsor. These appeared in *The Architectural Sketch Book* in 1875, the same year in which Ware, along with his partner Henry Van Brunt, also began collaborating with Winsor on the design for the new stack wing at Gore Hall (see 2-031–2-033). Henry Hobson Richardson designed his first public library for the town of Woburn, Massachusetts, the following year.

5-011. Designs for a memorial library. W. C. Richardson and H. G. King, 1875. In *The Architectural Sketch Book*, vol. 2, no. 9 (May 1875). P&P,LC-DIG-ppmsca-15587.

The classical demeanor of these student projects reflects the French Beaux-Arts pedagogy that Ware had introduced into the curriculum at MIT and pre-sciently portends the form of hundreds of small libraries that arose in America following the turn of the century. As was not uncommon at the time, the program asked the students to combine the functions of a small public library with "that of doing honor to the memory of the town's people who fell during the war." In addition to having "a library-room, for keep-ing about twenty thousand books," this structure was to be designed to house a delivery area, reading rooms and workspaces for the librarians. Following the precepts of Boston librarian Justin Winsor, the book room was "not to be used by the general pub-lic, but by the librarian and his assistants only." This space was "accordingly for use, and not for show; and the books must be arranged in as compact and conve-nient a manner as possible."

5-012. Designs for a memorial library. R. S. Atkinson and F. W. Stickney, 1875. In *The Architectural Sketch Book*, vol. 2, no. 9 (May 1875). P&P,LC-DIG-ppmsca-15588.

F. W. Stickney's plan focuses on a large central delivery area that opens directly into the book room, which has been extended axially from the rear of the building to form one leg of a T.

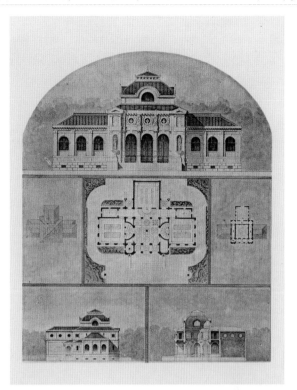

5-013. West front, City Library, Newburgh, New York. John A. Wood, 1876–1877. Jack E. Boucher, photographer, 1970. P&P,HABS,NY,36-NEWB,9-2.

In spite of the rise of a more educated architectural profession, many American libraries continued to exhibit a wide variety of eclectic, picturesque, and ecclesiastical features during the late 1870s and 1880s. These included high-pitched gables, steeples, and nave-like book and reading rooms. Others were represented by commercial storefronts, reflecting the as yet unformed iconography of this young public institution.

5-014. Southeast view showing first and second additions, Hubbard Free Library, Hallowell, Maine. Alexander C. Currier, 1878–1879; new west wing, 1898. Mark Bisgrove, photographer, 1971. P&P,HABS,ME,6-HAL,3-4.

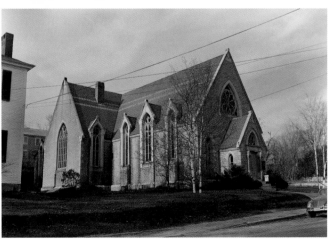

5-015. Interior of the original building shortly after completion in 1879, copy photo, Hubbard Free Library, Hallowell, Maine. Alexander C. Currier, 1878–1879. Mark Bisgrove, photographer, 1971. P&P,HABS,ME,6-HAL,3-1.

5-016. Northeast front and southeast side, Thomas Hughes Public Library, Rugby, Tennessee. Cornelius Onderdonk, 1882. Jack E. Boucher, photographer, 1983. P&P,HABS,TENN,65-RUGBY,2-4.

Named for a popular English author and social reformer, this library, which formed the center of a utopian English agricultural colony founded in 1880, still retains its original furnishings and its entire collection of seven thousand volumes published before 1899. Its simple, slightly ecclesiastical gestures and its small reading room surrounded by shelves of books seem to summarize the democratic yet spiritual aspirations of both the Rugby commune and of American public libraries during the nineteenth century.

5-017. View of interior from northeast, Thomas Hughes Public Library, Rugby, Tennessee. Cornelius Onderdonk, 1882. Jack E. Boucher, photographer, February 1983. P&P,HABS,TENN,65-RUGBY,2-8.

# THE PUBLIC LIBRARIES OF HENRY HOBSON RICHARDSON

It was not until Henry Hobson Richardson introduced his seminal designs for libraries in Woburn, North Easton, Quincy, and Malden, Massachusetts (1876–1885) that the American library began to attain a clearly recognizable form. More than any other architect of the nineteenth century, Richardson formed a new identity for this institution. With their prominent book wings, welcoming entryways, and ecclesiastical associations both outside and in, the form of his buildings would have a profound impact on library planning and design for more than a decade and a half. The most immediate influences of his work can be witnessed in the rapid popularization of his signature Romanesque Revival (or Richardsonian Romanesque) style, with its quarry-faced masonry and prominent round arches, and in the proliferation of the type of linear, two-story alcove book wing that he introduced in his first building of this type.

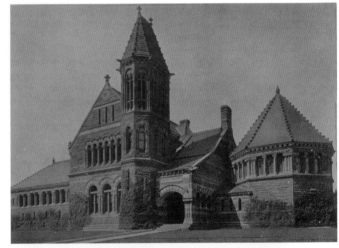

5-018. Woburn Public Library, Woburn, Massachusetts. Gambrill and Richardson, 1876–1879. Unidentified photographer, ca. 1880. P&P, LOT 8908, LC-DIG-ppmsca-15349.

Following the directives of Charles Bowers Winn, who left a bequest of $140,000 for the construction of a public library in his native town, five prominent Boston architectural firms were invited to submit proposals for the building in 1876. The program for the structure included a book room and delivery area, at least two reading rooms, an art gallery, and a natural history museum.

5-019. Book room, Woburn Public Library, Woburn, Massachusetts. Gambrill and Richardson, 1876–1879. Unidentified photographer, ca. 1880. P&P, LOT 8908, LC-DIG-ppmsca-15350.

With a clear eye towards function rather than form, American librarians, led by men such as Justin Winsor and William Frederick Poole, vociferously objected to the type of two-story, linear alcove book storage employed by Richardson in all of his libraries. Winsor defended compact storage, as is indicated by the metal bookstack he advocated at Harvard (see 2-031–2-033), while Poole lobbied for open rooms with freestanding, wooden bookcases no taller than the reach of the average person.

5-020. East front view, Oliver Ames Free Library, North Easton, Massachusetts. Henry Hobson Richardson, 1877–1883. Jack E. Boucher, photographer, 1987. P&P,HABS,MASS,3-EATON,2-2.

The Woburn library had been designed to hold 100,000 volumes; the North Easton book room was projected to accommodate just 25,000. Neither it nor Richardson's third library at Quincy included an art gallery or museum, and their public reading areas were reduced in size, so he was able to progressively simplify and refine his library typology in these two later buildings.

5-021. Detail view of Romanesque east entry, Oliver Ames Free Library, North Easton, Massachusetts. Henry Hobson Richardson, 1877–1883. Jack E. Boucher, photographer, 1987. P&P,HABS,MASS,3-EATON, 2-5.

At North Easton, the entry is now marked with a simple yet imposing arch that replaces Woburn's porch and has been absorbed into a multistory, gabled block—a maneuver that Richardson's early biographer, Mariana Griswold Van Rensselaer, felt imparted a "due dignity" to the entrances, furnishing the buildings with "a true centre of interest."

5-022. General view of barrel-vaulted stack room, from north, Oliver Ames Free Library, North Easton, Massachusetts. Henry Hobson Richardson, 1877–1883. Jack E. Boucher, photographer, 1987. P&P,HABS,MASS,3-EATON,2-8.

5-023. Reading room, Oliver Ames Free Library, North Easton, Massachusetts. Henry Hobson Richardson, 1877–1883. Unidentified photographer, ca. 1905. P&P, LOT 8908, LC-USZ62-104270.

The small reading room to the right of the entry at North Easton was finished with black walnut paneling and an open timber ceiling. The space is dominated by a great hearth with a bas-relief of the library's patron, Oliver Ames II, executed by the American sculptor Augustus Saint-Gaudens, set into the overmantel. The luxurious oak leaves and acorns that surround Saint-Gaudens's bas-relief, and the pomegranate bushes that flank it, have been attributed to the brilliant ornamentalist Stanford White, who was in Richardson's employ at the time this library was being designed.

5-024. Crane Memorial Library, Thomas Crane Public Library, Quincy, Massachusetts. Henry Hobson Richardson, 1880–1882. Detroit Publishing Co., ca. 1900–1906. P&P, DETR, LC-DIG-det-4a11326.

The Crane Library, observed *Harper's Weekly* in 1883, "is the third Village library that Mr. Richardson has designed in Massachusetts, and, upon the whole, the most successful; and saying that is pretty safely saying that it is architecturally the best Village library in the United States."

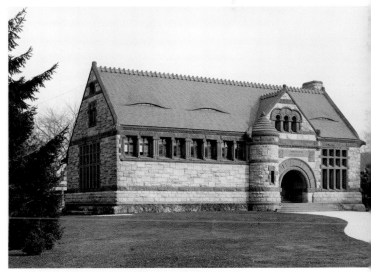

5-025. Converse Memorial Library, Malden, Massachusetts. Henry Hobson Richardson, 1883–1885. Detroit Publishing Co., 1906. P&P, DETR, LC-DIG-det-4a13206.

Completed at the very end of his short career, Richardson's Malden library was erected by Elisha Slade and Mary Diane Converse as a memorial to their son Frank, who had been murdered twenty years earlier during a robbery at his father's bank. The library was dedicated on October 1, 1885, the thirty-ninth anniversary of Frank's birth. At a cost of some $125,000, this monument was far and away the most expensive public library designed and built by Richardson. The arrangement of the interior of the building is related to Richardson's Billings Library at the University of Vermont, the design of which was in the office at the same time (see 2-017–2-019).

5-026. Converse Memorial Library, Malden, Massachusetts. Henry Hobson Richardson, 1883–1885. In *American Architect and Building News* 18 (October 3, 1885). GEN COLL, LC-DIG-ppmsca-15585.

The wide-ranging influence of Richardson's libraries can be seen in a variety of interpretations in the form and planning of more than three dozen such institutions erected across the United States from the early 1880s until about 1900, when the popularity of his Romanesque Revival style would begin to be eclipsed by the growing influence of classicism.

5-027. Howard Memorial Library, New Orleans, Louisiana. Henry Hobson Richardson and Shepley, Rutan, and Coolidge, 1886–1888. Detroit Publishing Co., 1900. P&P, DETR, LC-DIG-det-4a04321.

Erected under the supervision of the successor firm of Shepley, Rutan, and Coolidge after Richardson's death in 1886, the Howard Memorial Library was based on designs that the architect had submitted to a competition for a public library in East Saginaw, Michigan, that same year, but had lost.

5-028. New London Public Library, New London, Connecticut. Shepley, Rutan, and Coolidge, 1889–1891. P&P, LC-DIG-ppmsca-15385.

Although the designers continued to adhere closely to Richardson's exterior forms, the growing criticism of his alcove book rooms pushed even Shepley, Rutan, and Coolidge to turn to metal-stack book storage in their subsequent libraries at Springfield, Ohio, and New London, Connecticut.

# RICHARDSONIAN ROMANESQUE

5-029. Perspective rendering, Scoville Institute, Oak Park, Illinois. Patton and Fisher, 1886–1887. P&P,LOT 8908,LC-DIG-ppmsca-15389.

At the time of his death in 1915, it was said that Normand S. Patton, principal of the firm Patton and Fisher (and after 1901, Patton and Miller), had been responsible for the design of more than one hundred public library buildings, the majority of which were Carnegie edifices constructed in the Midwest (see 6-067–6-069). The Scoville Institute represents the first of these.

5-030. First floor plan, Scoville Institute, Oak Park, Illinois. Patton and Fisher, 1886–1887. P&P,LOT 8908,LC-DIG-ppmsca-15370.

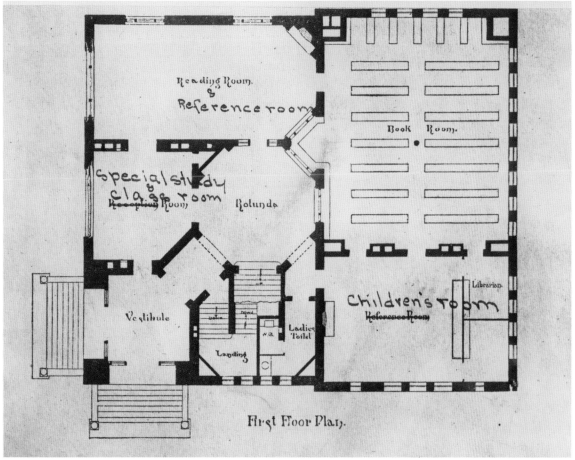

5-031. Delivery desk, Scoville Institute, Oak Park, Illinois. Patton and Fisher, 1886–1887. Unidentified photographer, ca. 1905. P&P, LOT 8908, LC-USZ62-104273.

5-032. Pasadena Public Library, Pasadena, California. C. W. Buchanan, 1887–1890. Unidentified photographer, [1890]. P&P, LOT 8908, LC-DIG-ppmsca-15384.

5-033. Bill Memorial Library, Groton, Connecticut. Stephen C. Earle, 1889–1890. Unidentified photographer, ca. 1890. P&P, LOT 8908, LC-DIG-ppmsca-15393.

Stephen C. Earle, whose office was in Worcester, Massachusetts, designed more than a dozen academic and public libraries between 1880 and the time of his death in 1913. Most of his libraries, like this small monument in Groton, were in the Romanesque Revival style.

5-034. James Prendergast Free Library, Jamestown, New York. A. J. Warner, 1890. Unidentified photographer, ca. 1905. P&P, LOT 8908, LC-USZ62-102429.

5-035. Entry arch, James Prendergast Free Library, Jamestown, New York. A. J. Warner, 1890. Unidentified photographer, [between 1891 and 1980?]. P&P, LOT 8908, LC-DIG-ppmsca-15429.

5-036. A. K. Smiley Public Library, Redlands, California. T. R. Griffith, 1898. Unidentified photographer, [1898]. P&P, LC-DIG-ppmsca-15379.

Following Shepley, Rutan, and Coolidge's earlier design for the campus of Stanford University (1887–1891), as it moved west, Richardson's Romanesque mode was often transformed into the popular Mission Revival style. This new regional fashion was characterized by plain stucco walls (meant to emulate the adobe construction of earlier Spanish missions), round arches supported on broad piers, and red tile roofs.

5-037. Perspective and plan, Brown Memorial Library, Clinton, Maine. John Calvin Stevens, 1899–1900. P&P, LOT 8908, LC-DIG-ppmsca-15364.

5-038. Book shelves with library counter in the background, A. K. Smiley Public Library, Redlands, California. T. R. Griffith, 1898. Everitt Photo, ca. 1905. P&P,LOT 8908,LC-USZ62-104258.

At Redlands, Griffith employed freestanding wooden bookcases of the type promoted for smaller institutions by librarians such as Justin Winsor and William Frederick Poole in the 1880s.

5-039. Reading room, A. K. Smiley Public Library, Redlands, California. T. R. Griffith, 1898. Unidentified photographer, ca. 1905. P&P,LOT 8908,LC-USZ62-104259.

5-040. Gale Memorial Library, Laconia, New Hampshire. Charles Brigham, 1901–1903. Detroit Publishing Co., 1908. P&P,DETR,LC-DIG-det-4a22682.

# WILLIAM FREDERICK POOLE'S LIBRARY PLAN

Before James Bertram began to distribute his suggested plans for Carnegie libraries (see 6-057) in 1911, the most influential model for the planning of small public libraries was published by William Frederick Poole in the *Library Journal* in 1885, in an article entitled "Small Library Buildings." In it, Poole observed that since the founding of the librarian's association in 1876, the discussion of library design had "been directed almost wholly to the requirements of large libraries," when for every library of "the larger class" that had been erected in America, "a hundred" small buildings were, in fact, needed. To fill this gap, his plan called for a structure that would cost in the neighborhood of $50,000 and would be capable of storing up to 30,000 books. The most prominent feature of Poole's plan was "a room for the storage of books *without alcoves or galleries*" (A in the plan). This was to be fifteen or sixteen feet in height, with eight-foot-high wall cases around its periphery and parallel rows of free-standing, double-sided, wooden shelves set in the center of the space. Extending as it did from the rear block of the building, this room could be illuminated with rows of windows set above the wall cases, and was capable, with minor modifications, of being expanded in any of three directions. In an era of closed stacks, a delivery desk separated the book room from a public delivery area (C). A general reference and reading room (E) was isolated at the front of the building. With some variation, Poole's plan was widely employed during the later nineteenth century by firms specializing in small library design, including Van Brunt and Howe and Patton and Fisher, and they often merged this new "modern" library arrangement with Richardson's distinctive Romanesque forms.

5-041. Floor plan for a small public library. William
Frederick Poole, 1885. In *Library Journal* 10 (1885),
p. 253. GEN COLL,LC-DIG-ppmsca-15576.

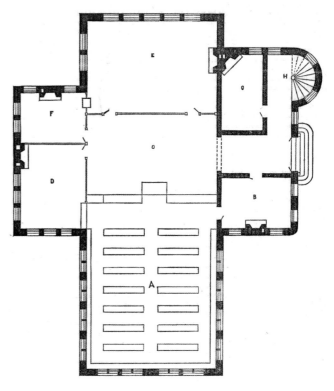

5-042. Dayton Public School Library, Dayton, Ohio. Peters and Burns, 1885–1888. In *American Architect and Building News* 19 (February 6, 1886). GEN COLL,LC-DIG-ppmsca-15586.

The plan in the upper-left-hand corner of this illustration bears a very close resemblance to Poole's 1885 plan, a fact the librarian noted in a discussion of library planning at the A.L.A. conference in 1886.

5-043. Dayton Public Library, Dayton, Ohio. Peters and Burns, 1885–1888. William Henry Jackson, photographer. Detroit Publishing Co., 1902. P&P, LC-DIG-det-4a09807.

5-044. Dedham Public Library, Dedham, Massachusetts. Van Brunt and Howe, 1886–1888. Unidentified photographer, between 1890 and 1920. P&P,LC-USZ62-102439.

While following Poole's plan, Van Brunt and Howe employed the type of metal stack shelving that Van Brunt and his former partner William Ware had pioneered a decade earlier at Gore Hall, Harvard (see 2-031–2-033). They would continue to use this system in their later libraries as well.

5-045. Reading room with delivery desk, Dedham Public Library, Dedham, Massachusetts. Van Brunt and Howe, 1886–1888. Unidentified photographer, ca. 1905. P&P,LC-USZ62-104264.

5-046. Free Public Library and Reading Room, Quincy, Illinois, Patton and Fisher, 1887–1889. P&P,LC-DIG-ds-06533

While slightly modified, with a small delivery room to the left and larger reference room to the right, Patton and Fisher's plan for Quincy is still closely related to Poole's scheme. It was constructed at a cost of $23,000, with a capacity to house 20,000 volumes and the potential to increase this number by adding an extension to the end of the book wing.

5-047. Kalamazoo Public Library, Kalamazoo, Michigan. Patton and Fisher, 1890–1891. In *Inland Architect and News Record* 17 (June 1891). GEN COLL,LC-DIG-ppmsca-15555.

Although the Richardsonian entryway has now been shifted to the center of the facade, Patton and Fisher's Kalmazoo plan was almost identical to that in Quincy, Illlinois. A third small library in this series, constructed in Muskegon, Michigan (1889–1890), has an arrangement that is identical to Poole's suggested plan. In spite of their exterior debt to Richardson, the editors of the *Library Journal* nonetheless approved of Patton's work, noting in 1891 that he had "the true theory of library construction; he thinks that the shell should be fashioned to accommodate the animal, not that the animal should be squeezed into the shell."

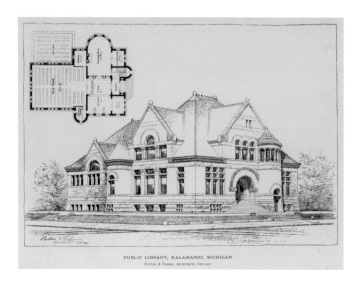

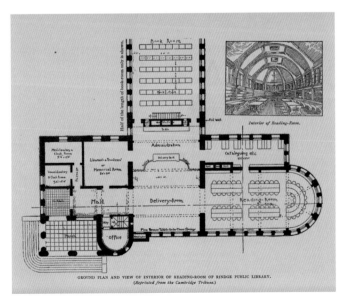

GROUND PLAN AND VIEW OF INTERIOR OF READING-ROOM OF RINDGE PUBLIC LIBRARY.
*(Reprinted from the Cambridge Tribune.)*

5-048. Hoyt Public Library, East Saginaw, Michigan. Van Brunt and Howe, 1886–1890. Detroit Publishing Co., ca. 1900–1920. P&P,DETR,LC-DIG-det-4a22437.

With William Poole as advisor to the competition for the design of this building, it is perhaps not surprising that Van Brunt and Howe's entry—which employed Poole's plan—triumphed over entries by firms such as that of Henry Hobson Richardson, and McKim, Mead & White. Richardson's successor firm of Shepley, Rutan, and Coolidge would reuse his losing entry in Saginaw in New Orleans (see 5-026) after his death in 1886, while Van Brunt and Howe employed a slight variation on their Saginaw plan two years later in Cambridge, Massachusetts.

5-049. Rindge Public Library, Cambridge, Massachusetts. Van Brunt and Howe, 1888–1889. Detroit Publishing Co., 1906. P&P,DETR,LC-USZ62-102442.

5-050. Ground plan and sketch of Rindge Public Library reading room, Cambridge, Massachusetts. Van Brunt and Howe, 1888–1889. In *Library Journal* 12 (1887), p. 552. GEN COLL,LC-DIG-ppmsca-15545.

5-051. Book wing, Hoyt Public Library, East Saginaw, Michigan. Van Brunt and Howe, 1886–1890. Unidentified photographer, ca. 1890. P&P,LOT 8908,LC-DIG-ppmsca-15387.

5-052. General view of southeast (front) facade, Pequot Library, Southport, Connecticut. Robert H. Robertson, 1887–1893. Jack E. Boucher, photographer, September 1966. P&P,HABS,CONN,1-SOUPO,23-1.

Elbert and Virginia Marquand Monroe erected the Pequot Library as a memorial to Virginia's uncle Frederick Marquand on the grounds of his estate, as a repository for a valuable collection of Americana. The library was donated to the Pequot Library Association by Virginia Marquand Monroe, Mary C. Wakeman, and the Reverend William H. Holman.

5-053. Probable restored floor plan based on a 1947 drawing by Roswell Barratt, Pequot Library, Southport, Connecticut. Robert H. Robertson, 1887–1893. John G. Waite, delineator, 1966. P&P,HABS,CONN,1-SOUPO,23-,sheet no. 2.

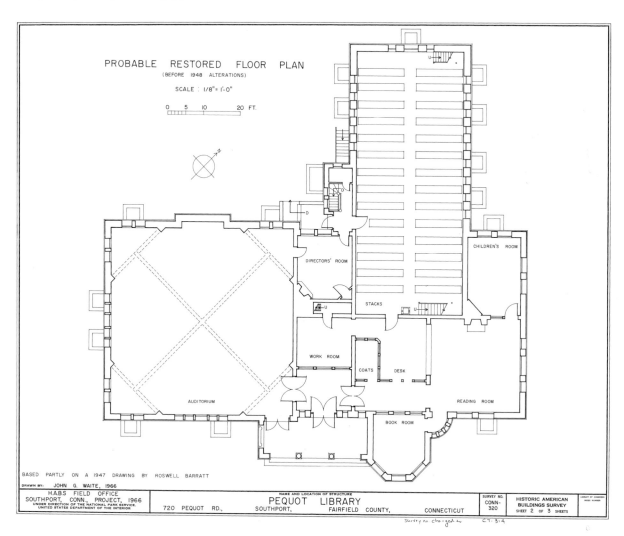

PROBABLE RESTORED FLOOR PLAN
(BEFORE 1948 ALTERATIONS)

SCALE : 1/8"= 1'-0"

0   5   10      20 FT.

DIRECTORS' ROOM

CHILDREN'S ROOM

STACKS

WORK ROOM

COATS    DESK

AUDITORIUM

READING ROOM

BOOK ROOM

BASED PARTLY ON A 1947 DRAWING BY ROSWELL BARRATT

DRAWN BY:   JOHN G. WAITE, 1966

H.A.B.S FIELD OFFICE
SOUTHPORT, CONN., PROJECT, 1966
UNDER DIRECTION OF THE NATIONAL PARK SERVICE,
UNITED STATES DEPARTMENT OF THE INTERIOR

720 PEQUOT RD.,

NAME AND LOCATION OF STRUCTURE
PEQUOT LIBRARY
SOUTHPORT,      FAIRFIELD COUNTY,      CONNECTICUT

SURVEY NO.
CONN-
320

HISTORIC AMERICAN
BUILDINGS SURVEY
SHEET 2 OF 3 SHEETS

Survey no. changed to      CT-314

5-054. Metal stacks in book room, Pequot Library, Southport, Connecticut. Robert H. Robertson, 1887–1893. Unidentified photographer, ca. 1893. P&P,LOT 8908,LC-DIG-ppmsca-15374.

The Winslow Brothers Company of Chicago manufactured the Library Bureau stack system pictured here. It consisted of single steel uprights to which were attached adjustable iron brackets that supported the cantilevered shelves. The Pequot Library system used the Library Bureau's "standard bracket, Bartlett design."

5-055. Detail of stack shelves, Pequot Library, Southport, Connecticut. Robert H. Robertson, 1887–1893. Jack E. Boucher, photographer, September 1966. P&P,HABS,CONN,1-SOUPO,23-10.

# A NEW CLASSICISM

Even as new Richardsonian libraries were appearing in the American countryside during the middle 1890s, his style was already being challenged by a renewed taste for the classical, one which was heavily driven by the growing influence of the École des Beaux-Arts in Paris. Prefigured by the MIT student designs of 1875 (see 5-011–5-012), this new fashion also was spurred by McKim, Mead & White's widely published designs for the new Boston Public Library (1887–1895; see 4-024–4-026) and the spectacular success of the Columbian Exposition in 1893. Even Shepley, Rutan, and Coolidge, whose early fealty to their mentor is manifest at New Orleans, and later in New London, Connecticut (1889–1891; see 5-027–5-028), rapidly succumbed to this growing classical movement. The shift in allegiance is more than apparent in their design for the Field Memorial Library, a building erected at the turn of the century by the Chicago merchandising magnate Marshall Field in his home village of Conway, Massachusetts (see 5-064). The move away from Romanesque Revival was as rapid as its ascension. Of sixty-seven library designs published in a special issue of the *Architectural Review* in 1902, for example, fifty-seven were classically inspired, and only five reflected the style of Richardson. The shift in taste is evident in the form of the hundreds of libraries constructed using Carnegie monies during the first two decades of the next century (see chapter 6).

5-056. Brooks Library Building, Brattleboro Free Library, Brattleboro, Vermont. J. M. Currier, 1886. Detroit Publishing Co., 1905. P&P,DETR,LC-DIG-det-4a12252.

By the mid-1890s, as the fashion for the Romanesque Revival began to wane, J. M. Currier's small library in Brattleboro, Vermont, with its broad Richardsonian arch but symmetrical facade and plan, seems to foreshadow the move toward the Classical Revival that would take the country by storm during the early years of the twentieth century. Other architects at the end of the century, such as Henry M. Francis in northern New England, seem likewise to have attempted to mediate between these two styles.

5-057. Ingalls Memorial Library, Rindge, New Hampshire. Henry M. Francis, 1894. Unidentified photographer, ca. 1905. P&P,LOT 8908,LC-USZ62-102432.

5-058. Benjamin M. Smith Memorial Library, Meredith, New Hampshire. George Swann, 1900–1901. Detroit Publishing Co., ca. 1900–1910. P&P,DETR,LC-DIG-det-4a22678.

5-059. James Blackstone Memorial Library, Branford, Connecticut. Solon S. Beman, 1893–1896. Unidentified photographer, ca. 1905. P&P,LOT 8908,LC-USZ62-102430.

Timothy E. Blackstone erected this building in his hometown as a memorial to his father, James, at a cost of $300,000. Timothy had moved some four decades earlier to the Midwest, where he made his fortune in the railroad industry and mixed with other Chicago philanthropists, such as Marshall Field. Solon S. Beman, the architect of this structure, is best known for his work at Pullman, Illinois, for George Pullman, a neighbor of the Blackstones.

5-060. Bookstacks, James Blackstone Memorial Library, Branford, Connecticut. Solon S. Beman, 1893–1896. Unidentified photographer, ca. 1905. P&P,LOT 8908,LC-USZ62-102431.

5-061. Hart Memorial Library, Troy, New York. Barney and Chapman, 1895–1896. Detroit Publishing Co., 1905. P&P,DETR,LC-DIG-det-4a30399.

5-062. Three-quarters view, Hearst Free Library, Anaconda, Montana. Frank S. Van Trees, 1897–1898. Unidentified photographer, ca. 1984. P&P,HABS,MONT,12-ANAC,1-K-1.

5-063. Scranton Memorial Library, Madison, Connecticut. Henry Bacon of Brite and Bacon, 1899–1900. Carol M. Highsmith, photographer, 2011. P&P,CMHA,LC-DIG-highsm-18890.

Mary Eliza Scranton gave this building, which was constructed at a cost of $30,000, to the Madison Library Association as a memorial to her father, Erastus Clark Scranton. In 1901 the association was dissolved and the library was incorporated as a public institution partially funded by the city of Madison.

5-064. Field Memorial Library, Conway, Massachusetts. Shepley, Rutan, and Coolidge, 1900–1901. Unidentified photographer, ca. 1900–1910. P&P,US GEOG,LC-USZ62-102438.

The Field Memorial Library, erected at a cost of almost $100,000, was given by Chicago merchandising magnate Marshall Field to Conway in memory of his mother and father. Field was a trustee of the Art Institute of Chicago, which was designed by Shepley, Rutan, and Coolidge and erected in 1891–1893, and the architects' almost contemporary Chicago Public Library was located just down the street from this institution (see 4-035–4-038).

5-065. Plan, Field Memorial Library, Conway, Massachusetts. Shepley, Rutan, and Coolidge, 1900–1901. P&P,LOT 8908,LC-DIG-ppmsca-15401.

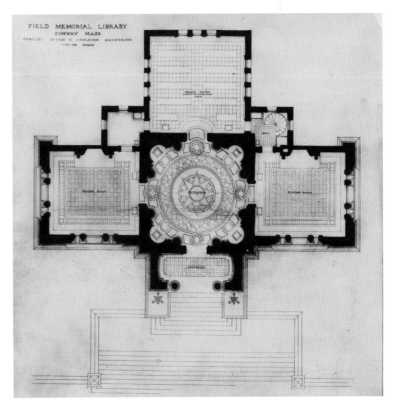

5-066. Case Memorial Library, Auburn, New York. Carrère and Hastings, 1899–1902. Unidentified photographer, [1902]. P&P,LOT 8908,LC-DIG-ppmsca-15362.

5-067. Book wing, Case Memorial Library, Auburn, New York. Carrère and Hastings, 1899–1902. Unidentified photographer, ca. 1902. P&P,LOT 8908,LC-DIG-ppmsca-15358.

5-068. Stickler Memorial Library, Orange, New Jersey. McKim, Mead & White, 1900–1901. Unidentified photographer, ca. 1902. P&P,LOT 8908,LC-DIG-ppmsca-15363.

Ironically, Andrew Carnegie's offer to build public libraries anywhere in the country, which began in earnest in 1898, would substantially stifle the type of locally focused philanthropy reflected by the Scranton, Field, Case, or Stickler family memorials. In 1899 and 1900, for example, Carnegie offered to endow thirty-seven new library buildings in the United States, and then during the following three years donated funds for an additional 463 structures of this type. Many local philanthropists thus began to look elsewhere to place their money.

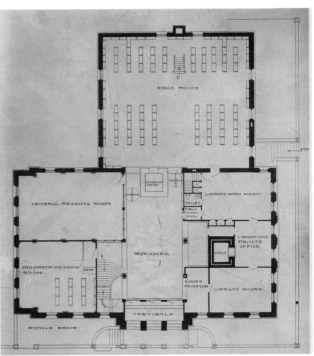

5-069. Public Library, St. Joseph, Missouri. Edmund Jacques Eckel, 1901–1902. Unidentified photographer, ca. 1903. P&P, LOT 8908, LC-DIG-ppmsca-15396.

This library was funded with a $100,000 school bond issue. The School District offices were located on the second floor.

5-070. Floor plan, Public Library, St. Joseph, Missouri. Edmund Jacques Eckel, 1901–1902. P&P, LOT 8908, LC-DIG-ppmsca-15369.

5-071. Circulation desk, Public Library, St. Joseph, Missouri. Edmund Jacques Eckel, 1901–1902. Unidentified photographer, ca. 1903. P&P, LOT 8908, LC-DIG-ppmsca-15410.

5-072. Book room, Public Library, St. Joseph, Missouri. Edmund Jacques Eckel, 1901–1902. Unidentified photographer, ca. 1900–1905. P&P, LOT 8908, LC-DIG-ppmsca-15419.

5-073. Ryerson Public Library, Grand Rapids, Michigan. Shepley, Rutan, and Coolidge, 1904–1905. Detroit Publishing Co., between 1905 and 1910. P&P,DETR,LC-DIG-det-4a23409.

This building was given to the city by native son Martin A. Ryerson after his move to Chicago. Ryerson also donated funds to the Art Institute, which was likewise designed by Shepley, Rutan, and Coolidge.

5-074. Peter White Public Library, Marquette, Michigan. Patton and Miller, 1902–1904. Detroit Publishing Co., 1905. P&P,DETR,LC-DIG-det-4a12347.

This library was named for Peter White, the founder of the Marquette Public Library in 1879. He also served as a member of the World's Columbian Exposition Commission, where he would have been introduced to the classicism exhibited by this building.

5-075. Handley Library, Winchester, Virginia. J. Stewart Barney and Henry Otis Chapman, 1908-1913. National Photo Co., [1920]. P&P,LC-DIG-npcc-02050.

Judge John Handley of Scranton, Pennsylvania, left $250,000 in 1895 for a library "for the free use of the people of Winchester." It is notable for its ornate Neo-Baroque ornament and dome.

5-076. General exterior, Finkelstein Memorial Library, Spring Valley, New York. George Munson Schofield, 1940–1941. Gottscho-Schleisner, Inc., July 25, 1941. P&P,GSC,LC-G612-T-40773.

While Colonial Revival in style, the Finkelstein library represents perfectly the type of open plan promoted by progressive librarians earlier in the century and touted by Wheeler and Githens in their 1941 treatise on modern library design. By the nineteen twenties it had become standard for America's smaller institutions.

5-077. Entrance detail, Finkelstein Memorial Library, Spring Valley, New York. George Munson Schofield, 1940–1941. Gottscho-Schleisner, Inc., July 25, 1941. P&P,GSC,LC-DIG-gsc-5a07460.

5-078. Interior, Finkelstein
Memorial Library, Spring
Valley, New York. George
Munson Schofield,
1940–1941. Gottscho-
Schleisner, Inc., July 25,
1941. P&P,GSC,LC-DIG-
gsc-5a07462.

5-079. Interior, Finkelstein
Memorial Library, Spring
Valley, New York. George
Munson Schofield,
1940–1941. Gottscho-
Schleisner, Inc., July 25,
1941. P&P,GSC,LC-DIG-
gsc-5a07461.

# THE GREAT DEPRESSION

In addition to the construction of new library buildings such as those undertaken by the Works Progress Administration (WPA) and the Public Works Administration (PWA), Roosevelt's New Deal attempted to make books available to constituencies that had been previously neglected. These included the rural poor and Depression-era refugees. Photographers working for another New Deal program, the Farm Security Administration (FSA), recorded these efforts, which contrast markedly with the opulence of elite private libraries, such as those founded by J. Pierpont Morgan or Henry Clay and Emily Jordan Folger (see 1-019—1-023).

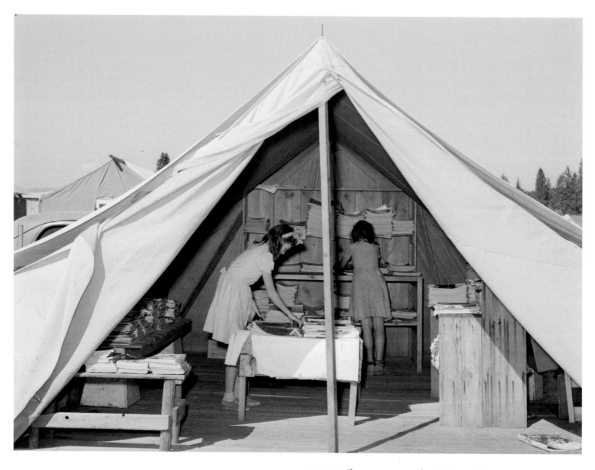

5-080. Library tent at the FSA mobile camp for migratory farm workers, Odell, Oregon. Russell Lee, photographer, September 1941. P&P, FSA, LC-DIG-fsa-8c22565.

5-081. In the library of the FSA (Farm Security Administration) farm families community, Yuma, Arizona. Russell Lee, photographer, 1942. P&P,FSA,LC-DIG-fsa-8c24228.

5-082. Books in a toolbox. Rockwood vicinity, Tennessee. Unidentified photographer, ca. 1935–1940. P&P,FSA,LC-USZ62-90715.

This small library represented an effort by the Tennessee Valley Authority to supply books to its employees in the most remote areas of its project.

5-083. Public library in the piney woods in the southwestern section of Mississippi. Dorothea Lange, photographer, July 1937. P&P,FSA,LC-DIG-fsa-8632222.

5-084. Public library in the piney woods of southwestern Mississippi. Dorothea Lange, photographer, July 1937. P&P,FSA,LC-DIG-fsa-8632221.

NORTH SIDE   PA.

# 6

# THE CARNEGIE ERA

The philanthropy of Andrew Carnegie had a profound influence on the rate of construction and the form of the American public library during the early years of the twentieth century. While his first gifts—primarily to cities and towns associated with his personal economic interests—began in 1886, the acceleration of his philanthropic endeavors at the turn of the century formed the real catalyst for change. Under the supervision of his personal secretary, James Bertram, Carnegie's gifting process was streamlined, and simple guidelines and sample plans were developed to assist recipient communities and architects in the development and planning of their local libraries.

By 1917, Carnegie himself and the Carnegie Foundation (which he established in 1911) had endowed 1,679 library buildings in what are now forty-seven of the fifty states, as well as in the District of Columbia and Puerto Rico, dramatically shifting the public library movement from the East Coast to the Midwest, West, and South. In addition to the widely recognized small libraries that articulate America's rural and suburban landscapes, Carnegie money funded the construction of central and branch libraries in America's larger cities, as well as many college and university facilities. According to Carnegie,

Opposite: 6-003, p. 243.

"the main consideration" of the philanthropist "should be to help those who will help themselves; to provide part of the means by which those who desire to improve may do so."

Carnegie first enunciated his philosophy of giving in an article entitled "Wealth" that appeared in the *North American Review* in 1889. He argued here that "the man of wealth" was "the mere trustee and agent for his poorer brethren, bringing to their service his superior wisdom, experience, and ability to administer, doing for them better than they would or could do for themselves."

While the vast majority of communities welcomed Carnegie's money, his largesse did not proceed without raising some suspicion of his motives—whether they represented an attempt by the industrialist to assuage his guilt over past actions, or to create a lasting monument to his own fame.

6-001. Andrew Carnegie. Marceau, N.Y.C., photographer, 1913. P&P,BIOG FILE,LC-USZ62-58581.

6-002. Andrew Carnegie. Albert Levering, illustrator. In *Life*, April 13, 1905, cover. GEN COLL,LC-USZ62-53268.

# THE EARLY CARNEGIE LIBRARIES

Before the commencement of his "wholesale" period of library philanthropy at the very end of the century, Carnegie erected Romanesque Revival institutions in half a dozen communities in the United States; most of these were related to his personal business interests. The two early exceptions were library buildings the philanthropist raised in Johnstown, Pennsylvania, where he belonged to a fishing and hunting club (see 6-017), and in Fairfield, Iowa, in 1891, when, at the behest of U.S. senator James Wilson, he donated $30,000 for a building, the first Carnegie library to be raised west of the Mississippi.

6-003. Carnegie Library and Music Hall, Allegheny City (now Pittsburgh), Pennsylvania. Smithmeyer & Pelz, 1886–1890. Detroit Publishing Co., 1905. P&P,DETR,LC-DIG-det-4a12727.

Employing a plan they derived from one published by William Frederick Poole in the *Library Journal* in 1885 (see 5-041), Smithmeyer & Pelz, who had designed the Library of Congress, were among the first architects employed by Carnegie.

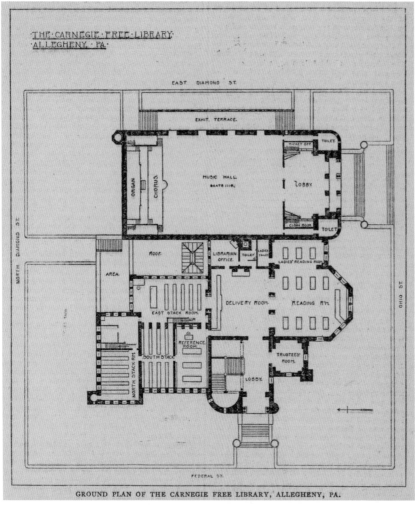

GROUND PLAN OF THE CARNEGIE FREE LIBRARY, ALLEGHENY, PA.

6-004. First floor plan, Carnegie Library and Music Hall, Allegheny City (now Pittsburgh), Pennsylvania. Smithmeyer & Pelz, 1886–1890. In *Library Journal* 18 (1893), p. 289. GEN COLL,LC-DIG-ppmsca-15544.

6-005. Reading room, looking into the delivery room, Carnegie Library and Music Hall, Allegheny City (now Pittsburgh), Pennsylvania. Smithmeyer & Pelz, 1886–1890. Unidentified photographer, ca. 1890. P&P,LOT 8908,LC-DIG-ppmsca-15378.

6-006. Women's Reading room, Carnegie Library and Music Hall, Allegheny City (now Pittsburgh), Pennsylvania. Smithmeyer & Pelz, 1886–1890. Unidentified photographer, ca. 1900. P&P, LOT 8908, LC-DIG-ppmsca-15405.

6-007. Children's reading room, Carnegie Library and Music Hall, Allegheny City (now Pittsburgh), Pennsylvania. Smithmeyer & Pelz, 1886–1890. Unidentified photographer, 1900–1905. P&P, LOT 8908, LC-DIG-ppmsca-15412.

6-008. Music hall, Carnegie Library and Music Hall, Allegheny City (now Pittsburgh), Pennsylvania. Smithmeyer & Pelz, 1886–1890. Unidentified photographer, 1890. P&P, LOT 8908, LC-DIG-ppmsca-15357.

Many of Carnegie's early libraries also housed other cultural and public amenities, such as art galleries, auditoriums, swimming pools, gymnasiums, and even billiard parlors and bowling alleys. This music hall, appended to one side of the Allegheny City plan, could seat 1,100 people.

6-009. Braddock Carnegie Free Library, Braddock, Pennsylvania. William Halsey Wood, 1887–1889; addition to right rear by Longfellow, Alden, and Harlow, 1893. Unidentified photographer, 1893. P&P, LOT 8908, LC-DIG-ppmsca-15382.

6-010. Gymnasium, Braddock Carnegie Free Library, Braddock, Pennsylvania. Part of the enlargement by Longfellow, Alden, and Harlow, 1893. Unidentified photographer, 1893. P&P, LOT 8908, LC-DIG-ppmsca-15372.

6-011. Carnegie Library of Homestead, Munhall, Pennsylvania. Longfellow, Alden, and Harlow, 1893–1898. Unidentified photographer, ca. 1900. P&P, LOT 8908, LC-DIG-ppmsca-15354.

Work was begun on this lavish facility just one year after the infamous Homestead Strike had paralyzed the Carnegie steel facilities in this community, resulting in the dissolution of the union as well as injury and death to numerous workers and the Pinkerton detectives who had been called in to forcibly end the walkout.

6-012. Delivery room, Carnegie Library of Homestead, Munhall, Pennsylvania. Longfellow, Alden, and Harlow, 1893–1898. Unidentified photographer, ca. 1900. P&P,LC-DIG-ppmsca-15356.

6-013. Adult reading room, Carnegie Library of Homestead, Munhall, Pennsylvania. Longfellow, Alden, and Harlow, 1893–1898. Unidentified photographer, ca. 1900. P&P,LOT 8908,LC-DIG-ppmsca-15355.

6-014. Gymnasium, Carnegie Library of Homestead, Munhall, Pennsylvania. Longfellow, Alden, and Harlow, 1893–1898. Unidentified photographer, ca. 1898–1905. P&P,LC-USZ62-86467.

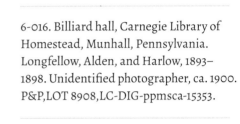

6-015. Swimming pool, Carnegie Library of Homestead, Munhall, Pennsylvania. Longfellow, Alden, and Harlow, 1893–1898. Unidentified photographer, ca. 1900–1905. P&P,LOT 8908,LC-DIG-ppmsca-15418.

6-016. Billiard hall, Carnegie Library of Homestead, Munhall, Pennsylvania. Longfellow, Alden, and Harlow, 1893–1898. Unidentified photographer, ca. 1900. P&P,LOT 8908,LC-DIG-ppmsca-15353.

6-017. North front and west side, Johnstown Public Library, Johnstown, Pennsylvania. Addison Hutton, 1890–1892. Jet Lowe, photographer, 1988. P&P,HABS,PA,11-JOTO,9-1.

While the Johnstown Public Library was not located in a community where he had factories, Carnegie pledged money to rebuild the Cambria library after it was destroyed in the great Johnstown Flood of 1889 caused by the collapse of a private dam owned by the South Fork Fishing and Hunting Club, an organization in which Carnegie was a prominent member. The building was rehabilitated in 1988–1989 for use as the Johnstown Flood Museum.

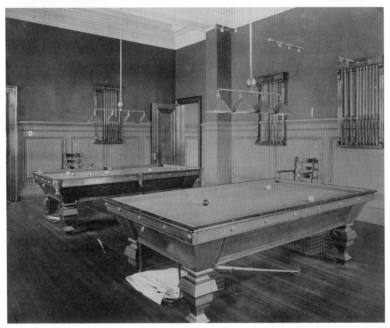

6-018. Carnegie Library, Schenley Park, Oakland, Pittsburgh, Pennsylvania. Longfellow, Alden, and Harlow, 1891–1895. Detroit Publishing Co., 1901. P&P,DETR,LC-DIG-det-4a09236.

This was the most ambitious of Carnegie's early libraries. The program called for a large music hall (between the towers to the left), a library, and an art gallery, as well as a science and natural history museum.

# CARNEGIE'S URBAN LIBRARIES, 1899–1921

In addition to his well-known gifts to small towns, Carnegie funded the construction of more than a dozen central library buildings in larger urban areas, though in these cities he also often insisted that a portion of his grant be expended on branch libraries that might better serve working-class and immigrant neighborhoods. The monumental classical form of many of the central libraries not only followed the example of the Columbian and other great American expositions of the era but, in response to the City Beautiful movement, occasionally took their place as integral elements of new civic center plans being developed for these communities. While the last of these central library buildings (the Detroit Public Library, which was given a grant in 1901) was not actually completed until 1921, Carnegie stopped making donations for these larger monuments after 1902.

6-019. Preliminary perspective drawing, Central Public Library, Washington, D.C. Ackerman & Ross, 1899–1903. Albert Randolph Ross, illustrator, 1899. P&P, LC-USZ62-114149.

In 1899, Carnegie pledged $682,000 toward the construction of a new central library and three branches in the District of Columbia. The central building served as Washington's primary library until Ludwig Mies van der Rohe's Martin Luther King Jr. Memorial Library (see AF-002) replaced it in 1972. Albert Randolph Ross was responsible for the design of half a dozen central Carnegie libraries, as well as numerous smaller buildings such as that in Nashville (see 6-043).

6-020. Central Public Library, Washington, D.C. Ackerman & Ross, 1899–1903. Detroit Publishing Co., 1906. P&P, DETR, LC-DIG-det-4a13170.

6-021. South front, Central Public Library,
Washington, D.C. Ackerman and Ross, 1899–1903.
Louise Taft, photographer, 1985. P&P,HABS,
DC,WASH,551-3.

Following the lead of Carrère and Hastings's design
for the New York Public Library (see 4-041–4-042),
Ackerman and Ross's Washington building employed
a triumphal arch motif for its entryway. It was ornamented with sculpture by Philip Martiny.

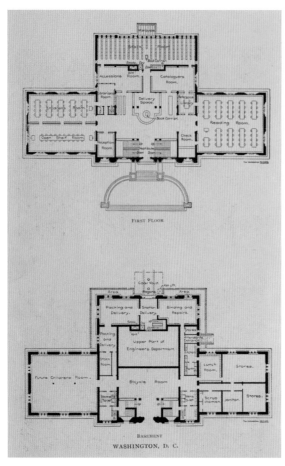

FIRST FLOOR

BASEMENT

WASHINGTON, D. C.

6-022. First floor and basement plans, Central Public Library, Washington, D.C. Ackerman & Ross, 1899–1903. In Theodore Wesley Koch, *A Book of Carnegie Libraries* (New York, 1917). GEN COLL,LC-DIG-ppmsca-15570.

6-023. North side, Central Public Library, Washington, D.C. Ackerman & Ross, 1899–1903. Louise Taft, photographer, 1985. P&P,HABS,DC,WASH,551-5.

Even though the plan incorporated a second entry, the architects clearly differentiated the utilitarian function of the rear bookstack with a wall of simple, unarticulated fenestration.

6-024. North front and east side, Carnegie Library of Atlanta, Atlanta, Georgia. Ackerman & Ross, 1899–1902. David J. Kaminsky, photographer, 1976. P&P,HABS,GA,61-ATLA,12-3.

In contrast to the more Roman or Baroque visage of the Washington, D.C., library, the paired Ionic columns, which rise through two stories to a flat entablature in Atlanta, evoke the much more spartan image of a Greek temple.

6-025. Interior, reference reading room, Carnegie Library of Atlanta, Atlanta, Georgia. Ackerman & Ross, 1899–1902. Photocopy of photograph, ca. 1903. Unidentified photographer. P&P,HABS,GA,61-ATLA,12-21.

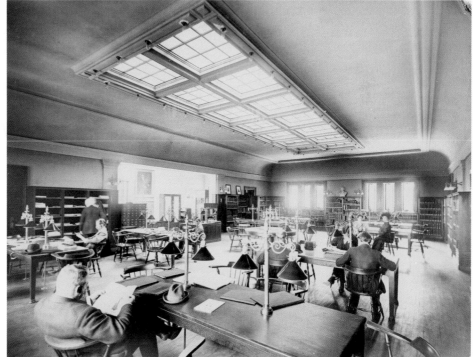

6-026. Free Public Library, Oakland, California. Bliss and Faville, 1899–1902. Unidentified photographer, ca. 1899–1902. P&P,U.S. GEOG FILE,LC-DIG-ppmsca-15432.

The Oakland Carnegie Library was recently rehabilitated for use as the African American Museum and Library.

6-027. Reading room, Carnegie Library, Oakland, California. Bliss and Faville, 1899–1902. Unidentified photographer, ca. 1900–1905. P&P,LOT 8908,LC-DIG-ppmsca-15417.

6-028. South front, St. Louis Public Library, St. Louis, Missouri. Cass Gilbert, 1907–1912. Jack E. Boucher, photographer, April/May 1986. P&P,HABS,MO,96-SALU,125-1.

In St. Louis, Cass Gilbert employed a variation on the triumphal arch motif that Carrère and Hastings used at the New York Public Library (see 4-042). Gilbert's library, however, is much less Baroque in character, owing more of a debt to the earlier Italian Renaissance palaces of the fifteenth century that had inspired McKim, Mead & White's Boston Public Library (see 4-025).

6-029. St. Louis Public Library (with Christ Church Cathedral and Lucas Garden), St. Louis, Missouri. Cass Gilbert, 1907–1912. Unidentified photographer, ca. 1890–1933. P&P,LOT 9643,LC-USZ62-57693.

The rear stack of the library can be viewed across the garden.

6-030. Springfield City Library, Springfield, Massachusetts. Edward L. Tilton, 1907–1912. Detroit Publishing Co., ca. 1900–1910. P&P,DETR,LC-DIG -det-4a22185.

Although conceived as an Italian Renaissance palace and similar in form to Gilbert's St. Louis library, the open plan of Tilton's Springfield library represents one of the most progressive interior arrangements to appear in a large public library prior to World War I.

6-031. First floor and basement plans, Springfield City Library, Springfield, Massachusetts. Edward L. Tilton, 1907–1912. In Snead & Company Iron Works, *Library planning, bookstacks and shelving, with contributions from the architects' and librarians' points of view* (Jersey City, NJ, 1915), figs. 238–39. GEN COLL,LC-DIG-ppmsca-15568.

6-032. Facade and interior views, Springfield City Library, Springfield, Massachusetts. Edward L. Tilton, 1907–1912. In Snead & Company Iron Works, *Library planning, bookstacks and shelving, with contributions from the architects' and librarians' points of view* (Jersey City, NJ, 1915), figs. 235–37. GEN COLL,LC-DIG-ppmsca-15569.

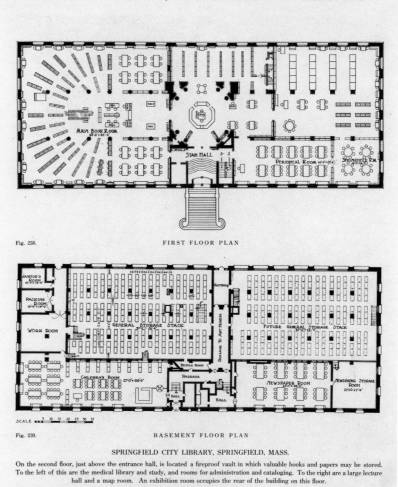

Fig. 238.    FIRST FLOOR PLAN

Fig. 239.    BASEMENT FLOOR PLAN

SPRINGFIELD CITY LIBRARY, SPRINGFIELD, MASS.

On the second floor, just above the entrance hall, is located a fireproof vault in which valuable books and papers may be stored. To the left of this are the medical library and study, and rooms for administration and cataloging. To the right are a large lecture hall and a map room. An exhibition room occupies the rear of the building on this floor.

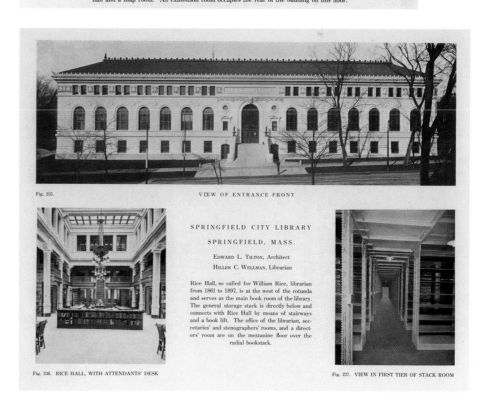

Fig. 235.    VIEW OF ENTRANCE FRONT

SPRINGFIELD CITY LIBRARY
SPRINGFIELD, MASS.

EDWARD L. TILTON, Architect
HILLER C. WELLMAN, Librarian

Rice Hall, so called for William Rice, librarian from 1861 to 1897, is at the west of the rotunda and serves as the main book room of the library. The general storage stack is directly below and connects with Rice Hall by means of stairways and a book lift. The office of the librarian, secretaries' and stenographers' rooms, and a directors' room are on the mezzanine floor over the radial bookstack.

Fig. 236. RICE HALL, WITH ATTENDANTS' DESK

Fig. 237. VIEW IN FIRST TIER OF STACK ROOM

6-033. Main building of the Detroit Public Library,
Detroit, Michigan. Cass Gilbert, 1913–1921.
Arthur S. Siegel, photographer, 1942. P&P, FSA,
LC-DIG-fsa-28591.

Although funded by Carnegie in 1901, Gilbert's design
for the Detroit Public Library was delayed until
1913. As part of Edward H. Bennett's City Beautiful–
inspired plan for Detroit's Center of Arts and Letters
Plan of 1915, the Detroit Public Library was located
several miles northwest of the central business
district. It was later joined by Paul Cret's Detroit
Institute of the Arts (1927), which was erected on axis
with it on the opposite side of Woodward Avenue.

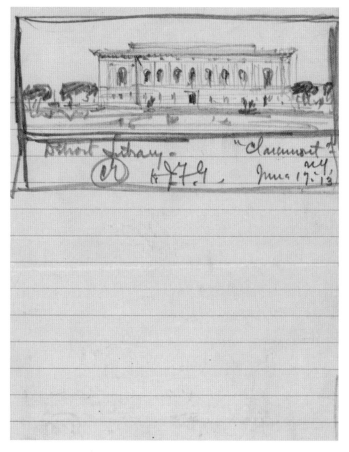

6-034. Sketch elevation, Detroit Public Library,
Detroit, Michigan. Cass Gilbert, June 17, 1913.
P&P,ADE 11-Gilbert,no. 38 (A size).

6-035. Sketch elevation and plan, Detroit Public
Library, Detroit, Michigan. Cass Gilbert, May 16, 1913.
P&P,ADE 11-Gilbert,no. 37 (A size).

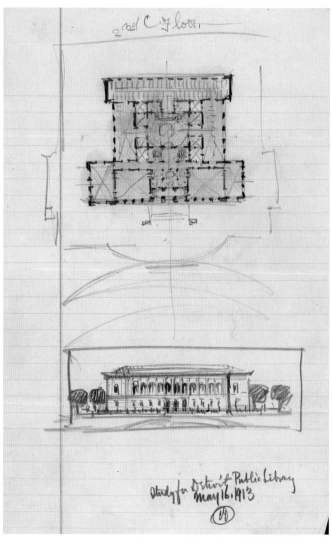

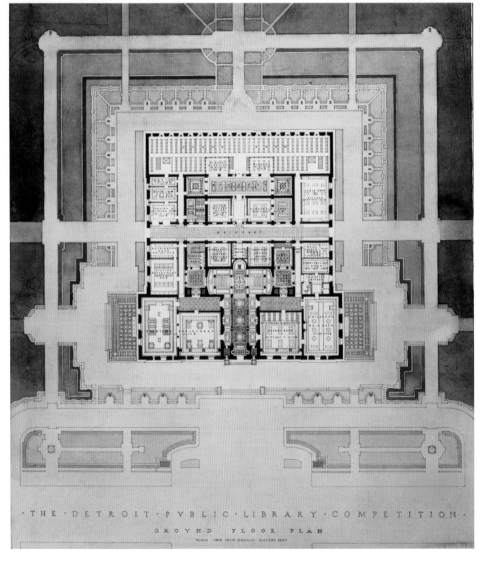

6-036. Rendering of the front elevation for the Detroit Public Library competition, Detroit, Michigan. Cass Gilbert, 1913. P&P,LOT 4484,LC-DIG-ds-06614.

This rendering depicts the second story arcade with standing sculptures that Gilbert later decided to eliminate from his design.

6-037. Ground floor plan, Detroit Public Library, Detroit, Michigan. Cass Gilbert, 1913, P&P,LOT 4484,LC-DIG-ds-06613.

6-038. Children's room, Detroit Public Library, Detroit, Michigan. Cass Gilbert, 1913–1921. Kenneth Clark, photographer, 1921. P&P,CGC,LC-DIG-ds-06567.

6-039. Fireplace, children's room, Detroit Public Library, Detroit, Michigan. Cass Gilbert, 1913–1921. Kenneth Clark, photographer, 1921. P&P,CGC,LC-DIG-ds-06568.

The children's room was situated on the ground floor of the building, across the main vestibule from the Newspaper and Periodical Department. This space was anchored by a colorful Pewabic tile fireplace, which depicted scenes from popular children's books.

6-040. Main reading room, Detroit Public Library, Detroit, Michigan. Cass Gilbert, 1913–1921. Kenneth Clark, photographer, 1921. P&P,CGC,LC-DIG-ds-06569.

Delivery was located in the center of the building at the top of a tall flight of stairs, and, as at the Boston Public Library, the main reading room ran across the front of the building behind its second story arcade. Other reading rooms flanked the delivery area and ran along the two sides of the building.

6-041. Main reading room, Detroit Public Library, Detroit, Michigan. Cass Gilbert, 1913–1921. Kenneth Clark, photographer, 1921. P&P,CGC,LC-DIG-ds-06566.

6-042. San Francisco Public Library, San Francisco, California. George W. Kelham, 1914–1917. Jet Lowe, photographer, 1981. P&P,HABS,CAL,38-SANFRA, 71-A-1.

The old San Francisco Public Library, which was part of Daniel Burnham's 1909 Civic Center plan, now houses the Asian Art Museum. The library occupies a new building, which opened across the mall from this structure in 1996.

# CARNEGIE'S BRANCH LIBRARIES

In addition to central libraries, Carnegie also subsidized the construction of some two hundred branch libraries in America's larger cities. This effort included buildings in New York, Pittsburgh, Denver, Philadelphia, Detroit, Los Angeles, and San Francisco, as well as in many smaller communities, such as Santa Monica, California. In New York alone, he contributed $5,200,000 for the construction of sixty-seven neighborhood libraries, which were constructed between 1901 and 1923 in Manhattan, Brooklyn, the Bronx, Queens, and Staten Island. He contributed another $1,500,000 for twenty-five branch buildings in Philadelphia, which were erected between 1904 and 1930. While Carnegie did not originate the idea of the branch library, his philanthropy did much to increase its acceptance as an integral element of the American public library system.

6-043. Perspective rendering, Carnegie Library, Nashville, Tennessee. Ackerman and Ross, 1898–1901. Albert Randolph Ross, illustrator, ca. 1902. P&P, LOT 8908, LC-DIG-ppmsca-15359.

Carnegie gave the city of Nashville $175,000 in 1901 for a main Nashville library building and three branches, including a "Negro Branch." In addition to many smaller buildings, such as branch buildings, Ross, of the firm of Ackerman and Ross, also designed a number of larger Carnegie libraries, such as those in Washington, D.C. and Atlanta, Georgia (6-019–6-025).

6-044. "How to run libraries." Felix Mahony, artist, 1901. P&P,CD 1-Mahony,no. 4 (B size).

Carnegie's generous offer to fund the construction of branch libraries in New York City met with some skepticism over how the money would be controlled by the Tammany political machine and its corrupt patronage system. There were no reported problems, however.

6-045. New York Public Library, branch at 328 East 67th Street, New York, New York. Babb, Cook, and Willard, 1904. In *Architectural Record* 17 (March 1905), p. 240. GEN COLL,LC-DIG-ppmsca-15556.

Unlike other Carnegie branches around the country, the New York buildings tended to be more urban in nature, often taking the form of small Italian Renaissance palaces. They were designed by many of the city's leading architectural firms.

6-046. New York Public Library, Branch at no. 224 East 125th Street, New York, New York. McKim, Mead & White, 1905. In *Architectural Record* 17 (March 1905), p. 242. GEN COLL,LC-DIG-ppmsca-15557.

6-047. Children reading in roof garden of the Rivington St. Library, New York, New York. McKim, Mead & White, 1905. George Grantham Bain Collection, ca. 1919. P&P,LC-USZ62-111297.

With a scattering of flower boxes and a broad striped awning, the rooftop terrace of this library appears to have been intended as an urban respite during the summer months for the city's tenement dwellers, especially its youth. It offered fresh air and sunshine, two fundamental elements on the agenda of urban reformers of the era.

6-048. Southeast front elevation,
looking northwest, Free Library of
Philadelphia, Thomas Holme Branch,
Philadelphia, Pennsylvania. Horace W.
Castor, 1906–1907. Joseph E. Elliott, pho-
tographer, 2007. P&P,HABS,PA-6754-1.

In 1904 Andrew Carnegie gave the city
of Philadelphia $1,500,000 for twenty-
five branch buildings. Since the central
library did not open until 1927, these
represented the first purpose-built
libraries in the city. As of 2016, sixteen
of the original Carnegie branch libraries
were still in use, although most of these
have been expanded and rehabilitated,
and all now contain rows of computers
to supplement their collections of books.

6-049. General view of interior, looking
east toward entrance, Free Library of
Philadelphia, Thomas Holme Branch,
Philadelphia, Pennsylvania. Horace W.
Castor, 1906–1907. Joseph E. Elliott, pho-
tographer, 2007. P&P,HABS,PA-6754-13.

6-050. Elevation of northeast front,
Free Library of Philadelphia, Richmond
Branch, Philadelphia, Pennsylvania.
Edward L. Tilton, 1908–1910. Joseph
E. Elliott, photographer, 2007.
P&P,HABS,PA-6763-1.

6-051. General view of interior, main reading room, looking southwest, Free Library of Philadelphia, Richmond Branch, Philadelphia, Pennsylvania. Edward L. Tilton, 1908–1910. Joseph E. Elliott, photographer, 2007. P&P, HABS, PA-6763-9.

This view of the reading room reveals changes made to upgrade the library since 1905.

6-052. Southwest front elevation, looking northeast, Free Library of Philadelphia, Kingsessing Branch, Phillip H. Johnson, 1918–1919. Joseph E. Elliott, photographer, 2007. P&P, HABS, PA-6755-1.

6-053. Denver Public Library, Sarah Platt Decker Branch Library, Denver, Colorado. Marean and Norton, 1913. Unidentified photographer, between 1913 and 1931. P&P,LOT 3752,LC-DIG-ppmsca-15339.

Although financed with Carnegie funds, this building was named for the suffragette and advocate for branch libraries Sarah Platt Decker. The structure's late medieval forms reflect the growing shift to a more eclectic historicism that began to engage the architectural profession during the second and third decades of the twentieth century, especially for smaller suburban and country libraries.

6-054. Denver Public Library, Sarah Platt Decker Branch Library, Denver, Colorado. Marean and Norton, 1913. Unidentified photographer, between 1913 and 1931. P&P,LOT 3752,LC-DIG-ppmsca-15340.

# LIBRARIES FOR AMERICA, 1898–1916

At the end of the nineteenth century, following his earlier donation of library buildings in Pennsylvania, Andrew Carnegie initiated the "wholesale" phase of his beneficence. Between 1899 and 1901, for example, he offered to build 138 public libraries in the United States, and he also began to shift his attention away from the erection of large central buildings to the funding of branch libraries in the cities and smaller institutions in the countryside. By 1917, he and the Carnegie Foundation (established in 1911) had promised to erect libraries in some 1,400 American towns and cities at a cost of more than forty million dollars, dramatically extending the American public library movement from the East Coast to the southern and western states.

The buildings erected during this period were designed under the direction of James Bertram, who introduced their architects to concepts of open planning and centralized administration. Following the dictums of professional librarians, Bertram promoted these ideas in his small pamphlet "Notes on the Erection of Library Bildings [sic]," which, after 1911, he distributed to all Carnegie grantees. Edward Tilton, one of the leading proponents of open planning during this era, collaborated with Bertram on the development of these "Notes." So influential were the "Notes" that the sketch plans and many of the suggestions concerning progressive library design that appeared in them were reproduced by Wheeler and Githens three decades later in their seminal publication on modern library design (see 6-057). As the authors noted in 1941, "The Carnegie leaflet was effective, not only because it was issued as a suggestion from the donor, but because of its common sense. Though written especially for small libraries, its warning applies equally to large. . . . Most of its principles are now accepted without question; it is still an active influence." (Both Carnegie and Bertram were also advocates of spelling reform, hence "Buildings" in the title of Bertram's pamphlet became "Bildings.")

Reflecting the growing influence of the City Beautiful movement and the nature of architectural education in the United States during the early twentieth century, classicism became the style of choice for the country's new civic monuments, especially public libraries. While never specified by Carnegie or Bertram, the majority of the structures the philanthropist endowed after 1900 reflected this newly revived taste, which vacillated among the classical forms of Greece, Rome, and the Italian Renaissance. While many architects across the country were involved in the Carnegie program, a handful of designers and firms, such as Ackerman & Ross (see 6-043), Patton and Miller (see 6-066–6-068), and William H. Weeks in California (see 6-057), were especially prolific.

6-055. Panoramic view of the main street, Perry, Iowa, with the Carnegie Library to the left. Liebbe, Nourse, and Rasmussen, 1904. F. J. Bandholtz, copyright claimant, 1907. P&P,PAN US GEOG,LC-USZ62-122838.

In many small communities on the Great Plains and in the West, South, and Midwest, the Carnegie Library was often the first monumental classical building to be erected in the town. In Perry, a 1903 Carnegie grant of $10,600 financed this library.

6-056. South (entrance) front, Gilroy Free Public Library, Gilroy, California. William H. Weeks, 1909–1910. Jane Lidz, photographer, 1980. P&P,HABS,CAL,43-GIL,3-1.

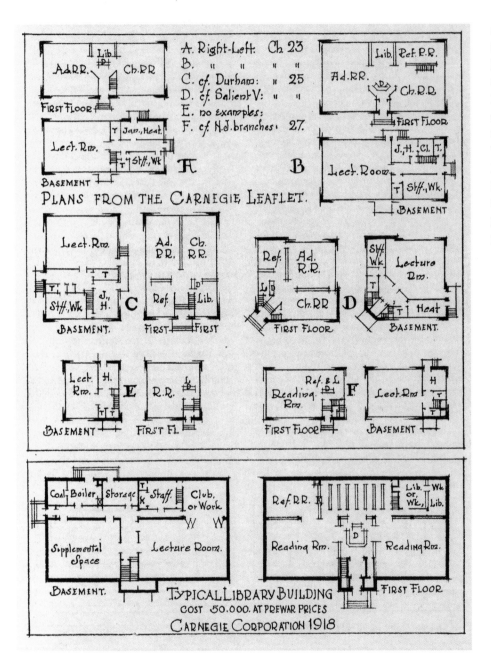

6-057. Suggested plans for Carnegie libraries. In James Bertram, "Notes on the Erection of Library Bildings (1918)," reproduced in Alfred Morton Githens and Joseph Lewis Wheeler, *The American Public Library Building* (New York: Charles Scribner's Sons, 1941), p. 218. P&P, LC-DIG-ppmsca-15822.

6-058. North and west facades from northwest, Carnegie Free Library, Connellsville, Pennsylvania. Jennings Moss McCollum, 1901–1903. Jet Lowe, photographer, May 1989. P&P,HABS,PA,26-CONL,1-5.

Carnegie gave the city of Connellsville $50,000 in 1899 for this building and later raised this amount to $75,000. Although Connellsville only had a population of 5,697 residents at the time, it was a major center of coke production for Carnegie's steel mills. The circulation, or delivery, desk, which is located in the center of the building, separates the bookstack from the delivery area. The general and children's reading rooms to either side of the desk could thus be readily supervised by the librarian. A small reference room and a periodical room flank the bookshelves, filling out what would otherwise be a standard T-plan of the type introduced at MIT some twenty-five years earlier (see 5-012). Variations on this type of plan were one of the most popular configurations for small Carnegie buildings.

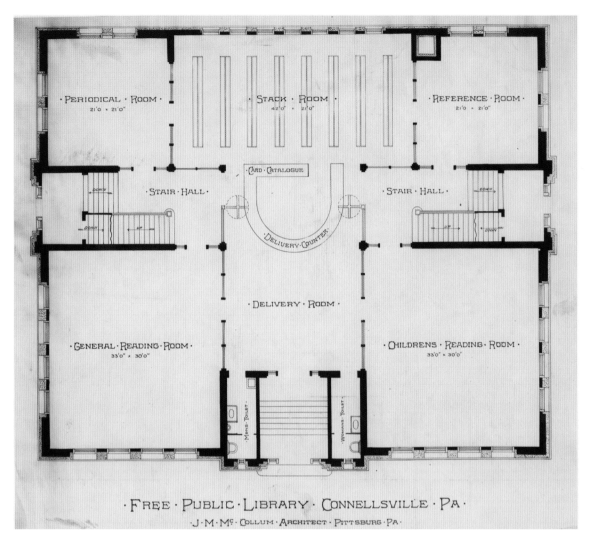

FREE · PUBLIC · LIBRARY · CONNELLSVILLE · PA
· J · M · Mc · COLLUM · ARCHITECT · PITTSBURG · PA ·

6-059. First floor plan, Carnegie Free Library,
Connellsville, Pennsylvania. Jennings Moss
McCollum, 1901–1903. P&P, LC-DIG-ppmsca-15398.

6-060. Interior, first floor, circulation desk and stacks, looking northeast, Carnegie Free Library, Connellsville, Pennsylvania. Jennings Moss McCollum, 1900–1901. Jet Lowe, photographer, May 1989. P&P, HABS,PA,26-CONL,1-6.

As historian Abigail Van Slyck has observed, the centrally situated circulation desk was a highly developed workspace for the librarian, who, in these smaller institutions, was often female and the only full-time attendant.

6-061. Auditorium, Carnegie Free Library, Connellsville, Pennsylvania. Jennings Moss McCollum, 1900–1901. Jet Lowe, photographer, May 1989. P&P,HABS,PA,26-CONL,1-10.

Like many buildings endowed by Carnegie, the Connellsville library included a community room or auditorium on its second-floor plan.

CARNEGIE LIBRARY. COSHOCTON. OHIO.
E. W. HART & CO., ARCHITECTS.
COLUMBUS, OHIO.

6-062. Perspective rendering, Carnegie Library, Coshocton, Ohio. E. W. Hart, 1903. C. E. Dykema, delineator. P&P, LOT 8908, LC-DIG-ppmsca-15395.

6-063. Plan, Carnegie Library, Coshocton, Ohio. E. W. Hart, 1903. P&P, LOT 8908, LC-DIG-ppmsca-15402.

This plan for the Coshocton Library is closely related to the plan for a "typical library building" that was published by James Bertram in 1918 (see 6-057, bottom right)

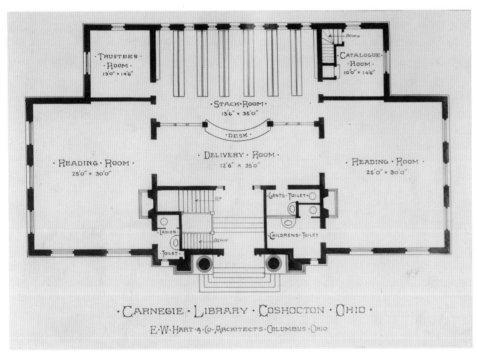

· CARNEGIE · LIBRARY · COSHOCTON · OHIO ·
E · W · HART · & · Co · ARCHITECTS · COLUMBUS · OHIO

6-064. Front and east side, facing northwest, Audubon Public Library, Audubon, Iowa. Proudfoot, Bird & Rawson, 1911. Michael Whye, photographer, 1991. P&P,HABS,IOWA,5-AUD,1-1.

The Audubon Carnegie Library was built with a $9,000 grant from the philanthropist given to the town in 1911, the year that Bertram's "Notes" first appeared. Designed by the Des Moines firm of Proudfoot, Bird & Rawson, it opened the following year. The librarian's desk is situated opposite the entry with a clear view of the entire space. As Bertram would insist by this date, a small lecture or community hall, previously situated on the second floor, was now located in the basement along with a workroom for the librarians, a washroom, and mechanical equipment.

6-065. First floor plan, Audubon Public Library, Audubon, Iowa. Proudfoot, Bird & Rawson, ca. 1911. Photographic copy of architectural drawing, in possession of Brooks Borg and Skiles Architects and Engineers, Des Moines, Iowa. P&P,HABS,IOWA,5-AUD,1-10.

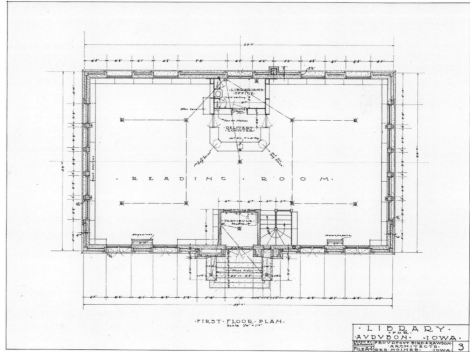

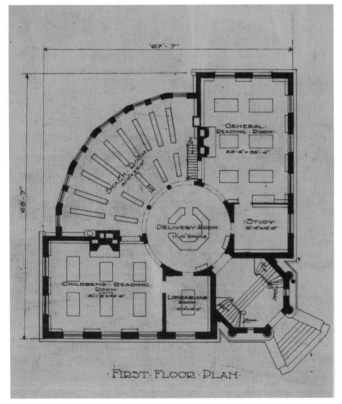

·FIRST·FLOOR·PLAN·

6-066. Interior, from rear of circulation desk facing southeast; atlas case on far left; vestibule entrance in right background, Audubon Public Library, Audubon, Iowa. Proudfoot, Bird & Rawson, 1911. Michael Whye, photographer, 1991. P&P,HABS,IOWA,5-AUD,1-5.

6-067. Carnegie Library, Marshalltown, Iowa. Patton & Miller, 1902–1903. Unidentified photographer, ca. 1910. P&P,U.S. GEOG FILE,LC-DIG-ppmsca-15431.

The Chicago architects Normand S. Patton and Grant C. Miller were perhaps the most successful designers of Carnegie libraries. They were said to be responsible for more than one hundred of these institutions, which were located primarily in the Midwest, but their buildings also stretched from Ohio to Cheyenne, Wyoming, and Waco, Texas. Patton began to develop his expertise in library design in the mid-1880s as a partner in the firm of Patton and Fisher (see 5-029–5-031, 5-047). This partnership was joined by Miller in 1899 and operated as Patton & Miller from 1901 until 1912. Some four dozen of their libraries may be viewed in their self-published booklet, Patton and Miller, *Library Buildings* (n.d).

6-068. First floor plan, Carnegie Library, Marshalltown, Iowa. Patton & Miller, 1901–1903. P&P,LOT 8908,LC-DIG-ppmsca-15366.

In Marshalltown, the bookstack shelves radiate like a fan from the central octagonal circulation desk, which was set between two wings housing a children's and a general reading room.

6-069. Central desk, Carnegie Library, Marshalltown, Iowa. Patton & Miller, 1901–1903. Unidentified photographer, 1897–1901. P&P,U.S. GEOG FILE,USZ62-118703.

Variations on a semi-panoptic plan, with shelves radiating outward from the circulation desk, became popular during the Carnegie era as a means of giving the librarian more control over activity in the bookstacks as well as the reading rooms.

6-070. Carnegie Library, Bayonne, New Jersey. Edward L. Tilton, 1903–1904. E. Eldor Deane, artist, ca. 1903. P&P,LOT 8908,LC-DIG-ppmsca-15352.

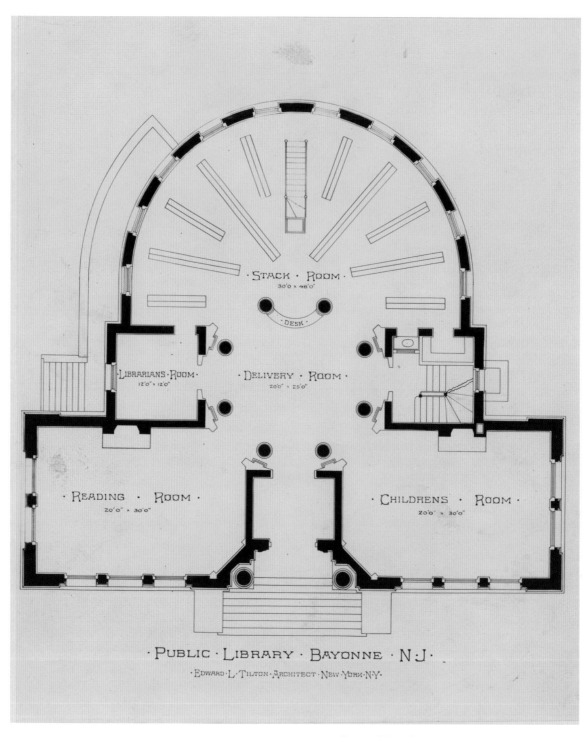

6-071. Plan, Public Library, Bayonne, New
Jersey. Edward L. Tilton, 1903–1904. P&P,LOT
8908,LC-DIG-ppmsca-15367.

# CARNEGIE'S ACADEMIC LIBRARIES

In addition to his more widely publicized benefactions for public libraries, Carnegie donated monies to several dozen smaller colleges and academic institutions for the erection of new library facilities.

6-072. Laying of the cornerstone of the Bethany Carnegie Library, Lindsborg, Kansas. C. F. Rosine, contractor, 1908. B. G. Gründal, photographer, 1908. P&P,LOT 9823,LC-DIG-ppmsca-15326.

6-073. Tuskegee Institute, Carnegie Library, Tuskegee, Alabama. Robinson Robert Taylor, 1901. Detroit Publishing Co., 1906. P&P,DETR,LC-DIG-det-4a13433.

At the request of Booker T. Washington, Carnegie donated $20,000 for this building at the pioneering educational institution founded by George Washington Carver in 1881 to educate freed slaves and their children. Robert R. Taylor, who was the school's Director of Industries, designed the building, which was constructed under his supervision by his students.

LAYING OF THE CORNER STONE OF THE BETHANY CARNEGIE LIBRARY, LINDSBORG, KANS.

6-074. Oblique view, Tuskegee Institute, Carnegie Hall, Tuskegee, Alabama. Robinson Robert Taylor, 1901. Duane Phillips, photographer, 1978. P&P,HABS,AL-868-C-1 (CT).

6-075. (Left to right) Robert C. Ogden, Tuskegee Institute trustee, Senator William Howard Taft, Booker T. Washington, and Andrew Carnegie, on the steps of the Carnegie Library at the Tuskegee Institute's twenty-fifth anniversary celebration. Frances Benjamin Johnston, photographer, 1906. P&P,Frances Benjamin Johnston Collection,LC-DIG-ds-01107.

6-076. Interior view of library reading room with students sitting at tables, reading, Tuskegee Institute, Carnegie Library, Tuskegee, Alabama. Robinson Robert Taylor, 1901. Frances Benjamin Johnston, photographer, ca. 1902. P&P,Frances Benjamin Johnston Collection,LC-DIG-ppmscd-00084.

6-077. Tufts College, Eaton Memorial Library. Whitfield & King, 1908. In *The Western Architect* 11 (June 1908). P&P, U.S. Treasury Dept. Office of the Supervising Architect . . . Collection, LC-DIG-ds-06521.

Carnegie donated $100,000 for this building to the college in 1904. His wife Louise requested that the new Tufts Library be named in memory of Charles Henry Eaton, a Tufts alumnus and graduate of the Tufts Divinity School. Eaton had officiated at the Carnegie's wedding in New York City in 1887.

6-078. Plan, Tufts College, Eaton Memorial Library. Whitfield & King, 1908. *The Western Architect* 11 (June 1908). P&P, U.S. Treasury Dept. Office of the Supervising Architect . . . Collection, LC-DIG-ds-06576.

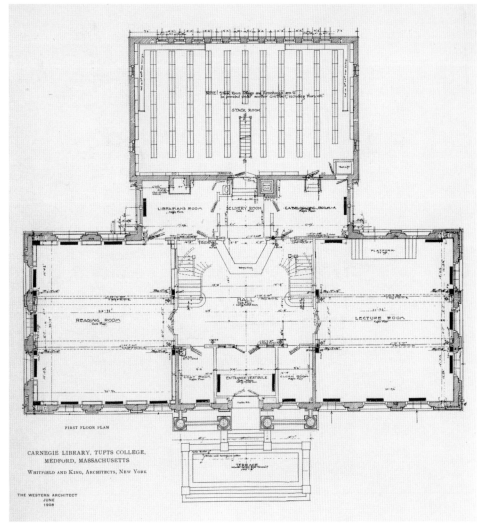

# LIBRARY WAR SERVICE BUILDINGS

Although World War I brought a close to the Carnegie Corporation's public library campaign, Edward L. Tilton continued to adapt Bertram's open planning in more than sixty army post libraries that he designed between 1918 and 1919 as part of the Library War Service. The American Library Association and the Carnegie Corporation sponsored this effort to make books available to American troops during the war.

In bookcase boxes 100,000 books a month are sent overseas from 6 Dispatch Offices.

Books on photography are in great demand by official photographers. A. L. A. Library, Camp Travis, Texas.

One day's delivery of magazines at the A. L. A. Library, Camp Custer, Michigan.

The workroom in an A. L. A. Camp Library, where hundreds of books and magazines are unpacked daily.

Typical interior of the A. L. A. Camp Libraries. Here the men learn why, where and how they are to fight.

The A. L. A. Library reading porch, one of the coolest and most popular places at Camp Kearny, California.

**AMERICAN LIBRARY ASSOCIATION**
LIBRARY WAR SERVICE

6-079. Activities of the American Library Association Library War Service. Published 1918. P&P, Poster Collection, LC-USZC4-7927.

6-080. Library War Service Library, Camp Bowie, Fort Worth, Texas. Edward L. Tilton, 1918–1919. Unidentified photographer, 1918–1919. P&P, LOT 13440-3, LC-DIG-ppmsca-15324.

6-081. Interior of library with soldiers reading, Chickamauga Park, Chattanooga, Georgia. Edward L. Tilton, 1918–1919. Stokes, photographer, 1918 or 1919. P&P, LOT 8871, LC-USZ62-105187.

Ironically, these simple wooden structures came closer to Bertram's ideal of architectural economy and utility than any of the classical "temples" that Carnegie's earlier philanthropy had financed.

6-082. Circulation desk, Camp Sevier Library, Greenville, South Carolina. Edward L. Tilton, 1918–1919. Unidentified photographer, 1918–1919. P&P, LOT 13440-3, LC-DIG-ppmsca-15325.

# AFTERWORD: THE LIBRARY POST–WORLD WAR II

As noted in the introduction to this book, European modernism came to dominate American library design after the middle of the twentieth century. Because open planning conformed to one of the primary tenets of the modern tradition then being embraced by American schools of architecture, it became the convention in library planning during the post–World War II era. While constrained budgets also contributed to the acceptance of this style, the modernist aesthetic was reinforced in academia by a shift in focus during the Cold War from a liberal arts to an engineering and science curriculum; this transformation further encouraged librarians, architects, and school administrators to embrace utilitarian forms as a reflection of America's postwar efficiency. These institutions were seen as a counterpart to the modern corporate office building: well organized and economically progressive.

Nowhere, perhaps, is the midcentury rejection of academic eclecticism and planning better exemplified than in the John Crerar Library at the Illinois Institute of Technology (IIT) (1962; AF-001) or the Martin Luther King Jr. Memorial Library in Washington, D.C. (1972; AF-002– AF-003).[1] At IIT, Walter Netsch, of Skidmore, Owings, and Merrill, continued the modernist vocabulary that Ludwig Mies van der Rohe (1886–1969) had introduced in his earlier buildings for the campus. Netsch employed exposed steel girders above the roof to eliminate the need for interior columns, and enclosed the structure with glass curtain walls. In his last completed building in the United States, and in stark contrast to the classical Carnegie Public

Opposite: AF-003, p. 289.

Library of 1899–1903 (see 6-021) that it replaced, Mies enclosed the open plan of this new central building with steel, glass, and brick curtain walls.

There were, of course, outstanding variations on this abstract modernist aesthetic. At Yale University. Gordon Bunshaft (1909–1990) transformed the Beinecke Rare Book and Manuscript Library (1961–1963; AF-004) into a luminous platonic cube. In contrast to the Crerar library by the same firm, Bunshaft created an elegant treasure vault at Yale to house a

collection of rare volumes donated by Edwin J. and Frederick W. Beinecke and their families (see 1-007–1-008). It is encased in a grid of granite and translucent Vermont marble that allows a luminescent glow of light to penetrate into the interior of the structure, where a six-story, freestanding stack is enshrined in the center of the room. This is encircled by a mezzanine and enclosed in its own glass box in order to maintain constant temperature and humidity levels to enhance the preservation of the books. At the

AF-001. John Crerar Library, Chicago, Illinois. Walter Netsch, Skidmore, Owings, and Merrill, 1962. Unidentified photographer, 1962–1975. P&P, LOT 11549, LC-DIG-ppmsca-15343.

AF-002. Facade, Martin Luther King, Jr., Memorial Library, Washington, D.C. Ludwig Mies van der Rohe, 1965–1972. Carol M. Highsmith, photographer, 2011. P&P,CMHA,LC-DIG-highsm-20534.

AF-003. Martin Luther King, Jr. Mural, Martin Luther King, Jr., Memorial Library, Washington, D.C. Donald Lloyd Miller, artist, 1986. Carol M. Highsmith, photographer, 2011. P&P,CMHA,LC-DIG-highsm-20536.

AF-004. Exterior, Beinecke Rare Book and Manuscript Library, Yale University, New Haven, Connecticut of Gordon Bunshaft of Skidmore, Owings, and Merrill, 1961–1963. Carol M. Highsmith, photographer, 2011. P&P,CMHA,LC-DIG-highsm-19230.

Phillips Exeter Academy Library (1969–1971) Louis Kahn (1895–1967) demonstrated his own mastery of light, and heroic geometry. Here he reintroduced the idea of the nineteenth-century hall library in the form of a six-story core that rises upward to a monumental X-frame and supports the surrounding stacks and study areas (AF-005).

In spite of the success of these modernist masterpieces, this austere aesthetic by the late 1960s began to come under the attack of critics such as Robert A. M. Stern (1939– ), Michael Graves (1934–2015), Robert Venturi (1925– ) and Denise Scott Brown (1931– ), who called for a return to more accessible—and to some degree more historically associated—precedents. New central libraries in Chicago (AF-006) and San Francisco reflect these Postmodern ideas, with

both buildings paying homage to the classical library tradition and Henri Labrouste's Bibliothèque Ste.-Geneviève in Paris (see IN-005). Of the two, Chicago's Harold Washington Library Center (1989–1991) by Hammond Beeby Babka is certainly the most exuberant. Constructed of brick with terra-cotta ornament, it features multistory arches meant to evoke earlier classical libraries as well as Chicago architectural icons such as the Rookery, Auditorium Theater, and Monadnock building. The library culminates in a glazed winter garden on the ninth story. In the Postmodern tradition, exaggerated, painted aluminum acroteria, designed by Kent Bloomer, with owls by Raymond Kaskey, embellish the corners and peak of the classical pediment.

This Postmodern sentiment led not only to a

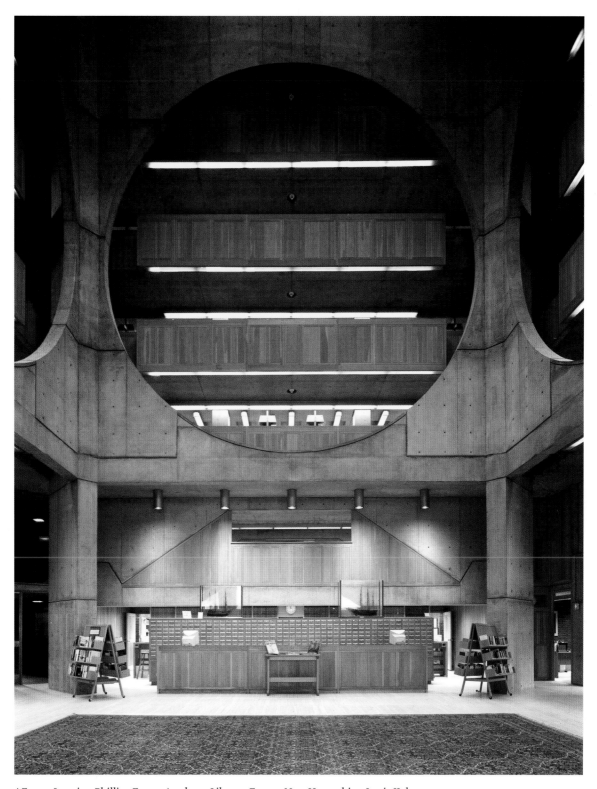

AF-005. Interior, Phillips Exeter Academy Library, Exeter, New Hampshire. Louis Kahn, 1969–1971. Carol M. Highsmith, photographer, 1980–2006. P&P,CMHA,LC-DIG-highsm-15570.

AF-006. Harold Washington Library Center, Chicago, Illinois. Hammond Beeby Babka, 1989–1991. Carol M. Highsmith, photographer, 1980–2006. P&P,CMHA,LC-DIG-highsm-12718.

return to historical forms and ornament but also to a rethinking of the open plan enclosed in a glass box, a paradigm that often proved cold and impersonal, qualities seen as antithetical to the type of domestic ambiance that had traditionally been employed to reflect the high-minded nature of these institutions and to encourage quiet reading and study, especially among younger patrons. And as earlier library build-ings have begun to age, many of them have become the focus of extensive rehabilitation projects rather than demolition and replacement. Included among these are the Jefferson Building of the Library of Congress and the Boston and Los Angeles public libraries, as well as scores of smaller libraries across the country.

# TECHNOLOGY AND THE MODERN LIBRARY

Alongside freestanding shelves of books and reading tables, new technologies—computers, wireless Internet access, automated sorting and checkout of books—have been introduced into libraries in order to maintain the level of service that the public has come to expect from this quintessentially American institution. But, contrary to popular belief, the impact of innovative technologies on library design is not new. Even in the nineteenth century, pneumatic tubes and telephones, conveyor belts, and elevators were already radically altering the way in which librarians ordered and disseminated knowledge (see 3-061–3-063). The invention of microfilm, which began to be marketed commercially by Eastman Kodak in 1928,[2] television, and then the mainframe computer (AF-007–AF-009) likewise intrigued librarians during the middle years of the twentieth century, and reoriented patrons and professionals. Before the turn of the twentieth century computer kiosks replaced the ubiquitous card catalog as a means of finding books, and personal computers began to appear on reading desks (see AF-003, 6-051). Books are now being barcoded to allow for self-checkout and the automated sorting of volumes upon their return. In some larger institutions high-density automated storage (ASRS) technologies allow the library's computerized system to locate, deliver, and track materials, which are now stored in bins, and permit patrons to request them from any computer with an Internet connection. Libraries continue, too, to experiment with new and innovative ways to deliver e-books, music, and videos directly to a patron's personal electronic device via high-speed and broadband Internet.

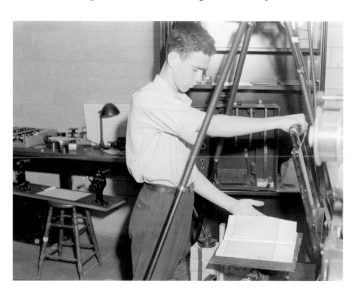

AF-007. Microfilming Chinese documents, Library of Congress, Washington, D.C. Royden Dixon, photographer, June 1942. P&P,FSA,LC-DIG-fsa-8d05577.

AF-008. Television in library, Grout Park School, Hamburg Street, Schenectady, New York. Skidmore, Owings, and Merrill, 1954. Gottscho-Schleisner, Inc., November 1954, P&P,GSC,LC-DIG-gsc-5a23195.

AF-009. "To the rescue, many librarians believe computers are the only means to effectively cope with their bulging bookshelves." Flatbush Branch, Brooklyn Public Library, Brooklyn, New York. Roger Higgins, photographer, 1966. P&P,NYWTS,LC-DIG-ppmsca-15437.

AF-010. "Supermarket comes to the library, Grand Rapids, Mich. Supermarket ideas are in evidence at the Grand Rapids Public Library as Mrs. Meyer Ginsberg (left) uses a wire cart and Sheila Tuller loads a shopping bag to solve the problem of taking home large numbers of books. The Library supplies the carts as a courtesy and sells the printed shopping bags for five cents." Grand Rapids Public Library, Grand Rapids, Michigan. United Press International Photo, 1955. P&P,NYWTS,LC-DIG-ppmsca-15436.

Likewise, librarians began to adapt modern merchandising strategies as early as the 1920s (see AF-010) and continue to look to large chain bookstores and even supermarkets and shopping malls to develop new methods of display, employing bright colors, supergraphics, and neon signs to attract the public. Coffee shops and cafes are now common components of library programs, along with expanded digital and literacy programs, interactive children's departments and dedicated teen activity areas. While they have always served as community centers—with auditoriums and lecture series—a renewed emphasis on the library as an active participant in the cultural and public life of the community is reanimating the institution.

At the Seattle Public Library (1999–2004; AF-011), designers Rem Koolhaas (1944–) and Joshua Ramus (1969–) of the Office for Metropolitan Architecture integrated print and digital resources in a plan that ascends upward to the tenth-floor reading room from what they call "the living room," through an information area and a four-story spiral book stacks (with a capacity to hold 1.4 million volumes). The library's ample glass curtain walls frame views of the city and the area's spectacular geography, further integrating it with its audience and place. As elsewhere, books are now scanned and sorted automatically, and the entire library is equipped with wireless Internet access. The incorporation of sustainable design features—the Seattle building was awarded a silver rating from U.S. Green Building Council—has also been embraced in many new library buildings that are now being showcased as exemplars of civic environmental responsibility.

Early in this century Google partnered with a number of major institutions to begin scanning their collections, and in 2012 the Digital Public Library of America was formed to make available online all of the digitized collections of the nation's libraries and archives. Other digital projects, such as the HathiTrust, are also enabling access to millions of books and articles online. As a result of these initiatives and the

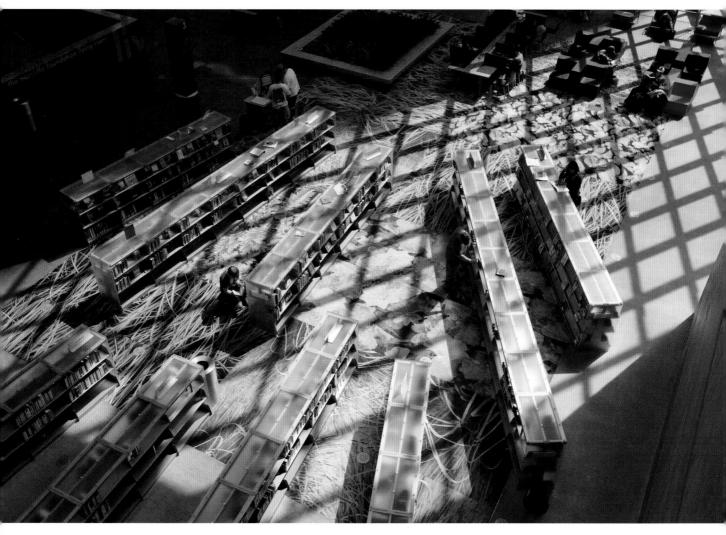

AF-011. Interior view, Seattle Central Library, Seattle, Washington. Rem Koolhaas and Joshua Ramus, Office for Metropolitan Architecture, 1999–2004. Carol M. Highsmith, photographer, 2009. P&P,CMHA,LC-DIG-highsm-04679.

invention and widespread accessibility of e-books, and the radical realignment of the traditional book market being fashioned by the rise of e-commerce, many are prophesying the demise of both the paper-based book and the public library. In 2013, for example, Bexar County, Texas, inaugurated its BiblioTech Digital Library, the first all-digital public library in the United States. And many other public libraries, as well colleges and universities, are dramatically diminishing their book acquisitions. In most libraries, users of personal computers and electronic tablets now compete with readers of books. In light of this information revolution, some images in this volume, especially those of the bookshop windows at the end of section one, might be viewed with nostalgia.[3] As Alexandrian efforts to digitize human knowledge expand, the distinctions examined here between public, private, academic, and commercial domains—as well as physical and virtual space—are becoming less and less clear. Yet in the face of these radical innovations, the public library, in particular, has undergone a renaissance during recent years. And it remains the most accessible and democratic of civic spaces within the urban fabric of the modern American city. As such, it will surely endure as one of the most significant inventions of the last two centuries. "I am perhaps misled by old age and fear," observed Jorge Luis Borges in 1941, in his often-referenced essay, *The Library of Babel*, "but I suspect that the human species—the *only* species—teeters at the verge of extinction, yet that the Library—enlightened, solitary, infinite, perfectly unmoving, armed with precious volumes, pointless, incorruptible, and secret—will endure."

*Notes*

1. For Mies's influence in the United States in general, see Phyllis Lambert, *Mies in America* (New York: Harry N. Abrams, 2001).

2. The Library of Congress was one of the early proponents of microfilm reproduction, which began to be marketed commercially by Eastman Kodak in 1928. This was just one of many technological innovations that preceded the introduction of the computer and affected the design of library spaces and the way patrons accessed library materials.

3. Nostalgia can, of course, work in many ways. Mireille Silcoff ironically observed in a recent article in the *New York Times Magazine* that just as the publication of books appears to be in some jeopardy, floor-to-ceiling shelves of books seem to be becoming newly fashionable decorator accessories. Mireille Silcoff, "Thy Neighbor's Floor-to-Ceiling Bookshelves," *New York Times Magazine*, April 27, 2014, p. 46.

# BIBLIOGRAPHY

Achilles, Rolf, ed. *Humanities Mirror: Reading at the Newberry, 1887–1987*. Chicago: Newberry Library, 1987.

*The Athenaeum Centenary: The Influence and History of the Boston Athenaeum from 1807 to 1907*. Boston: Boston Athenaeum, 1907.

Battles, Matthew. *Library: An Unquiet History*. New York: W. W. Norton, 2003.

Bauman, Charles H. *The Influence of Angus Snead Macdonald and the Snead Bookstack on Library Architecture*. Metuchen, NJ: Scarecrow Press, 1972.

Belding, Patricia W. *Where the Books Are: The History and Architecture of Vermont's Public Library*. Barre, VT: Potash Brook, 1996.

Bélier, Corinne, Barry Bergdoll, and Marc Le Coeur. *Henri Labrouste: Structure Brought to Light*. New York: The Museum of Modern Art, 2012.

Benjamin, S. G. W. [Samuel Greene Wheeler]. "Libraries." *Harper's New Monthly Magazine* 29 (September 1864): 483–88.

Billings, John Shaw. "The New York Public Library." *Library Journal* 36 (May 1911): 233–37.

Bobinski, George. *Carnegie Libraries: Their History and Impact on American Public Library Development*. Chicago: American Library Association, 1969.

Boll, John. "Library Architecture 1800–1875: A Comparison of Theory and Buildings with an Emphasis on New England College Libraries." PhD diss., University of Illinois, 1961.

Borges, Jorge Luis. *The Library of Babel with Etchings by Erik Desmazières*. Boston: David R. Godine, 2000.

Bostwick, Arthur E. *The American Public Library*. New York: Appleton, 1910.

Breisch, Kenneth A. *Henry Hobson Richardson and the Small Public Library in America: A Study in Typology*. Cambridge, MA: MIT Press, 1997.

———. *The Los Angeles Central Library: Building an Architectural Icon, 1872–1933*. Los Angeles: The Getty Research Institute, 2016.

———. "Small Public Libraries in America 1850–1890: The Invention of a Building Type." PhD diss., University of Michigan, 1982.

———. " 'A Source of Sure Authority': Library Building in Los Angeles during the Twentieth Century," in *The World from Here: Treasures from the Great Libraries of Los Angeles*, edited by C. Burlingham and B. Whiteman, 35–56. Los Angeles: Armand Hammer Museum and J. Paul Getty Trust, 2002.

———. "William Frederick Poole and Modern Library Architecture," in *Modern Architecture in America: Visions and Revisions*, edited by R. G. Wilson and S. K. Robinson, 52–72. Ames: Iowa State University Press, 1991.

Brenneman, David A. "Innovations in American Library Design," in *Thomas Alexander Tefft: American Architecture in Transition, 1845–1860*, 61–76. Providence, RI: Department of Art, Brown University, 1988.

Bunting, Bainbridge. *Harvard: An Architectural History*, completed and edited by Margaret Henderson Floyd. Cambridge, MA: Belknap Press of Harvard University Press, 1985.

Burchard, John, Charles W. David, and Julian Boyd, eds. *Planning the University Library Building*. Princeton: Princeton University Press, 1949.

Burton, Margaret. *Famous Libraries of the World*. London: Grafton, 1937.

Campbell, James W. P. *The Library: A World History*. Chicago: University of Chicago Press, 2013.

Cannons, Harry G. T. *Bibliography of Library Economy, 1876–1920*. Chicago: American Library Association, 1927.

Carnegie, Andrew. *The Gospel of Wealth and Other Timely Essays*. New York: Century, 1901.

*Carpenter Memorial Library: Dedication Exercises, November 18, 1914*. Concord, NH: Rumford Press, 1916.

Chanchani, Samiran. "Architecture and Central Public Libraries in America, 1887–1925." PhD diss., Georgia Institute of Technology, 2002.

*Change and Continuity: A Pictorial History of the Boston Athenaeum*. Boston: Boston Athenaeum, 1976.

Clark, John W. *The Care of Books: An Essay on the Development of Libraries and Their Fittings, from the Earliest Times to the End of the Eighteenth Century*. Cambridge: Cambridge University Press, 1909.

Clemons, Harry. *The University of Virginia Library, 1825–1950: Story of a Jeffersonian Foundation*. Boston: Gregg Press, 1972.

Cole, John Y. "Storehouses and Workshops: American Libraries and the Uses of Knowledge," in *The Organization of Knowledge in Modern America, 1860–1920*, edited by A. Oleson and J. Voss, 364–85. Baltimore: Johns Hopkins University Press, 1976.

Cole, John Y., and Henry Hope Reed, eds. *The Library of Congress: The Art and Architecture of the Thomas Jefferson Building*. New York: W. W. Norton, 1997.

Conway, James. *America's Library: The Story of the Library of Congress, 1800–2000*. New Haven: Yale University Press in association with the Library of Congress, 2000.

Cramer, Clarence Henley. *Open Shelves and Open Minds: A History of the Cleveland Public Library*. Cleveland and London: Press of Case Western Reserve University, 1972.

Crosbie, Michael J. *Architecture for the Books*. Mulgrave, Australia: The Images Publishing Group, 2003.

Dain, Phyllis. *The New York Public Library: A Universe of Knowledge*. New York: New York Public Library, 2000.

Daly, César. "Bibliothèque Sainte-Geneviève." *Revue générale de l'architecture et des travaux publics* 10 (1852): cols. 379–81.

Dana, John Cotton. *Libraries: Addresses and Essays*. Freeport, NY: Books for Libraries Press, 1966.

———. *A Library Primer*. Chicago: Library Bureau, 1899.

Davies, David William. *Public Libraries as Culture and Social Centers: The Origin of the Concept*. Metuchen, NJ: Scarecrow Press, 1974.

Davis, Donald. *Libraries and Culture: Proceedings of Library History, Seminar VI*. Austin: University of Texas, 1981.

De Poli, Aldo. *Biblioteche, 1995–2005*. Milan: Federico Motta, 2002.

Delessert, Benjamin. *Mémoire sur la Bibliothèque Royale, où l'on indique les measures à prendre pour la transférer dans un bâtiment circulaire, d'une forme nouvelle, qui serait construit au centre de la Place du Carrousel*. Paris: H. Dupuy, 1835.

Della Santa, Leopoldo. *Della costruzione e del regolamento di una pubblica universale biblioteca con la pianta dimostrativa*. Firenze: Trinita, 1816.

Dickinson, Donald C. *Henry E. Huntington's Library of Libraries*. San Marino, CA: Huntington Library, 1995.

Dickson, Paul. *The Library in America: A Celebration in Words and Pictures*. New York: Facts on File Publications, 1986.

Dierickx, Mary B. *The Architecture of Literacy: The Carnegie Libraries of New York City*. New York: The Cooper Union for the Advancement of the Sciences and Art and the New York City Department of General Services, 1996.

Ditzion, Sidney. *Arsenals of a Democratic Culture: A Social History of the American Public Library Movement in New England and the Middle States, 1850–1900.* Chicago: American Library Association, 1947.

Du Mont, Rosemary Ruhig. *Reform and Reaction: The Big City Public Library in American Life.* Westport, CT: Greenwood Press, 1977.

Eastman, William R. *The Library Building.* Chicago: American Library Association, 1912.

Edwards, Edward. *Memoirs of Libraries, Including a Handbook of Library Economy.* 2 vols. London: Trübner, 1859.

Fletcher, William I. *Public Libraries in America.* Boston: Roberts Brothers, 1894.

"Free Access of the Public to Shelves in Public Libraries." *Library Journal* 13 (September 1888): 309–10.

Fussler, Herman H. *Library Buildings for Library Service.* Chicago: American Library Association, 1947.

Garrigus, Carle E., Jr. "The Reading Habits of Maryland's Planter Gentry, 1718–1747." *Maryland Historical Magazine* 92 (Spring 1997): 37–53.

Garrison, Dee. *Apostles of Culture: The Public Librarian and American Society, 1876–1920.* New York: Free Press, 1979.

Gelernter, Mark. *A History of American Architecture: Buildings in Their Cultural and Technological Context.* Hanover and London: University Press of New England, 1999.

Githens, Alfred M. "The Army Libraries and Liberty Theaters." *Architectural Forum* 29 (July 1918): 15–19.

———. "Libraries," in *Forms and Functions of Twentieth-Century Architecture*, edited by T. Hamlin, vol. 3, 675–715. New York: Columbia University Press, 1952.

Goodrum, Charles A. *The Library of Congress.* New York: Praeger, 1974.

*Gore Hall: The Library of Harvard College, 1838–1913.* Cambridge, MA: Harvard University Press, 1917.

Green, Samuel S. *The Public Library Movement in the United States, 1852–1893.* Boston: Boston Book, 1913.

Gromly, Dennis M. "A Bibliographic Essay of Western Library Architecture to the Mid-Twentieth Century." *Journal of Library History* 9 (January 1974): 4–24.

Hadley, Chalmers. *Library Buildings: Notes and Plans.* Chicago: American Library Association, 1924.

Hamlin, Arthur T. *The University Library in the United States: Its Origins and Development.* Philadelphia: University of Pennsylvania Press, 1981.

Harris, Michael H., ed. *The Age of Jewett: Charles Coffin Jew-*

ett and American Librarianship, 1841–1868. Littleton, CO: Libraries Unlimited, 1975.

———. "The Purpose of the American Public Library: A Revisionist Interpretation of History." *Library Journal* 98 (September 15, 1973): 2509–14.

Harris, Neil. "Cultural Institutions and American Modernization." *Journal of Library History* 16 (1981): 28–47.

Hesse, Leopold August Constantin. *Bibliothéconomie; ou, Nouveau manuel complet pour l'arrangement, la conservation, et l'administration des bibliothèques*, new ed. Paris: Roret, 1841.

Hilker, Helen-Anne. *Ten First Street, Southeast: Congress Builds a Library, 1886–1897.* Washington, DC: Library of Congress, 1980.

Hill, L. Draper, Jr. *The Crane Library.* Quincy, MA: Thomas Crane Public Library, 1962.

"Hints upon Library Buildings." *Norton's Literary Gazette and Publishers' Circular* 3 (January 15, 1853): 1–2.

Hofer, Candida, with an Essay by Umberto Eco. *Libraries.* Munich: Schimmer/Mosel, 2006.

Jones, Theodore. *Carnegie Libraries across America: A Public Legacy.* New York: John Wiley, 1997.

Jordy, William H. *American Buildings and Their Architects: Progressive and Academic Ideals at the Turn of the Century*, vol. 3. New York: Doubleday, 1972.

Kallisch, Philip Arthur. *The Enoch Pratt Free Library: A Social History.* Metuchen, NJ: Scarecrow Press, 1969.

Kaser, David. *The Evolution of the American Academic Library Building.* Lanham, MD, and London: Scarecrow Press, 1997.

Koch, Theodore W. *A Book of Carnegie Libraries.* New York: H. W. Wilson, 1917.

Kruty, Paul. "Patton & Miller: Designers of Carnegie Libraries." *Palimpsest* 64 (July/August 1983): 110–22.

Lancaster, Jane. *Inquire Within: A Social History of the Providence Athenaeum since 1753.* Providence, RI: The Providence Athenaeum, 2003.

Lane, William C. "The New Harvard Library." *Library Journal* 38 (May 1912): 259–62.

Leupp, Harold L. "The University of California Library." *Library Journal* 37 (May 1913): 267–70.

Levine, Neil. "The Book and the Building: Hugo's Theory of Architecture and Labrouste's Bibliothètheque Ste. Geneviève," in *The Beaux-Arts and Nineteenth-Century French Architecture*, edited by R. Middleton, 139–73. Cambridge, MA: MIT Press, 1982.

———. "The Romantic Idea of Architectural Legibility: Henri Labrouste and the Neo-Grec," in *The Architec-*

ture of the Ecole des Beaux-Arts, edited by Arthur Drexler, 325–416. New York: Museum of Modern Art, 1977.

Library Builders. London: Academy Editions, 1997.

Lowe, John A. Small Public Library Buildings. Chicago: American Library Association, 1939.

Lydenberg, Harry. History of the New York Public Library. New York, 1923.

Malmstrom, R. E. "Lawrence Hall at Williams College," in Studies in the History of Art, Number 2. Williamstown, MA: Williams College Museum of Art, 1979.

Massachusetts Public Library Commission. Ninth Report: Free Public Libraries of Massachusetts, 1899, Public Document No. 44. Boston: City of Boston, 1899.

Mattern, Shannon, The New Downtown Library: Designing with Communities. Minneapolis: University of Minnesota Press, 2007.

Maturi, M. B., and R. J. Maturi. Cultural Gems: An Eclectic Look at Unique United States Libraries. New York: 21st Century Publishers, 1996.

McDonald, Angus Snead. "Comments on Library Planning," in American Public Buildings Today, edited by R. W. Sexton. New York: Architectural Book Publishing, 1931.

McMullen, Haynes. "Prevalence of Libraries in the Northeastern States before 1876." Journal of Library History 22 (1987): 321–26.

Mearns, David C. The Story up to Now: The Library of Congress, 1800–1946. Washington, DC: Library of Congress, 1947.

Metcalf, Keyes D. Planning Academic and Research Library Buildings. New York: McGraw-Hill, 1965.

Miner, Curtis. " 'The Deserted Parthenon': Class, Culture and the Carnegie Library in Homestead, 1898–1937." Pennsylvania History 57 (April 1990): 107–35.

Murray, Stuart, A.P. The Library: An Illustrated History. Chicago: American Library Association, 2009.

Nourse, Henry. "The Public Libraries of Massachusetts." New England Magazine, new series 5 (1891–92): 139–59.

Oehlerts, Donald. Books and Blueprints: Building America's Public Libraries. New York, Westport, and London: Greenwood Publishing, 1991.

———. "The Development of American Public Library Architecture from 1850 to 1940." PhD diss., Indiana University, 1974.

Ojeda, Oscar Riera. Phoenix Central Library: Bruder DWL Architects. Gloucester, MA: Rockport Publishers, 1999.

Papworth, John Woody, and Wyatt Papworth. Museums, Libraries, and Picture Galleries, Public and Private: Their Establishment, Formation, Arrangement, and Architectural Construction. London: Chapman and Hill, 1853.

Patton, Normand S. "Architects and Librarians." Library Journal 14 (1889): 159–61.

———. "Library Architecture." Public Libraries 6 (June 1901): 200–4.

Perry, Everett R. Handbook of the Central Building, Los Angeles Public Library. Los Angeles: Los Angeles Public Library, 1927.

Person, Roland Conrad. A New Path: Undergraduate Libraries in the United States and Canadian Universities, 1949–1987. Westport, CT: Greenwood Press, 1988.

Petroski, Henry. The Book on the Bookshelf. New York: Alfred A. Knopf, 1999.

Pevsner, Nikolaus. A History of Building Types. Princeton: Princeton University Press, 1976.

Poole, William Frederick. "The Construction of Library Buildings." American Architect and Building News 10 (September 17, 1881): 131–34.

———. "Newberry Library." Library Journal 15 (1890): 107–11.

———. "Progress of Library Architecture." Library Journal 7 (1882): 130–36.

———. Remarks on Library Construction. Chicago: Jansen, McClurg, 1884.

———. "Small Library Buildings." Library Journal 10 (1885): 250–56.

"Problem XVI.—A Memorial Library." The Architectural Sketch Book 2 (1875), plates xliv–xlvi.

Proceedings at the Dedication of the Building for the Public Library of the City of Boston, January 1, 1858. Boston: City of Boston, 1858.

Redmond, Kathleen Moltz, and Phyliss Dain. Civic Space/Cyberspace: The American Public Library in the Information Age. Cambridge, MA: MIT Press, 2001.

Reed, Henry Hope, and Francis Morrone. The New York Public Library: The

Architecture and Decoration of the Stephen A. Schwarzman Building. New York:

W. W. Norton & Company, 2011.

Rhees, William. Manual of Public Libraries, Institutions, and Societies in the United States and British Provinces of North America. Philadelphia: Lippincott, 1859.

Roth, Leland M. American Architecture: A History. Boulder, CO: Westview Press, 2001.

Sanford, Charles B. Thomas Jefferson and His Library. Hamden, CT: Archon, 1977.

Schmidt, J. A. F. Handbuch der Bibliothekwissenschaft, der Literatur- und Bücherkunde. Weimer: Voigt, 1840.

———. *Handbuch der Bibliothek-Wissenschaft, besonders zum Gebrauche der Nicht-Bibliothekare, welche ihre Privat-Büchersammlungen selbst einrichten wollen.* Vienna: Beck, 1834.

Schrettinger, Martin. *Versuch eines vollständigen Lehrbuchs der Bibliothek-Wissenschaft; oder, Anleitung zur Vollkommenen Geschäftfuhrung eines Bibliothekars, in wissenschaftlicher Form abgefasst.* 2 vols. Munich: Lindauer, 1810–1829.

Sharp, Katherine L. "Illinois Libraries." Whole issue, *University (of Illinois) Studies* (1906–1908).

Shera, Jesse H. *Foundations of the Public Library: The Origins of the Public Library Movement in New England, 1629–1855.* Chicago: University of Chicago Press, 1949.

Shores, Louis. *Origins of the American College Library, 1638–1800.* Nashville: George Peabody College for Teachers, 1934.

Shurtleff, Nathaniel B. *A Decimal System for the Arrangement and Administration of Libraries.* Boston: privately printed, 1856.

Silver, Joel. "Thomas Jefferson as a Book Collector." *AB Bookman's Weekly* 100 (September 15, 1997): 586–94.

Small, Herbert. *The Library of Congress: Its Architecture and Decoration*, edited by H. H. Reed. New York: W. W. Norton, 1982.

Snead and Company. *Library Planning, Bookstacks and Shelving.* Jersey City, NJ: Snead & Co. Iron Works, 1915.

Soule, Charles C. *How to Plan a Library Building for Library Work.* Boston: Boston Book, 1912.

Stevenson, Gordon, and Judith Kramer-Greene, eds. *Melvil Dewey: The Man and the Classification.* Albany, NY: Forest Press, 1983.

Stone, Elizabeth. *American Library Development, 1600–1899.* New York: H. W. Wilson, 1977.

Streeter, Burnett Hillman. *The Chained Library: A Survey of Four Centuries in the Evolution of the English Library.* London: Macmillan, 1931.

"The Sterling Memorial Library at Yale." *Library Journal* 51 (February 15, 1926): 183–84.

Sturgis, Russell. "The Carnegie Libraries in New York City." *Architectural Record* 17 (March 1905): 237–46.

Tilton, Edward L. "Library Planning." *Architectural Forum* 47 (December 1927): 497–506.

———. "Library Planning and Design." *Architectural Forum* 56 (June 1932): 567–72.

———. "Scientific Library Planning," in *Library Planning, Bookstacks and Shelving*, Snead and Company, 113–17. Jersey City, NJ: Snead & Co. Iron Works, 1915.

Trezza, Alphonse F., ed. *Library Buildings: Innovation for Changing Needs: Proceedings.* Chicago: American Library Association, 1972.

Turner, Paul Venable. *Campus: An American Planning Tradition.* Cambridge, MA: MIT Press, 1984.

United States Department of Interior, Bureau of Education. *Public Libraries in the United States of America: Their History, Condition and Management.* Special report, part 1. Washington, DC: U. S. Government Printing Office, 1876.

Van Slyck, Abigail A. *Free to All: Carnegie Libraries and American Culture, 1890–1920.* Chicago: University of Chicago Press, 1995.

———. "Free to All: Carnegie Libraries and the Transformation of American Culture, 1886–1917." PhD diss., University of California at Berkeley, 1989.

———. "The Lady and the Library Loafer: Gender and Public Space in Victorian America." *Winterthur Portfolio* 31 (Winter 1996): 221–41.

———. "'The Utmost Amount of Effectiv [sic] Accommodation': Andrew Carnegie and the Reform of the American Library." *Journal of the Society of Architectural Historians* 50 (1991): 359–83.

Van Zandt, David. "The Lenox Library: What Hunt Did and Did Not Learn in France," in *The Architecture of Richard Morris Hunt*, edited by S. Stein, 90–106. Chicago: University of Chicago Press, 1986.

Veit, Fritz. *Presidential Libraries and Collections.* Westport, CT: Greenwood Press, 1987.

Wadlin, Horace. *The Public Library of the City of Boston: A History.* Boston: Boston Public Library, 1911.

Wall, Joseph F. *Andrew Carnegie.* New York: Oxford University Press, 1970.

Webb, T.D., ed. *Building Libraries for the 21st Century.* Jefferson, North Carolina: McFarland, 2000.

Wetherold, Houghton. "The Architectural History of the Newberry Library." *Newberry Library Bulletin* 6 (November, 1962): 3–23.

Wheeler, Joseph L., and Alfred Morton Githens. *The American Public Library Building: Its Planning and Design with Special Reference to Its Administration and Service.* New York: Scribners, 1941.

Whitehill, Walter Muir. *Boston Public Library: A Centennial History.* Cambridge, MA: Harvard University Press, 1956.

Wiegand, Wayne A. "American Library History Literature, 1947–1997: Theoretical Perspectives?" *Libraries and Culture* 35, no. 1 (Winter 2000): 4–34.

"Williams College Library." *Norton's Literary Gazette and Publishers' Circular* 3 (March 13, 1853): 1.

Williamson, William Landram. *William Frederick Poole and the Modern Library Movement.* New York: Columbia University Press, 1963.

Wilson, Douglas L. *Jefferson's Books, Monticello Monograph Series*, preface by D. J. Boorstin. Monticello, VA: Thomas Jefferson Memorial Foundation, 1996.

Winsor, Justin. "Library Buildings." U.S. Department of Interior. Bureau of Education. *Public Libraries in the United States of America: Their History, Condition and Management.* Special report, part 1, 465–75. Washington, DC: U.S. Government Printing Office, 1876.

Woelfel, Roger H. *The Story of the Los Angeles Public Library.* Los Angeles: Los Angeles Public Library, 1987.

Wolf, Edwin. *"At the Instance of Benjamin Franklin": A Brief History of the Library Company of Philadelphia.* Philadelphia: Library Company of Philadelphia, 1976.

# INDEX

[References are to pages of text and illustration captions. Architects and photographers are identified, respectively, by the abbreviations *arch.* and *ph.*]